Re/Constructing
Elementary Science

Studies in the
Postmodern Theory of Education

Joe L. Kincheloe and Shirley R. Steinberg
General Editors

Vol. 177

PETER LANG
New York · Washington, D.C./Baltimore · Bern
Frankfurt am Main · Berlin · Brussels · Vienna · Oxford

Wolff-Michael Roth,
Kenneth Tobin, and Steve Ritchie

Re/Constructing
Elementary Science

PETER LANG
New York · Washington, D.C./Baltimore · Bern
Frankfurt am Main · Berlin · Brussels · Vienna · Oxford

#45166650

Library of Congress Cataloging-in-Publication Data

Roth, Wolff-Michael.
Re/constructing elementary science /
Wolff-Michael Roth, Kenneth Tobin, Steve Ritchie.
p. cm. — (Counterpoints; vol. 177)
Includes bibliographical references (p.) and index.
1. Science—Study and teaching (Elementary)—Case studies.
I. Title: Re/constructing elementary science. II. Tobin, Kenneth George.
III. Ritchie, Steve. IV. Title. V. Counterpoints (New York, N.Y.); vol. 177.
LB1585 .R55   372.3'5044—dc21   00-048749
2001   ISBN 0-8204-5200-9
ISSN 1058-1634

Die Deutsche Bibliothek-CIP-Einheitsaufnahme

Roth, Wolff-Michael:
Re/constructing elementary science /
Wolff-Michael; Roth, Kenneth Tobin; Steve Ritchie.
–New York; Washington, D.C./Baltimore; Bern; Frankfurt
am Main; Berlin; Brussels; Vienna; Oxford: Lang.
(Counterpoints; Vol. 177)
ISBN 0-8204-5200-9

Cover design by Lisa Dillon

The paper in this book meets the guidelines for permanence and durability
of the Committee on Production Guidelines for Book Longevity
of the Council of Library Resources.

© 2001 Peter Lang Publishing, Inc., New York

Printed in the United States of America

Table of Contents

within groups and manipulate materials, there is little evidence of participation that will lead students toward appropriate understandings of science. A third and still all-too-common scenario is that science is the first subject not to be taught when elementary teachers find themselves pressed for time. Related to these tendencies are the efforts of teacher educators to address only the first and third of them. Professional development programs for elementary teachers tend to address perceived limitations in the science background of elementary teachers and tendencies to either base programs on textbooks or to fail to teach science to an acceptable extent. One solution is materials-centered science, and in many instances programs are based around the use of commercially available kits. My experience with teacher education programs such as these is that they frequently lead to the second of the problems listed above, that teachers enact a curriculum that has many hands-on activities but little in the way of discussion that leads to the emergence of a science-like discourse.

S[tephen Ritchie]: Your categorization is interesting but does not entirely cover the spectrum of reasons. I want to start with a personal experience that somewhat but not entirely falls into your third category. In the early 1990s I was doing some research in an experienced elementary teacher's classroom. He was a very well respected teacher and I enjoyed many of the mathematics, language, and social studies lessons I observed. After some weeks I asked if I could observe a science lesson when next it was scheduled. Willing to oblige, the teacher promptly planned a lesson on electric circuits for my next visit. The children enjoyed the activities and were able to describe for me the difference between open and closed circuits as they demonstrated the steadiness-tester they had just constructed. But the teacher later admitted that this had been a "one-off" lesson put on for me as a personal favor. He then declared that he didn't like teaching science that much because it was too difficult and time-consuming to organize the equipment. Typically science in this class was done via television broadcasts or the occasional but engaging "one-off" lesson. This experience reinforced for me the conclusion reached by the Panel for the Discipline Review of Teacher Education in Mathematics and Science that science in Australian primary schooling was in a state of crisis. The panel painted a dismal picture of primary classrooms where, if children encountered any form of science instruction, their experiences were mostly unrewarding. Since then we have seen the production of national statements of science and technology for Australian schools (*e.g., A Statement on Science for Australian Schools*) that each state is beginning to address in their respective syllabi. These blueprints for change promise better times ahead, especially now that such helpful support materials as Primary Investigations are becoming more widely used. Of course, there have always been some enthusiastic and dedicated science teachers in primary classrooms. In earlier times, they might have focused on the "processes" of science associated with hands-on science activities. However, these activities have the potential to offer much more than process development. Through the various case studies we present in this book, practicing teachers might see new possibilities for science activities in their own classrooms.

M: Ken's categorization and your personal example cover the spectrum of constraints faced by many elementary teachers when it comes to science. However, in my experience, I have found many elementary teachers who really wanted to become better teachers, but who also felt that they did not have the background to envision and bring about the changes that they really wanted. They did not have the background to know what these changes might look like. It has been an interesting experience to work with such teachers. For the past six years, I have been engaging in coteaching: Virtually at the elbow of the regular classroom teacher, we have enacted curriculum innovations by playing off each other's strengths. Elementary teachers usually have developed tremendously efficacious practices when it comes to organizing classrooms, schools, and parents; they also understand how to bring about a sense of community, foster collective activities, and deal with the minor and major crises in the lives of children. They transport these practices into their science lessons. My strengths have been a solid background in the science, open-inquiry learning environments, and experience in science curriculum design. Together, we enacted tremendous science lessons and allowed learning by teachers.

But let us talk about the second question.

Why Did I Do the Case Studies?

K: My initial interest was to explore a science classroom in which students used a materials-centered approach as a basis for developing a science-like discourse. I wanted the students to correlate data from their investigations with materials to patterns and ideas. The negotiation of a science-like discourse was a rare phenomenon in elementary classes and I believed that in Ms. Scott (Chapter 7), I had a rare individual who would be able to motivate her students and facilitate their learning. However, this is not what happened and although I learned a great deal from the study, a second study was needed to see what teachers can do to connect materials-oriented investigations to an emerging science-like discourse. Ms. Mack is a teacher who has made a transition from not teaching science to teaching science that was factually oriented to teaching in much the same way as Ms. Scott. Spurred on by her goals to improve the learning of her students and an obligation to overcome her subject matter limitations Ms. Mack continued to learn about the teaching of science as inquiry and about how to employ the added roles as co-researcher and co-learner into her enacted science curriculum. Together the two studies provide what I consider to be rich insights into the way that science can be taught. The first study shows how a strong elementary teacher enacts a materials-centered curriculum but does not yet know how to build an interactive environment in which science-like language games occur. The second study portrays the changes in a teacher and an enacted science curriculum as she learns how to emphasize investigations that are inquiry oriented. The value in both studies being presented together is that they show how teachers such as Ms. Scott can become teachers such as Ms. Mack by engaging in ongoing professional development programs and undertaking research in their own classrooms.

S: A few years after my first study of primary classrooms I was invited to sit in on a not-so-experienced teacher's (i.e., Mr. Hammett) Grade 6 class. Upon entering this classroom, I was stunned by the visual impact of the thematically decorated room. This space was more like a rai forest than a classroom. It was a living laboratory; rock pools in one corner, aquaria in another. But there were samples of students' poems, artwork, and technological artifacts on display too. There were no "one-off" science lessons in this class. Sure, there were clearly identifiable science activities, but these generally were linked to the theme underpinning language, social studies, and art activities. After class, the children frequently stayed behind. There were always extra ideas for them to try out and projects in progress. Because this class was so different from the others I had seen, I became excited about the possibilities my new experience might offer. I wanted to find out about Mr. Hammett's personal practical theories and the nature of the students' scientific learning in this classroom. I felt the need to write about what was happening in this class to encourage other teachers to try to create their own stimulating science learning environments. Over a two-year period, I observed many science and technology lessons in Mr. Hammett's classes. Most of these lessons were related to design activities where students worked together in teams to produce artifacts for particular purposes. Chapters 4 and 5 focus on different issues that I identified from my observations of Mr. Hammett's classes. Apart from showing how Mr. Hammett's design activities were enacted, I wanted to demonstrate that the children's experiences in these activities provided opportunities for sharing ideas through their own language games[3], and that these ideas could then be transformed into canonical discourse with peer and teacher support. For some time now, I have been concerned about the views expressed by my own teacher education students. Somehow, several of my students have come to believe that the move toward student-centered pedagogies diminishes the significance of the teacher's classroom interactions. So I also wanted to demonstrate how vital the teacher's role is in introducing students to the language games of canonical science. This is a major thrust of Chapter 5.

M: As I indicated earlier, I was interested in testing new ideas about enacting curriculum while at the same time documenting in detail the knowing and learning of children who co-participate in enacting the curricula. In this, my particular interest was in understanding the process of children's designing; the constraints arising from the social, material, historical, and cultural contingencies of their activities; and how new and formal discourses arise from the engagement with the artifacts that they create. In the first case study (Chapter 3), I present a conversation from a classroom where Gitte, a graduate student who worked as a curriculum developer and who had previously taught four years in elementary schools, cotaught a unit she had designed with Tammy, a twelve-year veteran in this school. This conversation shows how, after two-and-one-half months, Grade 4–5 children had developed a competent science discourse, supported by gestures, to talk about aspects of the structures they had designed. In this conversation, we not only see the students maintain a conversation almost without teacher intervention, but the interactions among students disclose deep understandings of structures, forces, and compound strength. My second case study comes from one of my own coteaching experiences in a Grade 6–7 class in Tammy's school (Chapter 4). There, I tested a new unit on simple machines in which the students spent a lot of time designing and presenting their own machines but every now and then engaged in teacher-designed activities that focused on specific scientific issues of particular simple machines. The conversation featured in Chapter 4 arose after I had challenged the class to a tug of war after rigging the competition with a block and tackle.

Out of the lost competition developed a conversation in which students were eager to develop alternative designs that would have helped them to win the competition.

But let us come to the third question.

What Role Can a Re/Constructed Science Curriculum Play?

K: I have a strong interest in education being an agent of both cultural production and cultural transformation. Let me unpack this sentence a little. I was astonished when key policy makers from Singapore announced to me that they were considering not teaching science in primary schools at all. They had decided that there were other priorities for primary education and that a science education could wait until students were competent in such areas as literacy in English and the children's native language, reading and writing, mathematics and civics. Although I could immediately think of many deleterious aspects of leaving science education until high school I could also understand their rationale. Even so, they did not seem to value just what could be attained from an elementary science program. Despite the success of Singapore children in international comparisons of science performance, the primary curriculum in that country is in need of re/construction just as it is here. The visions of science contained in the classes taught by Ms. Mack can catalyze marked changes in what children know and can do, and it is to be anticipated that what is learned can be socially and culturally transformative.

M: It strikes me that a major problem not only in Singapore but also in our own countries lies in the subdivision of children's school lives into subject areas. When our children do mathematics, they use some root language to communicate. When children do science, they not only communicate in their mother tongue (or some other chosen language), but they also manipulate a variety of representations that fall into the domain of mathematics. It is easy to seek out situations where science can be studied from historical and social perspectives. If schools were to begin to focus on topics that serve as vehicles to engage in practices that are normally associated with subject matter domains, we would not only achieve subject matter integration but also a greater continuity than the current timed, hourly switches from one domain to another, from one teacher to another.

K: I agree, but I also want to point out that we need to start with topics that are closely related to children's lives. In the suburban areas of much of the United States, the enacted curricula seem to be much more successful than in urban schools where social factors associated with poverty, crime, and poor health are often problems. What are the characteristics of a science program that can make a difference in urban schools as well as in suburban schools and countries such as Singapore? My recommendation is to select science content that is linked closely to the lived worlds of children, that is, associated with society and technology, and that consciously evokes passions related to lived experiences. The emotions, interests, values, and characteristics such as curiosity ought not be suppressed in learning, and efforts can be made to connect the science curriculum with the social, cultural, historical, and gendered experiences of elementary school learners. If elementary science can be re/constructed in this way, then there is every possibility that students who learn science will have a richer array of options awaiting them in their lives in and out of school.

M: Furthermore, as Penny Eckert showed in *Jocks and Burnouts,* children and students who come from poor and working-class neighborhoods have a much deeper sense of the social fabric that gives sense to their lives.[4] These lived experiences are possible starting points for an integrative approach to school subjects such that it permits students to engage in transformations of their lifeworlds.

S: I think that we already have a related example in this book. In Chapter 6 there is a wonderful excerpt that shows the excitement generated within a team that explored the electrical conductivity of salt water. The children thought that their apparatus caused the separation of salt from water and that this invention would lead to useful desalination applications. Without understanding the process in terms of canonical science, these children nevertheless linked their classroom activity with social practices. The thought that their activity might lead to cultural transformation was uplifting for them. At this stage they did not have access to the discourse that would help them understand electrolysis, nor did the teacher introduce this discourse. One can only speculate about the impact that the teacher might have made, for example, by linking their work to William Nicholson and Anthony Carlisle's discovery of electrolysis nearly 200 years ago. Such a link might have contextualized the children's activity within the cultural practices of the nineteenth-century scientific community and introduced them to appropriate language that could lead to a deeper understanding of the phenomena.

M: And while doing a historic study of the discovery of electrolysis, children may begin to ask (or can be encouraged to ask) questions about the social and historical fabric of the society that allowed Nicholson and Carlisle to pursue the activities they did while large parts of the population labored hard simply to eat and stay alive. In this sense, I see in a re/constructed elementary science not only opportunities for children to learn "science-speak," but also opportunities that allow children and students to engage in a transformation of their own lifeworlds. If Ken's inner-city children were to begin to investigate garbage and health, they might become interested in cleaning up their neighborhoods or engaging in political action to get the city help build new parks—as some neighborhood groups in Baltimore have begun to do.

S: So what we are saying then, is that a re/constructed science curriculum would encourage children to link their classroom activities to social and cultural practices. Mr. Hammett frequently assigned mini-design projects that served this purpose. Apart from the design activities described in Chapters 5 and 6, I remember seeing other activities where classroom social practices became the focus for design. For example, practical problems such as reducing the afternoon glare within the classroom and opening the upper window louvers without standing on desks all required engineering solutions. The children could see the direct benefits of their inquiries, and most required the use of canonical language games. In Mr. Hammett's classroom, design activities were integrative devices drawing together the language games of canonical science, available resources, and authentic classroom and community practices.

M: On the surface, these design activities may not seem to lend themselves to a re/constructed elementary science. In this respect, I want to make two comments. First, there are a numerous historical and sociological analyses of architecture and civil engineering that would lend themselves to reflexive and transformational activities. For example, in the article "Do Artifacts have Politics?," Langdon Winner analyzed bridges on Long Island that were so low that the they prevented the buses used by working-class people in the early part of the twentieth century to have access to the beaches.[5] Furthermore, we can read from Schön's analysis of architectural design processes and from Eckert's analysis of space use by middle and high school students that there are political, social, and cultural implications of designing artifacts.[6] This is to say that there are many opportunities to engage children not only in talking about the engineering and science sides of designbut also in the political, social, and cultural aspects. Although the teachers in the Grade 4–5 class (Chapter 3) did not encourage such reflections, the children already asked questions such as "What is the purpose of this bridge?" Such a curriculum in inner-city schools may engage children in asking questions about the structures in their neighborhoods. Second, the case studies on engineering constitute but one example of the kind of structural organization of lessons such that, whatever the topic, children have the opportunity to build discursive resources that allow them to participate in conversations in which science is a relevant context.

S: Before we provide an overview of the book we should tell readers more about metalogues and why we use them in this book.

What Is a Metalogue?

M: As far as I know, it was Gregory Bateson who introduced metalogues.[7] A metalogue is a conversation about some problematic subject. But it is not just a conversation. Rather, in the ideal case, the structure of the conversation in its entirety is also relevant to the subject; that is, a metalogue exemplifies its subject matter in its form. Jacques Désautels also pointed out to me that metalogues have an evolutionary structure in that they constitute earlier parts as new conversational topics.[8] Here we use metalogues in the way Mary Catherine Bateson constructed them, not as stand-alone texts but as conversations that occur in a context. Our metalogues are constructed as continuing conversations about elementary science. The metalogues take one case study as a starting point for highlighting important issues that are not addressed by the studies themselves but that are important considerations in the re/construction of elementary science. As the metalogues unfold, the results of previous metalogues become themselves topics of the conversation.

K: In a sense, our metalogues also reflect our argument. Throughout the book, we suggest that for learning to occur, elementary children and their teachers need to engage in conversations around artifacts. Children learn science and engineering by talking about, explaining, critiquing, and defending design choices. Teachers learn when they engage each other in ongoing professional conversations about pertinent events from their own classrooms and the classroom of others.

Chapter 2

Learning Science through Design Activities

Students should have control over where to go and what to do when they are learning. Allowing students to determine which activities to pursue and when to pursue them provides students with a greater feeling of being in control of their learning. Moreover, this level of control better engages students' interest and allows them to follow paths of inquiry relating to their individual interests. (Schank, 1994, p. 453)

There currently exists a small number of educators who concur with Schank that design activities provide many advantages for learning in school. Most generally, designing allows students to set and therefore appropriate goals and to learn as they work to achieve these goals. A subset of these educators, who are often science educators, is concerned with design activities in the context of technology. Because technology has some—yet-to-be-determined—relationship to science, technological design or, as it is often referred to, engineering design has some promise as a context within which students can learn science (e.g., Fensham & Gardner, 1994). Despite the enthusiasm of some science educators for engineering design activities, there are different views of the nature of professional design and, consequently, different ways of viewing children's design. We begin this chapter, by providing overviews of professional design and the relationship between science and technology (which will determine how children learn science through engineering design activities). We then outline our view of the nature of the design process and provide a map for the analysis of design activities. This is followed by a detailed description of the nature of children's designing. The chapter closes with a section that addresses some benefits and constraints of learning science through engineering design activities.

Professional Design

Design Traditions and Theories of Designing

Theories of designing (e.g., by professional designers) and execution of design (e.g., the processes by which craftsmen convert designs into artifacts) were, at one time, integrated. Important engineering feats such as Gothic cathedrals emerged from the contingent collective work of master masons and armies of craftsmen they commanded (Turnbull, 1993). Designing and constructing was one integrated activity, based on the use of templates, string, and geometry, from which magnificent cathedrals emerged as design artifacts. However, from the thirteenth to the sixteenth century, design was separated from execution, resulting in a division of labor between engineer-architects and subservient masons. This division is institutionally embodied in the division between design theory and technique and the application of such ideas to instrumental problems of practice (Schön, 1983). Design was treated as a more or less linear, logical process of applying well-established knowledge to existing problems, a view promoted by the engineer in the following quote:

> Engineering requires a large knowledge base to make choices and those choices are not made by chance, but logical reason based on previous experience. . . . A building cannot be designed or constructed in real life without logical reasoning using basic engineering principles. (Aerospace engineer, personal communication, June 12, 1994)

Underlying this view of engineering as the logical application of pre-existing knowledge bases is a technical rationality, a view of knowledge as symbolic information on which some parts of the mind operate. Such views of engineering knowledge arise from analyses of engineering design that are re/constructed with hindsight from the perspective of completed and functioning artifacts (Bucciarelli, 1994). Analysts inspect such artifacts, analyze their internal logic, and isolate the set of design decisions that explain how the artifact came to be as it is. Stories of artifact design constructed in this way will most often sound rational but have little to do with what people experienced during the design process. Much like the rational-sounding histories of science (Kuhn, 1970), rational stories of engineering design are re/constructed, deterministic, and heroic accounts.

Others disagree with a characterization of the design process as linear, straightforward problem solving (Brown & Duguid, 1992, 1996; Norman, 1991; Winograd, 1996). Rather than re/construct histories of design by departing from finished artifacts, these authors base their accounts of design on the daily experience or research of the everyday work of designing. Both empirical and theoretical work on design in the workplace emphasizes the integration of theory and practice. For example, Swedish system designers used cardboard mock-ups to design the workplace for a new computer-supported newspaper production unit. Mock-ups allowed them to design, evaluate design, construct modifications, and even radically change designs and engage in collaborative exchanges with users (Bucciarelli, 1994; Ehn & Kyng, 1991). Here, the ultimate design artifacts, the finished workplace, emerged from the interaction of multiple elements that include designers, users, computers, cardboard mock-ups, and existing technology. In this example of "situated design," formerly separated domains of design theory and construction practice were reintegrated (Greenbaum & Kyng, 1991).

To overcome the limitations of linear models of design, researchers interested in cognition developed cyclical models that include some or all of the following stages: sensing problems, defining problems, deriving solutions, implementing solutions, and evaluating outcomes (Starling, 1992). However, many studies indicate that most engineering design is not modeled well by cyclical models. Rather, evolution appears to be a more viable concept for design processes and concomitant changes in social, physical, and technological design environments. This is evidenced in detailed analyses of the Challenger disaster (Starling, 1992), the development of gas pipelines from Texas to New England (Constant, 1987, 1989), the invention of Bakelite plastic (Bijker, 1987), and the design of high-energy physics detectors (Knorr-Cetina, 1995). Consequently, designing is no longer regarded as a simple, additive process of knowledge integration and application. Instead, there are

> disorderly problem-solving negotiations, in which different kinds of knowledge are juxtaposed and checked, and where the outcome also depends on the persuasive abilities of the engineers involved. The problem often changes. Consequently, what counts as relevant expertise and equipment is rather "open." (Sørensen & Levold, 1992, p. 27)

Such studies point out that in technology, when designing and building an artifact of some complexity theoretical knowledge is almost never sufficient to make things work. Engineering design cannot be reduced to an application of general rules or theories. Rather, situated, tacit, and practical knowledge built up through experience is a key ingredient to successful design (Faulkner, 1994; Schön, 1983).

Clearly in some instances, designing practice has come full circle from an integrated process to the separation of theory and practice to reintegration. Anthropologists and sociologists have recently acknowledged that actual design is more than a straightforward, linear and logical process of applying basic knowledge. Workplace studies of design in architecture, various fields of engineering, and artificial intelligence document that design is (a) similar to everyday practical reasoning, (b) situated in social and physical contexts, and (c) influenced by numerous factors never entirely under the designers' control (Bijker, 1987; Bond, 1989; Callon, 1987; Constant, 1989; Henderson, 1991, 1998; Latour, 1992; Law & Callon, 1988; Luff & Heath, 1993; Pinch & Bijker, 1987; Schön, 1983; Sørensen & Levold, 1992; Starling, 1992; Suchman & Trigg, 1993; Woolgar, 1985). The following quote from a study on aerospace engineering contrasts with the view of the previously cited aerospace engineer:

> When the messiness of the job is finished, it is not the pure logic, clean formulas, or computer-generated drawings, all of which are too often singularly credited in technological achievement, that get a new turbine package built. It is, rather, social construction accomplished through the use of rough drawings and sketches acting as conscription devices and boundary objects that get the job done. The tradition of sketches, the building blocks of technical design . . . facilitate the capture, formation, negotiation, and final cognitive and physical structure of shared knowledge embedded in the official drawing set. (Henderson, 1991, p. 468)

Engineering designs such as ARAMIS, VEL, or VAL (all urban transport systems in France; only VAL reached the full implementation stage) are conceived as general ideas with few specific details (Latour, 1992). In the process of testing more and more components, increasingly complex prototypes, and first public implementations, initial ideas eventually become concrete artifacts—literally by means of a process of "concretion." Moreover, in the same process, engineers must go through numerous design stages on paper, with models, and with first prototypes. Meanings that are attributed by various stakeholders in the project to ideas and emerging artifacts differ. Negotiations over these differences change meanings and subsequent designs. While engineers like to blame politicians, public officials, or potential users for irrational demands on the design of transport systems, Latour (1992) showed the reciprocal influences on the emerging design posed by various engineering communities. Latour also showed that the progress in the design of these urban transport systems could not be modeled by rational conceptions of design. Rather, designing was a fundamentally non-linear and situated activity.

The cultures of prototyping are based on the same phenomenon of iterative evolution of the design artifact (Schrage, 1996). In the process of designing, new elements may emerge in and contribute to existing design languages. Designing is thereby an open-ended process in which new design options unfold in indeterminate ways before an open horizon of possibilities. Goals, while relatively enduring through time, must themselves be seen as subject to mangling in practice (Pickering, 1993, 1995). Practical goals are constructed in a temporally emergent cultural field, and their detailed substance is itself emergently constructed in that field.

Design and designing are in a deep sense social. During the design process, designers communicate in their teams and with future users of the design artifacts. The design team is not independent but functions in a social, institutional, economic, organizational, and cultural context. To communicate effectively, there need to be design languages that can be used by and make sense to a variety of concerned interlocutors. Finally, design has social consequences in that it changes the setting in which objects are incorporated after completion.

Analysis of Design Activities

To analyze design activities, we need something like maps to guide our observations and data collection. Maps are formal analyses of any practice. The basic patterns of human actions and interactions should include, at a minimum, standard practices, ready-to-hand tools and equipment, linguistic distinctions, sets of breakdowns,[1] and sets of ongoing concerns (Denning & Dargan, 1996). Such maps are also referred to as the ontology of the domain. That is, ontology constitutes a conceptual frame for interpreting the recurrent actions in a particular domain (cf. Winograd & Flores, 1987). In each domain, there exist:

- Standard practices enacted by members, by means of which the characteristic activities of the domain get done. In engineering design, these include specifying goals, reading books, writing articles, writing grant applications, interpreting graphs, talking to customers (cf. Bucciarelli, 1994).
- Ready-to-hand material resources, such as tools and equipment, that members use as part of their standard practices; a tool is ready-to-hand if a member uses it transparently, focusing on the task rather than the tool. Among the tools of a designer we may find pencil and paper, a CAD program, measuring instruments, or modeling clay.

- Linguistic resources that members use to make distinctions important to the competent and efficient activities of the field. Among the linguistic distinctions of an architect, one may find "screwy site," "maximum height for a kid," "nook," "differential potential," "fifteen feet max," "working slightly," "pass-through," and "interval" (Schön, 1987, pp. 50–52, 96).
- Breakdowns, interruptions of standard practices, and slowdown of an activity's progress that evolve from the breaking and absence of tools or changing of familiar contexts. For example, in the process of designing bridges, the lack of resources (e.g., absence of materials and machinery in remote parts of the world) or familiarity with practices may lead to problematic situations. (In a "screwy site," traditional practices of design may lead to unsuitable designs.)
- Sets of ongoing concerns of members, including common missions, interests, and fears. For example, many software designers are concerned with the usability and transparency of their products. Their design practices therefore will include careful investigations of the workplaces for which they design and many cycles of field-testing. Among architects' ongoing concerns are the livability of the houses and neighborhoods they design.

This ontology constitutes a topology that provides a useful set of guidelines for our analyses of children's designing, increasing competence in design practices, obstacles to learning, and interactions with each other and teachers. In the past, schools have almost exclusively focused on (directly) teaching linguistic resources. Because this usually happened outside the context of authentic practices and ongoing concerns of the domain, all students could do was memorize definitions and engage in constructing answers to rather simplistic word problems. Furthermore, the material resources (tools, instruments, and devices) often were not authentic in the sense that engaging with them would have allowed students to traverse a trajectory of increasing participation in the practices of a domain (Brown & Duguid, 1992).

The important role ongoing concerns play in the choice of practices and resources is highlighted in the following example of soccer (other team sports would do equally well). Goalies, defenders, mid-fielders, and forwards are all part of a team whose goal is to win (shoot more goals than you receive). However, the activities of each player are different, depending on a set of ongoing concerns with a particular position. A defender, for example, is primarily concerned with preventing a ball in her own net. Her choice of practices and resources to achieve this is driven by a set of ongoing concerns, such as covering a particular forward, covering open spaces, and so forth. This does not prevent a defender from engaging in an attack. But even while marching toward the opponents' goalie, defenders attend to concerns that are inherent in their assigned roles.

To change school science, students need to be able to engage in the construction of goals over which they feel ownership. In the process of pursuing these goals, there need to be opportunities for students to be enculturated into sets of ongoing concerns characteristic for the domain. These concerns usually are the driving forces for the selection of resources and practices for the tasks at hand. That is, once appropriate goals are chosen and sets of concerns are evident, students will almost inevitably draw on resources and practices characteristic of the domain with which they are to develop familiarity. Among the most significant aspects of any practice is the language in use, because it mediates agents' interactions with the natural and social world, resources that can be perceived, and the ongoing concerns any agent experiences.

Design Languages

Language is the primary human (social) practice and is central to the way we experience the world and ourselves (Heidegger, 1977; Wittgenstein, 1994/1958). With the term "language game" Wittgenstein meant to highlight that the speaking of language is part of an activity or lifeform. Consequently, he viewed the meaning of words not as something inherent but as emergent from their use. Design languages are like natural languages, but in their specificity they are useful for creating and interacting with things in the world (Rheinfrank & Evenson, 1996). Similar to natural languages, their communicative functions and structures are evolving semiotic systems that are increasingly adapted to allow description and experience in design worlds. Building scientific knowledge can be considered as a process in which aspects of design languages seek explanation of general patterns in materials and artifacts. Schön (1983, 1987) provided some detailed analyses of an architectural design language, a language game for doing architecture consisting of drawings and talk. Schön provided the example of an architectural studio master who explains to his student, "The kindergarten might go over here. . . then you might carry the gallery level through—and look down in here. . ." while drawing a kindergarten "here" and making a line that "carries the gallery level through." In this example, drawings and words are both part of the language of designing. Each element in such a design language creates coherence in people's experienced world and creates relevance by highlighting some things over others and thereby rendering them important. Each element also sets up a situation, a design move that has consequences for future design moves. When the studio master draws a geometric shape "here" and labels it "kindergarten," he shapes the emerging design. This has consequences for subsequent moves such as where the hallway can be put. Thus, the design language—words and drawn symbols—shape what can be designed and therefore shape the lived experience of the world in which designing takes place.

In this example, an architectural student had come to see and talk to the studio master. Important to this conversation is that the design language is sensible to both participants. Here, the design context offers opportunities for learning because student and teacher engage each other in the joint inquiry. There are design traditions in which the notion of design as learning environment is even more explicit; for example, in Scandinavian-born "participatory design" (Bannon & Bødker, 1991; Ehn, 1992; Ehn & Kyng, 1991). In participatory design, designers of computer-based workplaces and future inhabitants of these workplaces come together for extended periods of time to build a common design language. Their interactions are organized around artifacts from the old workplaces, mock-ups of potential new artifacts, drawings, and photographs. As they develop a new design language, designers and workers come to understand the lifeworld of the other. That is, participatory design is a learning environment in which participants build and learn new language and come to understand another community of practice.

Children's Design

Courses need to be created within a context that enables students to pursue their own interests as long as they want to without disallowing the possibility of switching interests at any time. (Schank, 1994, p. 432)

A number of recent studies provided us with deep insights into the kinds of learning that design activities provide for children. Of particular interest to schools is children's increasing competence in the formal representation of a domain's knowledge: the development of competence of the domain's language game. Several recent studies also provided detailed understandings of the social, material, and cultural nature of children's designing.

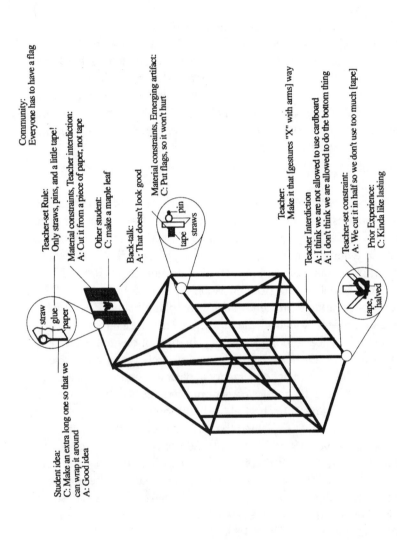

Figure 2.1 The many elements that contributed to the emergence of Arlene and Chris's twin tower. Because of the multitude of the influences, the design artifact is a heterogeneous assemblage. The design process is not something that can be thought of as a mental thing; it needs to be seen as a multi-leveled, situated, and heterogeneous

construction of a flag was not independent of the community. Rather, in this community there was a trend to use Canadian flags because (a) "everyone is using them" and (b) "otherwise it doesn't look good" (Roth, 1995d, 1998a).

Although we wrote for the moment about different elements that influenced the design, these elements did not exist in some absolute sense with determinate effects and meanings. As the example of a teacher-set constraint "use only a specific set of materials" shows, the way an element comes to bear on a specific design can differ quite dramatically not only between but also even within design groups. That is, each tool, material, teacher-set constraint, student utterance, and artifact is interpretively flexible or, in other words, has an unstable ontology.

Ontology of Setting

Most science, design, and technology educators assume that tasks, materials, instructions, teacher-set constraints, and tools have the same meaning for students as they have for themselves. Several recent studies with students in different countries, of different ages, and in different subject matters showed that this assumption is often untenable (Roth, 1995b, 1996a; Roth & Duit, 1996; Roth, McRobbie, Lucas, & Boutonné, 1997a, 1997b). These studies provided many examples of situations in which students and teachers viewed the "same" events in different ways, and there were differences among students. The upshot of such different experiences of what are taken to be the same events is the emergence of misunderstandings of what conversational partners are talking about. For example, in a Grade 12 physics classroom, students watched the teacher perform an experiment (Roth et al., 1997b). Subsequently, the teacher developed a theory that explained the motion observed during the demonstration. However, 19 of 24 students did not observe the type of motion that the teacher's theory explained. Thus, the entire theoretical elaborations made very little sense to the students because of the conflicting observations and the lack of communication about what has been observed.

In another situation, students investigated various moving objects using a computer simulation (Roth, 1995a). In his interaction with one group, the teacher listened to students' observational and explanatory talk. He quickly realized that students must have had a different perceptual experience of the computer display than he had. He therefore engaged students in a conversation about a series of different representations that he created on the computer screen. In the course of these interactions, students came to see the events in the way of the teacher. Once they were at this stage, students modified their observational descriptions that entailed changes in their explanatory descriptions. Students' descriptions converged to resemble the currently accepted scientific canon.

These observations have important implications for engineering design classrooms because tools, materials, community standards, teacher-set constraints, the current state of the design artifact, individual preferences, and past discursive achievements cannot be taken as stable entities. These elements are indeterminate and do not exist in any absolute sense. One could also say that the meanings of these elements are interpretively flexible and that the degree of their salience is contingent on specific local developments. Tools, materials, artifacts, teacher interdictions and constraints, the history of activity and design artifacts, and plans do not have stable ontologies. Because of the different meanings that they can have for different children, they lead to different design actions and, ultimately, different learning. In the following, we provide illustrative examples from a Grade 4–5 engineering design curriculum that show that various elements of the children's learning environment do not have stable ontologies but take different meanings for different actors, locations, and times.

Andy, Simon, and Tim had decided to design an earthquake-proof tower using drinking straws as a material. After their emerging design included two stories, one of the two teachers conducting the class asked the three boys whether they could enlarge their existing tower. The students heard the question as an instruction, so Tim decided to make a cone top. He designed a triangular pyramid from the same straws and then offered it to his peers as the solution to the problem of the missing top which the teacher appeared to have framed: "Here's the cone top." Andy immediately constructed a problem.[2]

01	Andy:	Don't make a triangle on the bottom (1.7) that's gonna be hard to put it on.
02	Tim:	⌈ I don't put it here. ⌉
03	Simon:	⌊ Make a pyramid, ⌋ make a pyramid, Andy.
04	Andy:	A pyramid. All these are squares, now (1.2).
05	Tim:	Yeah, but we can put just a few supports like that and put it on (1.3).
06	Andy:	⌈ No. ⌉
07	Simon:	⌊ Not ⌋ really, that is too hard, Tim.
08	Andy:	It's too hard.
09	Tim:	No it isn't.
10	Simon:	Yes it is.

11	Tim:	You only ⌈need.
12	Andy:	⌊It won't⌋ look good then.
13	Tim:	You don't know.
14	Simon:	No it won't work.

Tim's cone top had a triangular base, whereas the existing tower had a square top face. Andy constructed this as a problem, because the two artifacts would be too hard to join. Thus, what could be considered the same physical situation was interpreted in different ways. What Tim considered to be a successful solution to a previous problem Andy interpreted as another, new problem. Both Andy and Simon proposed a solution to this new problem: Tim should construct a square pyramid. But Tim did not agree, he reframed Andy and Simon's problem of the mismatched faces to be one of missing supports (line 05). Again, Andy and Simon rejected this proposition as a feasible solution (lines 06–08, 10). Tim refused to accept their frame so Andy suggested another problem: If they were to follow Tim, they would end up with an artifact that would not look good.

In this conversation, the different participants made their cases whether a particular situation was a problem or a solution. The relationship between the "same" artifacts was interpreted in different ways: it was either problematic and unproblematic, an advance in their design project, or an impediment to their ultimate goal. The entire design project was in this way a constant negotiation of alternative perspectives of what the design was all about.[3] Even individual modules were interpreted in different ways. In one situation, Simon had just completed a small cubical shape and Tim held a large cube. Simon thought that his module would constitute the bottom part of their earthquake tower design, whereas Tim thought he had constructed the bottom part. Simon based his assessment on a design precedent, an existing earthquake-proof tower in the downtown area of the city for which the body of the building hangs from a narrow base. Tim based his assessment on the experience that a larger base usually provided more stability to a structure. But they had pursued their activities, each thinking that he was designing the bottom part of the tower. During the episode it became clear that Tim and Simon interpreted their current artifact in different ways; thus, whether the design was the "same" depended on the point of view. The group accepted Tim's frame of the situation and deferred to a future moment the decision that would remove the interpretive flexibility of the artifact. In this way, the design of their tower was repeatedly reinterpreted as expressed by their labels, which

Resources for Mediating Conversations

Students' design conversations are not only about but also over the emerging artifacts. That is, the artifacts—as do any other material aspect in their phenomenal world such as tools, equipment, and the physical setting—provide frames within which otherwise meaningless utterances do conversational work. Any material aspect in the setting can be referred to by means of pointing so that it does not need to be symbolically represented in students' utterances: These aspects serve as their own representation. The following examples illustrate this function of the emerging artifacts.

Stan and Tim had agreed to design a bridge from cardboard. At one stage, Tim proposed that they should add some material to support the bridge deck from the central pier. When he returned from the table with the materials, he suggested:

```
01   Tim:    Stan, why don't we connect some straws like
02           ⌈this? (0.8)
             ⌊Holds straws [Figure 2.3a]
03   Stan:   No, we are not allowed to use straws! (7.1) We are not allowed to use straws.
04   Tim:    I know. (2.2) Go get some cardboard so we can
05           go ⌈like that.
                ⌊Gestures diagonally [Figure 2.3b]
```

Here, the straws that Tim held in his hands and the currently existing artifact were not represented in the discourse but were used as their own representation. He simply held the two straws (line 01, Figure 2.3a) next to the existing artifact and questioned whether they should connect them in a particular way. After Stan's reminder that they were not allowed to use straws, Tim suggested they stabilize the bridge deck by adding some cardboard. Again, rather than expressing his design in the form of a verbal description, he used a gesture (line 05, Figure 2.3b). In both situations, Stan could understand Tim's utterances or gestures because they were made against the existing structure as the background which served as a frame within which the gesture and utterance took meaning.

Although the materials and artifacts are resources in these situations, they are not enough to clearly communicate words and gestures with any predictable certainty. What it is that people say or gesture is always interpretively flexible and open to reinterpretation and change as soon as frames are changed. As the following excerpts illustrate, Tim's gesture of how the cardboard was to be placed turned out to be interpretively flexible.

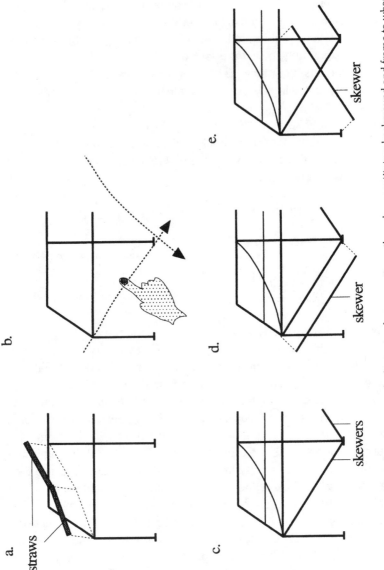

Figure 2.3 Design artifacts are not only the topic of conversations, they also constitute a background and frame to what student designers say and do. In this way, design artifacts decrease the interpretive flexibility of words and gestures and contribute, as a framing ground, to an efficient multi-modal communication.

After the above conversation, Tim negotiated with one of the adults to use skewers for stabilizing his bridge. As Tim began to attach one of the two skewers in front of him, he asked Stan to get two more. Stan questioned why they needed additional skewers and Tim responded that they needed to "put them the opposite direction." Although this utterance was consistent with his earlier gesture, analytic hindsight shows that the utterance and gesture were not enough to guarantee a shared understanding. While Stan went to get additional skewers, Tim attached those in front of him such as to make a diagonal brace between each of two piers (Figure 2.3c).

```
01   Stan:   Why do you need two more?
02   Tim:    Because we put them the opposite direction on each side, see look.
03           (15.4) [ While Tim tapes initial two skewers, Stan gets two more. ]
04   Stan:   [ Stan holds skewers parallel to the existing ones as in Figure 2.3c. ]
05   Tim:    The wrong way Stan, ⌈put them      ⌉
06   Stan:                        ⌊I don't (these⌋ doesn't?)
07   Tim:    And now we're gonna make ⌈it crisscross.
08                                    ⌊Holds skewer [Figure 2.3d]
```

As Stan returned, he held the new skewers parallel to the existing ones in the structure (line 04, Figure 2.3d). But Tim suggested that this was not what he meant; took one of the skewers from Tim, suggested they make the skewers "crisscross," and held the new skewer in front of the existing one so that they formed an "X" (Figure 2.3e). Here, talk and gesture did not completely result in making utterances unambiguous. Stan and Tim acted as if they shared a common definition of how the design would develop. The differences in their visions of how the new skewers should be placed to provide additional support became apparent only at the moment that Stan gestured one position. Because he held the skewer in a particular way, Stan's understanding became accountable and inspectable. Tim was able to look at the skewer and engage in a repair sequence with Stan in which their different understandings of the future design became apparent.

The lesson we can draw from these examples is that the material world is full of explanatory resources. The richness arises, in part, because the material world exists in discourse so that most of our explanations involve the material world (Brown & Duguid, 1996). The artifacts students construct contribute to their definition of the situation, which does not have to be made explicit unless trouble in communication becomes apparent. As long as it appears that indexical terms ("this," "that") and gestures are used in the same way, design artifacts and the material world more generally serve as a common frame. If trouble becomes apparent, the artifacts can actually be used, as in the present case, to elaborate new meanings.

Material Grounding of Emerging Discourses

In the previous subsections, we illustrated how two pairs of students used artifacts (a) to think with and (b) as a peripheral resource to their conversations that helped them make sense of each other's utterances and gestures. Our account still leaves open the question of how thinking with artifacts and using artifacts as conversational support leads to learning. The following examples illustrate that thinking with and interacting over artifacts led to the material grounding of students' newly emerging discourses. These examples are consistent with existing research in linguistics (Johnson, 1987; Lakoff, 1987), artificial intelligence (Agre, 1995; Brooks, 1995), philosophy (Heidegger, 1977), and neurobiology (Varela, 1995) that finds that all cognition—including language—ultimately bottoms out in physical experience.

Earlier we described how Jeff and John developed their bridge deck in successive cycles of prototyping and testing. In the course of these cycles, Jeff and John first used triangular braces in response to what they had constructed as a weakness in their earlier designs (Roth, 1996c). These structural problems were visible to the pair when their bridge decks began to bend and collapse during the tests. As Figure 2.4a shows, this experience grounded Jeff's verbal and diagrammatic descriptions of braces. Recapitulating the design history of his own bridge (see the structural similarity of the bridge deck with that displayed in Figure 2.2), the "before" and "after" depictions contrast increased load capacity arising from the added braces. His sentence links braces with the support his additional straws provided and with the prevention of failure of later designs. In a similar way, Tim's explanation of the "X shape" was grounded in his experience of searching for increased structural strength of his bridge. He first talked about the need to strengthen the structure when the bridge gave in to a slight pressure he had applied onto the deck. As we saw earlier, he developed the X-shaped braces in the course of designing additions to the bridge that would enhance its structural strength. Afterward, he explained the X shape in part with a drawing that depicts his bridge in an iconic way. His text makes explicit reference to the "compression" to which the X shape resists. In the process, his understanding was

curriculum during her four-year teaching career and had later developed the unit as part of her work as a curriculum designer. She had presented more than 40 workshops on teaching this curriculum.

During the EfCS unit, children spent much of their time on practical design activities with a partner of their choice. Both teachers went from group to group to talk with the students at length about engineering issues, technical problems arising from the children's work, how to work in groups, and how to deal with frustrations. In each lesson, time was set aside to talk with the whole class about the children's work. During this time, one of the teachers pointed out features in children's joining or strengthening techniques that are also used by professional engineers or students presented what they had done to date, the problems they had encountered, and how they had solved their problems. These sessions were also occasions for children to compliment their peers, ask questions, or provide suggestions for improvement of structures of their peers. Over time, the children developed an engineering language game that the adults present in the room (teachers and researchers) and several visiting elementary teachers considered very sophisticated for their age level.

Presenting and Defending a Bridge Design

We use one whole-class conversation as an anchor to introduce the elements of a relatively successful curriculum in which Grade 4–5 children learn scientific discourse through engineering design activities. The following whole-class conversation was recorded during Week 11 of the EfCS unit. At this time, the children had developed considerable experience with the process of presenting and then answering questions or reacting to comments.

"Our bridge was made of straws and spaghetti . . ."

As usual, Tammy and Gitte asked each student group to present what they had designed and then opened the forum for comments, questions, and critique from other students. Here, John (Grade 4) and Jeff (Grade 5) presented their bridge to the whole class. Several other individuals also contributed significantly to the exchange, including Tom (Grade 4), Ron (Grade 5), and both teachers. Four other students contributed to a lesser degree, including Grade 4 students Tim, Dennis, Doug, Andy, and Stan.[2]

Jeff and John began the presentation by showing the bridge (for a sketch see Figure 3.1) and reading a prepared text:

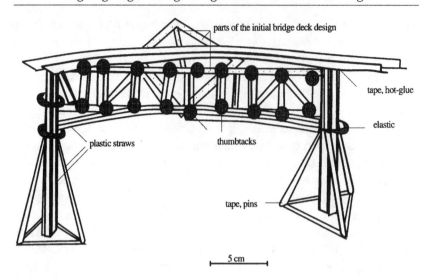

parts of the initial bridge deck design

tape, hot-glue

elastic

plastic straws

thumbtacks

tape, pins

5 cm

Figure 3.1 Jeff and John's bridge design made from drinking straws, spaghetti, adhesive tape, needles, and thumbtacks. The shaded straws indicate the very first design tested by the two boys. Other parts of the bridge were added in repeated cycles of designing and testing. This process of designing shares a lot of similarity with prototyping by professional designers.

01	Jeff:	Our bridge was made of straws and spaghetti to strengthen the straws.
02		Our bridge has the class record of 346 wooden blocks. And we only used
03		glue thumbtacks and tape for the joints. (7.0)
04	John:	Our difficulties were to strengthen it. We solved that problem by using
05		braces. Luckily we didn't get any catastrophic failure. It took us 8 days and
06		we hope you like our bridge.
07	Tammy:	Ahm::, does anybody have any questions about the bridge? (4.8) Why do
08		you think it held so many blocks? 346 is a fairly large number, I'd say. We
09		go to the questions first and see if that comes up along with it. Tim?
10	Tim:	I like the way they strengthened, the idea how to strengthen the straws, and
11		the way you put the straws in the middle to strengthen it, and the pins
12		attached to them. (6.1)
13	Dennis:	Were you happy when you started and got the straws?
14	Jeff:	Well, actually, we started off with spaghetti, and then we wanted to change
15		to straws. Then we said, "We have to"
16	John:	We couldn't figure out how to put the spaghetti together.
17	Jeff:	And so we said "Gitte, can we change?," and she said "Well, you can use
18		straws and then you have to use a handful of spaghetti too," about this
19		much.

After Jeff and John's presentation, Tammy invited others to ask questions (lines 07–09). Although she waited a considerable time, nobody volunteered a question, so she followed up with a second question concerning the "class record" of 346 wooden blocks of load that Jeff and John's bridge supported during a test. Tim then commented upon a strengthening technique the two presenters had included in their bridge design without explicating which specific aspects of the bridge he was talking about (lines 10–12). Dennis then posed a question about the materials. In their response, Jeff and John provided an account of how they had negotiated a different set of materials than they initially had received (lines 14–19).

In this first excerpt, four issues are worth highlighting: (a) the presentation is evidence of the considerable number of linguistic resources (engineering terms) that students developed during this unit; (b) Tammy (as did Gitte) often allowed a great deal of time for students to reflect on potential answers before actually asking one student to respond; (c) some of the students' comments and questions are illustrations of concerns different than those of canonical engineering design and science; and (d) students' accounts provide evidence of the great flexibility with which students negotiated the curriculum with teachers and designed their artifacts. We briefly elaborate on each of these four issues.

First, in their presentation, Jeff and John provided a list of the building materials (straws, spaghetti) and joining materials (glue, pins, tape) that they had used. John referred to the braces they had used (Figure 3.1). Using braces was the most central concept in this unit for the teachers. Another word in Jeff's description, catastrophic failure, had also been cherished by Gitte, and she had spent much time enrolling children in this language game (Roth, 1995d). Toward the end of the unit, as the glossary entries attested, a considerable number of children used various elements of this language game on a regular and unprompted basis. On the day of this presentation, however, there were still few students who used this term for their own purposes. After this show and tell, the teachers encouraged comments, critique, and questions.

Second, a large amount of research in the late 1970s and early 1980s about classroom questioning strategies indicated that teachers never really waited long enough for students to provide answers. In this research, the "wait time" teachers provided often was less than one second (e.g., Tobin, 1984). Contrary to this practice, Tammy frequently waited, as in the present case, for several students to frame answers, ready themselves to speak, and provide their answers. She also addressed a second type of wait time in that she permitted the entire question-and-answer session to extend for more than 10 minutes.

Third, there is a considerable contrast between the sample question Tammy proposed (line 07–08) and Tim and Dennis's contribution to the conversation. Tammy's question "Why do you think [the bridge] held so many blocks?" is about design. It challenged students to provide an explanation for the type of structure that could support a great load—the second strongest bridge, constructed by Tim and Stan, held 151 blocks. The concerns of children, however, were frequently different. Tim commented that he liked the strengthening without specifying which aspect of the bridge he referred to. Jeff and John had added spaghetti in the center of the straws and had various ways of reinforcing materials and structure that brought about the high load capacity. However, these aspects were not made explicit in Tim's comment. Furthermore, because he sat in the audience and could not point to specific parts of the bridge, he could not point to the parts of the bridge he described. (We show in the next chapter how such distances between speaker and thing talked about make communication difficult.) Dennis's comment was even further removed from the technical question about strength Tammy had asked. Dennis' question, like many questions and comments children asked, especially in the beginning, characteristically dealt with issues that were not the concerns of canonical engineering design and science. Such comments and questions related to the adornments of the artifacts, including small cars, color, additional figures, and flags, or comments related to the stories that frequently accompanied the artifact.

This initial part of the conversation therefore already showed the tension that existed even in this classroom between cultural production and cultural reproduction. On the one hand, both teachers wanted children to take ownership of their designs and develop their understandings around issues of their concern. On the other hand, the canonical concerns of engineering design and science—including material strength, structural strength, stability—were not initially the concerns of the children. Introducing canonical concerns is therefore an aspect of a classroom environment to which the teachers have to attend lest science not be addressed in an explicit form. Here too, one could think that a teacher concerned with technical issues might have asked Tim to elaborate on his comment and make explicit what he described as an aspect of the bridge.[3] His elaboration could have then been a starting point for a discussion of the question that Tammy had asked earlier.

Fourth, Jeff and John's answer to Dennis's question provided an account of how they dealt with a problem. Here, they "couldn't figure out" how to produce a bridge. In their assessment, they would not have had the same problem with straws, so they negotiated with Gitte to use a different set of materials. This part of the conversation highlights two aspects of the classroom environment. First, teachers held students accountable not only for the structures they actually built, how they used strengthened and stabilized structuresbut also for the process of designing, problem frames, and solutions. Frequently, teachers explicitly asked students "What was your problem and how did you solve it?" Later, and following the example of the teachers, students asked the same and similar questions. Because they often knew about problems their peers had encountered, their questions were elliptic, taking the problem for granted. Dennis also had received spaghetti as material, but he had not been successful in negotiating different materials. His question revealed his own unhappiness and experience of frustration with the spaghetti. Jeff and John's account provided evidence of the flexible nature of the enacted curriculum. Students framed and reframed their problems, thereby changing the design tasks initially outlined by the teachers. This was possible because there appeared to be an implicit agreement that if students argued their case convincingly, they could get additional materials, change materials, or change the nature of the task. ("If you want more [materials] you have to give us a really good reason")

"It would have held a little bit less . . ."

Tom began this next episode by voicing a subtle critique of the fact that Jeff and John had tested their bridge upside down, that is, with the piers pointing upward. He had been one of the spectators during Jeff and John's last testing cycle and had seen that the bridge rested upside down during this test. As evidenced in a later episode, Jeff had decided to test the bridge in this way because the piers had shown signs of weakness in a previous test. This critique became the starting point for many of the subsequent exchanges during which other students repeatedly questioned the legitimacy of testing the bridge in a particular way without making that practice explicit.

20	Tom:	Well, I think that it would have held a little bit less, well, if it had been the
21		right side up. (1.4)
22	Tammy:	Oh, interesting, so it had more when it was upside down?
23	Jeff:	⌈Yeah we ⌉ know ⌈that. ⌉
24	Tom:	⌊Yeah, it did ⌋ Like, it ⌊would⌋ have been better if your bridge hadn't been
25		like between the desks, it would have held a lot more, I mean
26	Jeff:	It was between two desks.
27	Tom:	No, maybe without legs maybe it would'a held more.

28	Jeff:	Well, we said, the legs were too flimsy so we tested it without.
29	Tammy:	Excellent thinking, Tom.
30	Tom:	I thought at first it was cheating putting it upside down, but then I realized it
31		is sort of like, like the same as mine and Andy's, because it was like
32		between two desks.

Tom's critique shows many features of a competent and sophisticated engineering discourse. First, Tom suggested that the bridge would have held less in the upright configuration (lines 20–21). He then attempted to elaborate the issue with his attempt to analyze and redesign the bridge and test. At first, it was not clear in which direction his suggestions were going (lines 24–26), but then he clearly stated that the bridge would have carried an even higher load in the upright configuration without the piers (line 27). Jeff implicitly agreed with this proposition and revealed that the test in the upside-down position was to test the bridge deck ("it") rather than the piers (line 28). Finally, Tom related Jeff and John's design of the bridge deck to his own bridge and hinted that it had a very similar symmetry: his deck was symmetrical in upside-down and upright positions (Figure 3.2).

A comparison of Figures 3.1 and 3.2 shows the similarities between the two bridges that Tom described. A double layer of materials was connected by systems of spacers and braces. But while the deck structure was symmetric, Jeff's bridge also had piers. When tested between two desks in the upside-down position, Jeff and John's bridge deck rested in the same way as Tom's, directly on the desk. Jeff's rejoinder (line 28) made clear that testing the deck rather than the piers had been his intent and therefore was the rationale for testing the bridge in the upside-down position.

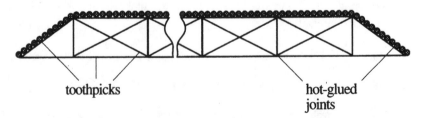

Figure 3.2 Tom and Andy's bridge design made from toothpicks joined by using a glue gun. During his critique of Jeff's design (Figure 3.1), Tom recognized that there were structural similarities between the two bridge decks.

Although Tammy uttered a closing, "Excellent thinking, Tom" he continued to elaborate his reflection on the historical development of his understanding, "I thought first . . . but then I realized . . ." (lines 30–32). His understanding arose from the tension of having a "real" bridge on piers and a bridge where the deck rested directly on the ground. He had, in a manner of speaking, "abstracted" the design of the bridge deck from the entire artifact. Here, it no longer mattered whether Jeff's bridge corresponded to real bridges resting on piers what was important was that Jeff had developed a bridge deck that showed properties similar to his own bridge. Tom's comments reveal the degree to which engineering principles had become an important aspect of many students' designs. Tom not only began a critique but also perceived a similarity between the two bridges at a higher level that transcended the surface-level differences.

Tom's comment was characteristic for this classroom, just as Jeff's earlier account of a problem and its resolution was: in this class, teachers encouraged children to account for learning whether it occurred because they had wrestled with a breakdown in their design or because they had been inspired by watching others. Tammy and Gitte's curriculum strove not only to develop an understanding for canonical engineering and science but also to develop an understanding of the learning process itself. As Faulkner (1994) pointed out, knowledge about knowledge is an important resource in the work of professional engineering design. Here, in the course of a 13-week unit, the children developed a great deal of discursive competence to account for the processes of designing, framing problems, finding solutions, and negotiating courses of action.

Tammy immediately followed Tom's comments with praise, "Excellent thinking" (line 29) and "Good thinking, I really like the way you changed your thinking on that one." Tammy always used such comments to attempt to defuse what she perceived as potentially problematic tensions arising from critical comments. She wanted to foster a frictionless and positive climate in which students—particularly girls—could safely develop their understandings. In this situation, she read Jeff's responses as somewhat aggressive. Here praise functioned as support for Tom and the critique he had contributed.

"Did you write anything about that it held that many, but upside down?"

After Tom ended his comments, Andy asked one of those questions that clearly drew upon students' interest rather than on the principles of canonical science: "Is it for people or for cars?" Subsequently, first Ron, then Stan questioned Jeff about the symmetry of the deck design and its relationship to the carrying capacity.

33 Ron: Did you write anything in the description thing about (0.8)
34   about that it held that many, but (.) upside down?
35 Jeff: No, we didn't write down "upside down."
36 Tammy: It would be an interesting thing to add. (1.4) Doug?
37 Doug: Is this a people bridge?
38 Jeff: We don't know. We were just concerned about the bridge
39   (2.5)
40   To us, it doesn't really matter if it is for people or cars.
41 John: Yeah, ⌈before ⌉
42 Tammy: ⌊It's the⌋ idea of a bridge, ⌈right? ⌉
43 Jeff: ⌊Yeah ⌋
44 John: Before we put the braces on, we were
45   gonna make people through there and cars go up on top, but it wouldn't be
46   strong enough, so we put the braces=
47 Jeff: ='Cause, 'cause like that it would be like an elevator to bring ⌈ people up ⌉
48 Tammy: ⌊ Oh, cool ⌋
49 Jeff: But now we say, well at least it's a bridge and we don't care what bridge it
50   is. (3.2). Stan?
51 Stan: When you will display it, are you going to put it upside down or the way
52   you got the 347 blocks or you're gonna put it? (.) The=
53 Jeff: =In the case, we are actually going to put ⌈ it like this (1.2)
54   ⌊ [Holds bridge upright]
55   I think (.) that would make it look better. (1.4) 'Cause if we have it like this
56   ⌈and you're just passing by, you probably think it is like a flight
57   ⌊Holds bridge upside down, as in Figure 2.3a]
58   control or something.

In this episode, both Ron (lines 33–34) and Stan (lines 51–52) expressed concern about the discrepancy between claims about the bridge's strength when it was tested upside down and their decision to display it right side up during an exhibit in the local science museum. Jeff's test in which the bridge was placed upside down had emerged as a contingent achievement during the series of tests he and John conducted. As they increased the load, the tests showed that the piers were the weakest part. The two, less concerned about the piers than about the bridge deck, decided to turn the bridge upside down. As the deck was initially designed symmetrically, this procedure appeared feasible. The symmetry was broken in the later stages of the development when Jeff and John added bent beams to the structure.

In response to the question about his bridge's purpose, Jeff suggested that he was concerned about the bridge design (line 38) rather than its ultimate purpose, whether it was for people or cars (line 40). John immediately reiterated this concern by accounting for the addition of braces in response to the earlier weakness they had noticed (lines 44–46). In these responses one can recognize that the two boys had gone beyond surface-level features and had begun to design based on structural features. In the traditional cognitive science literature, this would have been an instance of "abstraction" because Jeff and John were concerned with the structural properties of their bridge rather than with a surface-level likeness with "real" bridges. This seeming abstraction arose from the deep familiarity Jeff and John had with their bridge because it arose from the repeated cycles of testing and redesigning. Their concerns were with attaining a class record; these concerns constituted the framing context for the activities of the two boys.

Stan returned to this issue (lines 51–52). He wanted to know whether Jeff would exhibit the bridge upside down or right side up when it was put on public display in the science museum. Although Jeff acknowledged that the bridge could be displayed either way, he suggested that in the upside-down position it left too much freedom for the interpretation of any onlooker—here, the shape of the bridge could be interpreted as the handle of an airplane control stick. Stan's concern, like Ron's, was with the discrepancy between the claim to have designed a bridge that could support a load of 347 blocks and the decision to display (and describe) it without reference to the differences used in the testing situation. Whereas Jeff and John were concerned with the structural properties, Stan and Ron's critique appeared to be concerned with realistic representation.

Doug's question (line 37) appeared to be a sideline in the questioning sequence by several students about the legitimacy of the testing procedure. His concern was with the ultimate use of the bridge, a concern that, for many children, became an important way of contextualizing their structures. Although the purposes of a design are important constraints in the development of design artifacts, Doug's question did not bring out the relationship between the structural differences that would frame the emerging design. Rather, his question appeared to be singularly concerned with surface-level appearances and building contexts. Other students, especially girls, were much more interested in building story contexts and elaborating these contexts by adding little figures, cars, and other adornments than in the structural aspects that were Jeff and John's concerns.

The issues in this episode have an important dimension at a different level. Jeff and John's canonical concerns with the structural properties and repeated cycles of testing make them "more" scientific than others who were concerned with surface-level features. Such differences are, in traditional science teaching, often emphasized and lead to the early separation of "science nerds" and those who lose interest in science. At the same time, if teachers are interested in allowing canonical science to emerge from design activities, they must foster the kinds of exchanges in which Ron, Stan, Jeff, and John were engaged.

Tammy's utterances (lines 36, 42, and 48) always came during what may have been interpreted by some participants as embarrassing or tense situations; their effect was to diffuse any problematic interpersonal situations. The important questions, however, were posed by students themselves (lines 33, 37, and 51). In terms of content, questions and answers addressed issues related to testing procedures, the design's purposes, and user specifications.

"Why do you think it's more flimsy with both legs on it?"

As we saw, students' questions did not always encompass scientific and engineering concerns. Although such concerns became an increasingly important feature of their questions and comments as the unit went along, teachers still needed to participate in the conversations so that canonical science and engineering design could emerge. Gitte and Tammy's attempt to take up one concern—the "flimsiness" of Jeff and John's bridge—characterizes this episode. It was typical of Gitte's questioning that it began with issues of interest to the children. By means of what we called "contingent queries" (Roth, 1996d), she used students' accounts, descriptions, and responses as starting points to ask a series of questions that focused on knowledge from all the domains that characterize professional engineering (Faulkner, 1994; Roth, 1996d). In this episode, Gitte and Tammy introduced canonical concerns to the classroom community by repeatedly asking students questions about how "real" engineers would deal with the problem at hand.

59	Gitte:	I was wondering why you think it's more flimsy with both legs on it?
60	Jeff:	'Cause ⌈ the
61	John:	⌊ It's just like to bring it up
62	Jeff:	To bring it up and it also got gravity on it, ⌈ plus these (1.9)
63		⌊ [Twists lower of pier]
64	John:	These are ⌈ not very strong
65		⌊ [Points to piers]
66	Gitte:	And how does that compare to a real bridge that would have those kind of
67		supports? What is different between your bridge there and, say, a bridge
68		you drive over?

69	Jeff:	(1.7) This bridge? (.) Most likely the bridge that I drive over doesn't have
70		⌈these (1.0)
71		⌊Grabs one pier with right hand]
72	Tammy:	But it has to be held up by something, it does have those. (1.0)
73	Jeff:	⌈Yeah
74	Gitte:	⌊Say, say there is a bridge that has those.
75	Jeff:	But see, ⌈it is too flimsy and will fall over like this. (3.1)
76		⌊[Rocks bridge sideways]
77	Tammy:	So in the real world, what would you do about that? (0.8)
78		If you ⌈were a real engineer? (.) You couldn't
79	Jeff:	⌊Put ⌈stays on.
80	John:	⌊we could tie it down, ⌈because it is.
81		⌊[Gestures toward stays from top of one
82		pier to ground]
83	Jeff:	Like a suspension.
84	John:	We could tie ⌈it there.
85		⌊[Gestures toward stays from the top of pier to the ground]
86	Tammy:	So that would be one way to ⌈do it.
87	Jeff:	⌊Yeah.
88	Tammy:	Because as an engineer you could not turn your bridge upside down, could
89		you?
90	John:	No. (1.0)
91	Tammy:	But if I'm just interested, in the real world, what would you do? (0.7)
92	Gitte:	Tom ⌈ has it.
93	John:	⌊ We would.
94	Jeff:	We would stick it down.
95	John:	Put stays into the ground and then take.
96	Jeff:	Yeah, or also, we would sort of make, put t ⌈hese (.) ahm, into like.
97		⌊[Points to the pier]
98	John:	Into a hole.
99	Jeff:	Into a hole=
100	Gitte:	=Yes, ⌈OK, that's great.
101	Jeff:	⌊Into a hole, and cover it up.
102	John:	Make strings down here
103	Jeff:	And we'd also make strings.
104	Gitte:	So what you are saying is that in a real bridge there is some kind of (.)
105		foundation ⌈(.) that is anchored or something, and you are not able to do
106	Jeff:	⌊Yeah
107	Gitte:	That because your bridge . . .
108	Jeff:	is free-standing.
109	Gitte:	is free-standing.

In this episode, both teachers repeatedly questioned John and Jeff. The effect of this questioning sequence (lines 59, 66–68, 72, 74, 77–78, 86, 88-89, 91, 92, 100, 104–105) was that the two boys were encouraged to describe a design option that would take care of the noted "flimsiness." As we saw (line 28), Jeff had described his bridge piers as "flimsy." Gitte asked a question that was designed to make the two presenters elaborate on the problems with the piers (line 59). She made an important move that brought canonical science into the discussion, for Jeff and John were asked to elaborate (and explain) an earlier utterance. In this way, they reintroduced to the conversation an issue that Jeff had mentioned earlier but that seemed to get lost among other concerns. As a by-product of this question sequence, new elements of a canonical language game were introduced and, more generally, students were given opportunities to use their current language game. Here, Jeff used the words gravity, stays,[4] and suspension. He had used the first two words during earlier lessons; his increasing familiarity with these terms permitted him to use them in canonical ways. In fact, it was Jeff who had proposed "stay," a word that even the adults in the room did not know. That is, Jeff and his peers appropriated existing language games beginning with observation sentences that constitute "the entering wedge in the learning of language" (Quine, 1992, p. 5). Jeff and John suggested that they could use stays to hold up the bridge or use the piers to attach cables in the way they are used in suspension bridges (lines 79–85, 95, 102–103). But he also described a stay as a form of "suspension" which is an inappropriate use.

Teachers as well as students introduced new words whenever the context appeared appropriate. In this episode, Jeff and John described a situation in which the piers would be stabilized by building them partly underground (lines 98–99). Gitte then supplied two words from canonical engineering that described the situation: foundation and anchor. As readers will see below, all these elements of a canonical engineering language became an active part of children's language game. The multitude of opportunities for appropriating and developing a language game and participating in conversations allowed students to make the language game their own. For a word is appropriated only when "the speaker populates it with his own intention, his own accent, when he appropriates the word, adapting it to his own semantic and expressive intention" (Bakhtin, 1981, p. 293). As we will see below, Jeff and Tom each took an opportunity in the next episode to use "foundation" for their intentions.

An important issue that got lost in the conversation was that Jeff had used the term "flimsy" in different contexts and therefore with different meanings. At first, "flimsy" was used as part of the description of the piers that "are not strong" (line 64). John expressed what Jeff's twisting of one of the piers seemed to indicate (line 63). Here, "flimsy" was associated with a structural weakness of the piers. Later (lines 75–76), Jeff used the same term while rocking the bridge sideways. There, "flimsy" was read as indicating a problem with the stability of the entire structure. This reading was confirmed when Jeff and John elaborated their solution to the problem: burying the bottom of the piers, that is, building a foundation. Teachers should be attentive to such differences in word use, because they introduce problems in communication. The use of a word in different ways—which boils down to the word having different meanings (Wittgenstein, 1994/1958)—gives rise to considerable misunderstandings and impediments to learning (Roth, 1996e). However, such differences in meaning are more easily uncovered in analysis that treats texts as stable and atemporal artifacts than in the real-time experience of an ongoing conversation.[5] The demands of following conversations in real time frequently leave uncovered alternative meanings and understandings that participants in the conversation do not recognize. It is only when conversational troubles become evident that participants engage in conversational repair until all partners can take mutual understanding for granted (Roth, 1995a).

This episode can be understood both as a critique on the teachers' parts and as an effort to scaffold students' development of competencies in arguing for and defending their design. By repeatedly questioning how engineers would deal with the problem, teachers allowed students to build a language game and to learn to argue in ways that characterize professional design (Coyne, 1995). Furthermore, by relating children's work to the "real world" and to professional engineering, teachers enabled children to become familiar with canonical concerns such as material and financial constraints, stability, and structural strength. But the teachers' comments can also be read as setting up a contrast between children's work and what happens in the "real world." In this case, children might experience their work as fake rather than authentic in the way the curriculum outlines it. Thus, here too, there exists a tension between relating to children what engineers do and devaluing their activities as non-authentic. One of the teachers with whom we had worked in the past resolved this tension by providing a classroom environment in which students experienced their work as being of the same type as that of professional science (Roth & Bowen, 1995). The teacher insisted upon telling students that they did what professional scientists do. During our interviews, students suggested that scientists looked at more variables and used bigger equipment, but that the nature of the investigations was very similar. In this situation, the teacher successfully dealt with a tension that was not sufficiently dealt with by Tammy and Gitte.

**". . . so it brings the weight down on the ends and then
it is easier for a force to go across here."**

In the next part of the conversation, Jeff illustrated further the depth of
his competencies in canonical science discourse. His descriptions and
gestures showed that he could analyze and describe the forces that acted
in the bridge structure. This episode presents further evidence of the
opportunities engineering design activities (and the accompanying conversations) provide to learn canonical science. (Figures 3.3a–d indicate
the positions of Jeff's hands and gestures during the presentation.)

```
110  Jeff:    Yeah, but you would, ahm, if it was an engineer, we, this also, this, we
111           couldn't have done it like that because this ⌈brings also the weight down on
112                                                        ⌊[Holds bridge, Figure 3.3a]
113           the ends, it brings the ⌈weight down on the ends, so it brings the weight
114                                    ⌊[Pushes down both ends, Figure 3.3b]
115           down on the ends and then it is easier for ⌈a force to go across here
116                                                       ⌊[Gestures, Figure 3.3c, d]
117  Tammy:  Tom⌈has a point. (.) I'm sorry.
118  Jeff:      ⌊as the weight goes here and the ⌈tension brings it down (0.9) so it
119           almost evens it out.                ⌊[Pushes as in Fig. 3.3b]
120  Gitte:  Yes, good, thanks Jeff. (2.0)
121  Tom:    Well, I was going to say as we found out, the foundation makes it stronger
122           but we weren't allowed to have a foundation.
123  Jeff:   I know.
124  Tom:    And we can't have a bridge attached to the table.
125  Jeff:   Yeah, but she asked us "What would you do as engineers?," ahm, and we
126           said "build a foundation."
```

Jeff provided a longer explanation of what he would do if he was a
"real" engineer. Rather than viewing his artifact as an image of something real, he constructed the artifact and activities that led to it as an
exploration of design principles.[6] Thus, it was not important whether or
not "real" bridges could be turned upside down. Holding the bridge in the
critiqued "upside-down" configuration and then gesturing, he elaborated
on the forces that acted in the structure.

What he had done was design a possible configuration and then construct an even stronger configuration by turning his artifact upside down.
From this perspective, if he had to construct a "real" bridge, all he would
have to do was use the design principles that made his current bridge in
its "upside-down" configuration as strong as it was. Jeff suggested he use
the design as he proposed it. The piers weighed down the ends of the
deck (Figure 3.3b), and additional suspension wires could be used to hold

up the bridge deck (increasing its carrying capacity). He also showed how the "piers" created tension in the straws. His gesture (Figure 3.3c, d) represented this tension as a dynamic entity. When he presented, there was a slight bend in the deck such that the pressure on the piers increased tension in the straws. Jeff's discursive competence relating to the forces acting within his structure was quite sophisticated; this will be further underscored in our discussion relating to his and other students' glossary entries. Jeff did not simply regurgitate teacher or textbook definitions; Tammy could not help him with the forces because she was not competently talking about them herself and they had no textbook to do further reading. Jeff had appropriated this discourse about forces, tension, and compression (possibly in part from an earlier visit with his parents to the

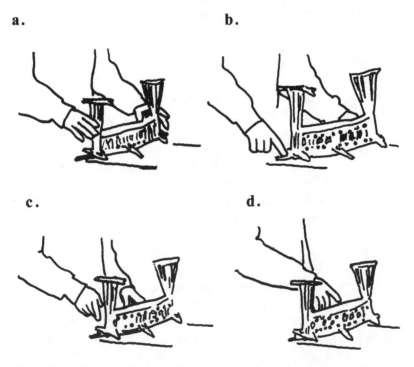

Figure 3.3 Jeff uses the bridge artifact extensively during the presentation to point to particular pieces, illustrate with gesture the direction of forces, and hold it in ways that elaborated his talk. a. Jeff holds the bridge in the position he tested it. b. Jeff shows how in the real world, the weight of the pillars would level the deck and increase the tension in the upper part of the deck. c. and d. Jeff uses gestures to demonstrate the direction and action of the tension.

bridge exhibit at the science museum) and used it here for his own purposes. Other students in this class learned from him.[7]

As in the previous episode, this was a situation in which students talked about two different issues. Here, Jeff had elaborated on the forces acting in the structure. He therefore addressed "flimsiness" in the sense of structural strength (lines 110–116, 118–119). Tom's comments (line 121–122, 124) also underscored this ambiguity in meaning. Foundations deal with stability that comes from anchoring the structure to the table (line 124), but Tom appeared to suggest that they also increased structural strength (line 121–122). As in the previous episode, neither students nor teachers pointed out the two different issues that were addressed in this part of the conversation.

Following the conversation and Jeff's gestures, we cannot but note the integration of hand gestures and discourse. Of course, on the part of the listeners, this requires watching as well as listening. Thinking is handwork (craft) that requires the integration of hands, eyes, and mind, an issue that we will elaborate more in Chapter 4. Representing thinking and discourse therefore necessitates not only a re-production of utterances but also that of pointing and gesturing. Manual activities, such as thinking and interacting with others, are in fundamental ways grounded in our experience of the material world. Jeff's swiping movement along a section of the bridge (Figure 3.3c, d) enacted the forces he used as analytical resources for describing his bridge and its performance. His earlier comment about interpreting the bridge model as the handlebar of an airplane control stick is elaborated and makes sense only with his associated gesture (Figure 3.3a). His gestures associated with the explanation of how the bridge could be stabilized by means of stays or strings (lines 81, 82, 96, 103, 104) re-enacted the lines the two boys had used to stabilize their tower in an earlier project.

Although Gitte and Tammy frequently waited until students had finished speaking, there were always situations in which they took their speaking turns too quickly and thereby interfered with, or took away, students' speaking turns. In this episode, Tammy clearly began to speak before Jeff considered his turn to be over (line 117). In an earlier episode, she clearly began to speak while John was explaining something (line 42); Gitte also sometimes began to comment before students had completed their turns (line 74, 101). In this situation, the two boys were not intimidated and frequently continued their turn despite the teacher's premature turn-taking. Such "boldness" is most frequently not the case, which allows teachers control over the discourse situation (Roth, 1993).

"If you took the legs . . . do you think it would hold the same as upside down?"

In this episode, Ron returned to the question of the bridge piers ("legs") and their relation to the strength of the bridge. Again, the effect of his interrogation was that it questioned Jeff's claims about the strength and pointed to details about the structure that would result in different strengths if the bridge design was tested right side up or upside down. Issues central to the portion of bridge design produce strength are the topic in this student-centered exchange. This episode is another example of the emergence of canonical science from engineering design activities.

Not satisfied with the previous explanations, Ron reiterated the questions and critique regarding the strength of the design, but he focused on the symmetry of the bridge deck (line 126–128, 131, 140).[8]

```
126   Ron:   I got a question. If you took the legs off (.) if you cut them off around the
127          bottom of the bridge, do you think it would hold the same as upside
128          down?
129   Jeff:  Yeah.
130          (1.6)
131   Ron:   Is it built the same?=
132   Jeff:  =Well actually, if you cut the legs off, you might, you might wanna try it
133          putting it down like ⌈this (.) without the legs. See how strong it would be.
134                            ⌊[Holds bridge upright, the deck resting on his hands]
135
136          (1.4)
137          ⌈You might try that.
138   John:  ⌊It would still be strong, sorry.
139   Jeff:  But we don't think it would hold any more, 'cause (1.4) . . .
140   Ron:   Is the bottom and the top built the same?
141   Jeff:  The bottom and the top, yes. 'Cause ⌈originally this was it,
142                                          ⌊[Points to center of bridge deck]
143          and then we ⌈built this under the bottom, to make it stronger.
144                     ⌊[Points to beams below deck]
145   John:  Initially we ⌈put in this.
146                       ⌊[Points to braces]
```

Ron read Jeff's response to the initial question (line 129) as another claim so that the latter followed up with another question. Here, Ron made a connection between "holding the same" (line 127) and being built the same (lines 131, 140). Jeff then provided the description of a possible test in which the bridge would have held the same in both positions. That is, one can hear his statements, "You might wanna try it" and "See how strong it would be" as acknowledgments that he did not actually conduct the test that would support his earlier claim. John chimed in also asserting that the bridge would be as strong as it was in the orientation in which they tested it (line 138). Jeff added that it would not hold more (line 139). Ron was not satisfied with these responses and queried whether the top and the bottom parts of the bridge deck were actually the same (line 140). Although the bridge did not appear to be symmetrical, which may have been at the source of Ron's questioning, Jeff maintained his claim that the bridge deck was designed symmetrically (line 141). He continued to explain that they added some straws below the deck, and John pointed out again the braces that they had included after the bridge collapsed during the first test.

Implicit in Ron's questioning was the notion of equal carrying capacity if the deck was symmetrical, for he followed the first question ("Would it hold the same?") with "Is it built the same?" Jeff responded that he did not think that there would be differences if the bridge deck alone could be tested right side up and upside down. Ron was not satisfied and continued to question the claims about symmetry. In response, Jeff pointed to the top of his double deck (Figure 3.1) and explained that they had begun with this part but that they added the bottom part to increase the carrying capacity of their bridge.

****

This conversation during Week 11 of the unit attests to the increasing complexity of the presentations. At issue here were basic principles of engineering design, the strength of a structure, and symmetry. Stan, Ron, and Tom questioned the legitimacy of testing the bridge in an upside-down orientation and presenting it right side up, which can be heard as a pretense that the class record was achieved in this orientation. In the process, Ron questioned the symmetry of the design that provided Jeff and John with opportunities to point out how they achieved structural strength by means of reinforcements and braces. The conversation was authentic because it was driven by the goals of students. Here, they addressed issues that really interested and concerned them. These conversations toward the end of the unit allowed canonical engineering and science to emerge. The episodes showed how Jeff explained the strength in terms of the direction that stresses and strains acted in his bridge. Finally, and most importantly, large parts of the conversation no longer needed teachers' questions to be sustained over considerable time.

Here, we are able to see the emergence of a community whose members engaged in recurrent conversations and the ways in which they produced, re-produced, and circulated an ever-evolving engineering discourse. Although there existed attempts on the part of the teachers to push certain issues despite students' reluctance, the learning conditions they fostered, by and large, facilitated the emergence of this community of engineering practice. This conversation clearly shows the students' competence in talking about the bridge designs they had developed during the three weeks prior to this conversation. Students' accounts, such as Jeff's explanation for the nature of his bridge deck, also show that they had learned about design through designing, an assessment that agrees with our observation of their design practice. Here, for example, Jeff and John had started the bridge design with little prior experience. With the materials given (straws, spaghetti, glue, tape, and pins) and the goal of making a bridge with high carrying capacity, they designed a very strong bridge deck (Figure 3.1).

Analysis of Children's Glossaries

Conversations such as the one analyzed provided us with a good deal of evidence that the children were using engineering design language games. We also recorded conversations during the actual design activities. There the talk was frequently more focused on getting details of the design done; issues related to design and science were spread over long periods of time because students spent much time with the practical aspects of designing. However, another form of evidence illustrated the children's competence related to engineering design. As pointed out earlier, Tammy and Gitte asked the children to construct glossaries with those engineering terms and techniques that they found useful during design and design conversations. These glossaries provided us with additional evidence for the deep understandings of engineering design and science that the children in this class developed in the course of the unit.

We used children's glossaries created between Week 11 to 13 of the unit to study children's language game in specific contexts. Teachers had asked the children to explain those engineering terms that they deemed relevant to their work in designing structures; they further suggested that the children use both words and sketches in their explanations. Children demonstrated quite complex descriptions that provided insights into their sense-making. There were a total of 21 different terms mentioned between 2 and 25 times:

catastrophic failure (25)	compression (22)	tension (21)
brace (18)	triangle (17)	pier (14)
foundation (12)	suspension (11)	X shape (11)
platform (10)	base (12)	bundle (10)
overlapping (9)	stay (7)	deadman (7)
cofferdam (5)	strengthening (5)	post (4)
anchor (3)	pillar (3)	footing (2)

The children's definitions are part of the evidence that in this class students developed their own ways of understanding and using engineering language rather than learning by means of all-too-often-standard definitions that are merely regurgitated (Poole, 1994). Examples from the children's glossaries (mostly from students who participated in the above conversation) and terms related to the conversation—can be found in Figures 3.4 to 3.6.

Three items from Jeff and John's glossaries indicate their understanding of "brace" and "compression," which by and large developed out of their activities during the bridge project. As readers saw earlier, Jeff's definition of brace included two frames in which he represented a bridge designed with and without braces (Figure 3.4a). At the beginning of the bridge project, Jeff and John (as were many of their peers) were not yet competent in the use of braces to produce structural strength despite Tammy and Gitte taught a special lesson on the topic and despite the fact that they scaffolded on this issue during the tower project. However, Jeff and John were among those students who began to use braces without teacher assistance as a contingent response to a structural weakness in their design (Roth, 1995d). Thus, their initial bridge design had only a simple deck (shaded part in Figure 3.1) and a rhombic structure that did not contribute to structural strength. In response to the bending of the bridge deck during the load test, Jeff and John began to redesign the deck to include a second deck connected by spacers and, again in response to testing, an increasing number of braces. The bent section in the center of the bridge deck he drew in frame 1 (Figure 3.4a) is just what Jeff had seen and experienced during the initial phases of designing his bridge. At the

Figure 3.4 Entries from Jeff and John's glossaries related to their experiences with the bridge design. a. For Jeff, bracing is a technique that, as his experience showed, "supports structures from failing." b. John's definition of brace includes an iconic reference to the bridge he designed. c. Jeff illustrates a dynamic understanding of the forces in an arch.

a.

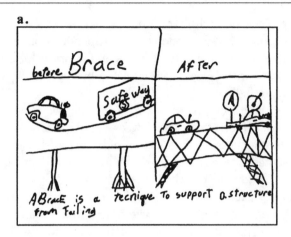

before **Brace**   AfTer

SafeWay

A BrucE is a tecnique To support a structure
from Failing

b.

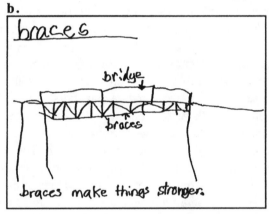

braces

bridge

braces

braces make things stronger.

c.

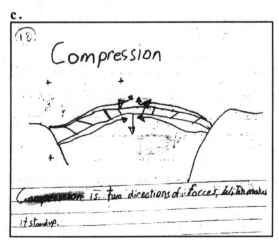

Compression

Compression is two directions of forces, which makes
it standup.

end of the project, he and his partner had set the class record with a bridge that supported 346 wooden blocks suspended from the center of the bridge deck. John's glossary entry regarding braces also features a stylized image of their bridge, including the braces that "make things stronger" (Figure 3.4b).

There is an interesting difference between the two glossary entries. John's verbal definition states what braces do. His is an object-centered perspective that focuses on the function of braces in structures. In contrast, Jeff's sentence takes a designer's perspective by defining braces as a technique—a resource—on which designers draw to "support a structure from failing." It is also interesting to note that both boys refer to structures that can be strengthened with braces rather than merely referring to bridges. This may indicate that Jeff and John use "brace" as a design resource that is no longer tied to the context of bridge design alone but can be applied in different contexts, that is, structures, more generally.

Jeff's definition of compression (Figure 3.4c) constitutes a complex rendering of the nature of this kind of force. The arrows along the structure render the direction of the forces along the structure. In the very center, there are two little arrows bent upward that, as his text states, "makes it stand up." Here, the upward arrow and the typological "stand up" are congruent, canonical descriptions of the arch. The observational description (arch) and the theoretical description (forces) are mapped onto the same drawing surface, much as one would find in physics or engineering texts. The arrows have an interesting parallel to Jeff's gesture when he explained tension during his presentation. The sweeping movement of his hand over the bridge structure is here captured in the sweeping arrow along the arch. Thus, we can see the grounding Jeff and John's engineering design language game—which includes the drawings—had in their experience of designing. Some of this experience is grounded in the physical manipulations and responses—or "talk-back" (Schön, 1987)—students experience from the materials.

Figure 3.5 provides further illustrations from the glossaries of students who participated in the critique of John and Jeff's design. In both instances, issues that were present during the whole-class conversation showed up again in students' definitions of terms. Tom's definition of piers is closely related to the piers that were at the center of the discussion following his critique. Readers will recall that Tom framed the difference between John and Jeff's design and his own in terms of the piers which, in Jeff's words, "bring [the deck] up" (line 62). When Jeff suggested that

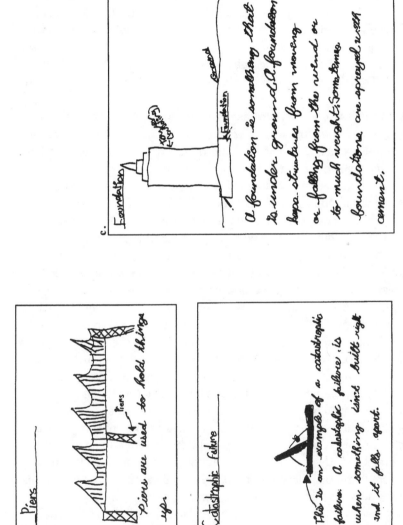

Figure 3.5 Glossary entries by other students who participate in the whole-class conversation. Tom's definitions of piers a. and catastrophic failure b. and Ron's entry under foundation c. contain elements apparent during the whole-class discussion.

a real bridge may not have piers as he designed them—in which case it would be a bridge deck like the one designed by Tom—Tammy objected, "but [the deck] has to be held up by something" (line 72). In both instances, Jeff and Tammy's language games refer to piers (or the synonymous "legs") as something that hold it up. This language game appears again in Tom's use, "Piers are used to hold things up." In this, his definition includes a bridge that contrasts with his own design but resembles the design he critiqued during the discussion. The structure of the sentence builds on the pragmatic way engineers use things (sharing similarity with Jeff's definition of braces). Piers are resources to get something done.

Tom's glossary entry for catastrophic failure (Figure 3.5b) includes alternative meanings that we already encountered in Jeff's use of "flimsy." Readers will recall that Jeff used the notion of flimsy to describe both structural weakness and the instability of a structure. Tom's drawing depicts a structure that had toppled over in the way Jeff described and gestured during the conversation (lines 75–76). The first sentence, which is declarative, simply refers to the toppled structure as an example of catastrophic failure. The second sentence suggests that catastrophic failure means that a structure "falls apart"; it therefore is similar to Jeff's definition of "flimsy" as structural weakness. In its structure, the sentence defines the term as the consequence of lack of correct action. Tom's sentence is based on the negative form of Jeff's brace definition which was of the type "This is what happens if you use a technique."

Ron's definition of "foundation" (Figure 3.5c) is related to the same part of the conversation as the part where Tom described his notions of piers and catastrophic failure. During the conversation, Tammy and Gitte asked a series of questions designed to elicit a solution to the problem of "flimsiness" (lines 59–109). In the course of this sequence, John and Jeff suggested that the toppling of a structure could be prevented if they would "stick [the piers] down," "put [the piers] into a hole," and "put stays into the ground." Gitte then described this situation as a "foundation" that "anchored" the piers (lines 104–105). Ron's definition picks up on this. First, he declares that a foundation is "underground," which is also shown in his drawing where "foundation" is literally under "ground." Second, the foundation "keeps structures from moving or falling from wind" and therefore provides a resource for dealing with the type of flimsiness Jeff illustrated during the conversation (lines 75–76) and as a result of which the term "foundation" was introduced to the classroom community by Gitte. Furthermore, Ron also suggested that the foundation would keep a structure "falling from . . . to[o] much weight" (Figure 3.5c). This resonates with the other type of "flimsiness" Jeff had described as a result of the force of gravity acting on a structure (line 62) and the structural weakness he demonstrated by twisting the piers (line 63).

We chose our final examples from the children's glossaries to illustrate an important aspect of designing and science from the children's perspective. Both Doug's (Figure 3.6a) and Renata's (Figure 3.6b)—as well as Jeff's (Figure 3.4a)—glossary entry for brace show the ways in which contextualizing their projects in familiar events and stories was important to many children. Some science educators may feel that these images contain a lot of gratuitous detail—detail that physics teachers, for example, want to exorcise from the diagrams they ask their students to do. Jeff's drawing accompanying "brace" included cars, a truck (even with inscription), and traffic signs. Doug's definition of a brace included cars and stories in bubbles (Figure 3.6a). Whereas his drawing and definition capture the essence of bracing, this definition appears to be a less important aspect of the drawings than the surrounding events.

In a similar way, Renata's definition of "tension" seems to be an appendix to the story her drawing tells (Figure 3.6b). These stories in which children embedded their structures were an important part of designing in this classroom (Roth, 1998a). Furthermore, whenever possible, children brought "micro machines" and figurines to adorn their structures. Some students also designed adornments from the materials at hand, including dolls, flags, and animals ("pets") that featured in the children's accounts of their work. The questions by Doug (line 37) and Andy about whether John and Jeff's bridge was for people or cars appear to have the same underlying concerns for a kind of context that is not relevant from a canonical perspective but may be crucial from the perspective of students.

Traditional science teaching often makes definitions a central goal. However, the definitions are those legitimated by teachers and memorized and regurgitated by (successful) students. Reproduction of the simplest form of knowledge, resources, is prized in such classrooms. On the other hand, the examples from the children's glossaries show that the definitions are not standardized and rigid; they indicate a variety of perspectives. In the EfCS unit, students appropriated engineering design and science language games based on their experience. This experience allows observations to be made. Observation sentences, grounded in students' experience, are a first step in the appropriation of a new discourse. "This is an example of a catastrophic failure," "A foundation is something that is underground," and "Piers [are used to] hold things up" are all

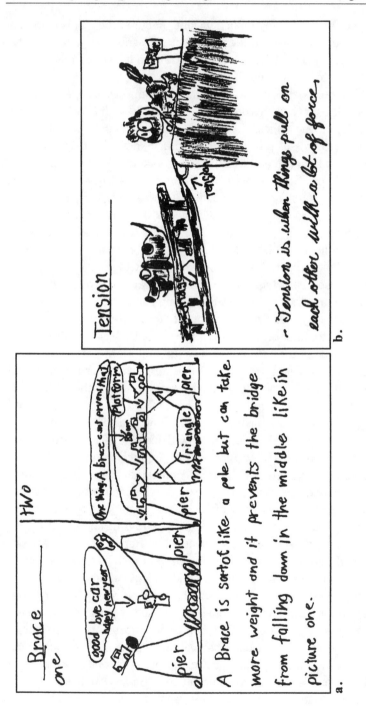

Figure 3.6 These glossary items show how important contextualization by means of detail was to students, although this detail was gratuitous from a canonical science and engineering perspective. a. Doug included cars, accidents, and comments to create stories. b. Renata's "pet bridge" illustrates her concern for animals, which sometimes came at the expense of science and engineering design.

observation sentences that are entry points to existing language games (Quine, 1992). Using the glossary as a vehicle, Tammy and Gitte engaged children in the cultural production of a language game related to science and engineering design. However, the glossaries also disclose[9] potential problems in learning canonical science and engineering design from curricula such as EfCS.

Potential problems arise from attention to detail extraneous to science and engineering, especially when this attention to detail comes at the expense of attention to canonical engineering design and science. Producing such detail takes considerable effort on the students' part. This sets up tensions for the teacher. Tammy—as probably many of her peers would have done—tended to provide positive comments when drawings were elaborate, although these glossary items were not always correct from a canonical perspective. In these cases, then, children's productions had taken over, were validated and celebrated ("Nice drawings," "I like it," and "You have lots of ideas"), but at the expense of canonical science and engineering design. In these instances, the children involved were deprived of the opportunity to engage in the cultural reproduction of science.

Metalogue

Issue 1: Representation of knowledge: epistemology

M: In these classroom conversations, the scientific knowledge appears to emerge from children's activities. That is, it may appear at first as if the children find the structure of the world, canonical scientific knowledge, through their physical engagement with the materials. But this is far from what I think to be the case; we are not advocating a discovery model, as was prevalent in the 1960s and 1970s. But knowing did not lie in the children alone either, or in their gestures. When Jeff used gestures to demonstrate the weight of the posts pushing down on the bridge deck and how this affected the tension forces in the deck and thereby provided the strength to the deck to hold up his 346 blocks, science was emergently enacted by the child, but in the presence of and with reference to the bridge artifact. Knowing lay in the relationship between the discursive, physical, and gestural actions against the bridge as a background, which brought forth the knowing about the bridge. Knowing therefore arose from the particular discourse, gesture, and physical pushing against the objects in the setting; that is, the setting served as a ground against in which knowing could become salient as a figure.

K: The epistemological point that I consider to be powerful is that the knowledge exists not only in the body of an individual but in the gestural space and associated artifacts. Without the artifacts the knowledge is not re/constructed in the same way. However, with the artifacts present an individual is able to engage in a discourse that can lead to learning and representations that extend beyond what is possible without those artifacts. The knowledge is not connected to the artifact in the same way that two separate entities connect to one another through the agency of a bridge. Rather the knowledge includes the discursive resources of an individual, the artifacts and the sociocultural contexts in which the artifacts were constructed. The science emerges from the efforts to coordinate claims about the artifacts with empirical data from tests on the structures. This is not a form of science that is abstracted and stripped of context. It is important that the science is connected to the artifacts and the qualitative experiences associated with the learners who built them to meet the constraints of solving a particular problem. Through an emotional attachment to the artifact as something that is built, a learner is able to create arguments about stability and strength that have personal relevance.

M: What you bring out here is an important but frequently misunderstood point about situated cognition. When people question this term, they seem to seek cognition qua neuronal activity in the environment. Of course, this makes little sense. Nobody who argues for situated cognition would suggest that this aspect of knowing is somehow transferred to the environment. Rather, what situated cognition does is expand the boundaries of what has to be included when we use terms such as "cognition," "knowing," and "learning." Jeff's gestures become significant in the physical context of the situation and in the sociohistorical and sociocultural context in which he uttered the words he used. Outside of the particularities of the context, the words do not have the meaning they have here, and therefore the kind of cognition we can infer does not have the same quality or nature. So situated cognition approaches simply make salient the ground against which human actions take on significance and therefore become objects for epistemological discourse.

S   From where does the canonical knowledge emerge? In this chapter we see evidence of canonical knowledge emerging through the discursive exchanges coordinated by the teachers. We discuss the mediational role of the teacher next, but there are two related issues that deserve attention now. First, Tom displayed a degree of skepticism with Jeff and John's practices and presentation that is typical of the exchanges between members of scientific communities. Tammy ensured that Tom's frankness didn't lead to a deterioration of communication channels by encouraging Jeff to articulate the criteria used to test fairly the strength of the bridge deck. Without such a successfully coordinated open discussion, the conversation may not have centered on canonical knowledge. This highlighted the significant role that student presentations and discussion play in allowing the emergence of canonical knowledge. Another strategy that fostered students' use of canonical knowledge was the glossary. When individual students are encouraged to construct glossaries of important words, canonical knowledge is foregrounded as a desired outcome. Also, this preparation seems to be essential when defending one's practices during whole-class discussions. There may have been more evidence of canonical discourse in Mr. Hammett's classroom (in Chapter 5) had he used glossaries.

K: What is happening when a person gestures toward a structure such as a bridge? The re/construction of knowledge is associated with a particular part of the structure and the recall of an event that was associated with an empirical test. This coordination of claim with evidence is made possible by the presence of the artifact, and the gesture probably involves more than merely pointing to a part of the artifact. It is possible that a gestural space consists of images of past experiences and tests and the pointing facilitates the re/construction of those images.

S: I agree; a gesture involves much more than the physical act of pointing to an artifact, for example. The term gestural space probably captures the essence of this for me. As we know, sometimes it is not necessary to talk with work partners to share ideas. Common experiences, knowledge of personal mannerisms (including use of gestures), conversations, and constructed artifacts create a shared gestural space. So the images and language evoked by the use of gestures in close-knit teams might not require further elaboration or clarification through talk. I experienced this gestural space for myself as a researcher working alongside and talking with Gavin in Chapter 5. His gestures, while not necessarily providing evidence that others might readily accept, were nevertheless convincing for me.

M: In this, I see different forms of evidence from the claims Mark Johnson (1987) made in his *The Body in the Mind* in the sense that that which we can speak, and which becomes representable in various expressive forms, is ultimately grounded in our physical experience of being-in-the-world. Also, Bourdieu suggested that living under similar (physical and social) conditions brings about particular forms of knowing. But at the same time, we must never forget that all representation is both fundamentally translation, reduction, and interpretation of lived experience and is in its form and structure arbitrary. Thus, there is no way that we can, from the physical experience alone, inductively arrive at the various expressive forms and their grammars.

K: From what you have said it is clear to me that the presence of the artifact points to use of a discourse that begins to look like canonical science. To begin with, there is an effort to link claim to evidence and the use of concepts from science to an argument about design. The artifacts and the context of an engineering problem facilitate the learning of science. Of course, the science did not just happen because of the materials. A presence of community permeates the interactions. The students know what to do and how to act with respect to the artifacts. The habitus of the community supports the emergence of a scientific discourse, and that is something we should unpack further.

M: And I think that therefore we need to look at the teachers' mediational role in all of this. Because even if Gitte and Tammy were not very present physically in the chapter, they were very present in the ways of describing, questioning, elaborating, arguing, and learning from design—that is, in the communicative habitus that shapes the practices in this small community—as we can observe it happening in the conversations surrounding Jeff and John's bridge project.

Issue 2: Teachers' Mediational Roles

M: In this chapter, the teachers appear to be almost completely absent. It therefore might appear that the Grade 4 and 5 students in this study could arrive at the kind of conversations on their own. But in the course of engaging children in the activities, the teacher also facilitated the bringing about of particular ways of engaging others, forms of presentation and argument, forms of question and critique. As the designing community began to form, the form of the questions asked by Gitte, the curriculum designer and 'expert' on engineering, and those asked by Tammy and the children were considerably different. But as time went by, the questions asked by Tammy and the children changed and increasingly sounded like those that Gitte might have asked in the situation if it had been her turn. That is, without making it an explicit focus of the instruction, or the focus of changing her questioning on Tammy's part, participating with Gitte in the engineering explorations allowed them to evolve what they considered and celebrated as new and more productive questioning strategies. The questioning of others' work became an aspect of the classroom culture, the ways of acting and interacting, the habitus. Thus, even if the teachers are not present physically or discursively, they are present in the practices that constitute the culture as it is enacted.

K: The habitus of this community is a most significant part of what is happening here. Although teachers are not seen as active in the interactions their presence is pervasive. It is not the case that the problem posed or the materials led to the emergence of science or science-like habits of mind. Rather, the participation of students and teachers in this community have obviously been honed over time, and students know what to do and how to do it because they have been acting in these ways over a period of time. Knowing when to actively interfere and when to fade into the background is an important part of being an effective science teacher. What is there in the text of this chapter to suggest that the teacher should have been a more active mediator of the learning of science? Are there missed opportunities that suggest that a more active teaching role would have been appropriate? I do not see any situations where teacher intervention would have resulted in higher-quality learning. What strikes me about this chapter is the pervasive presence of the teachers even though in the telling of what happened the teaching is very much in the background. It is important for readers to realize that activities like these will not happen without teachers and without careful attention to the building of an appropriate habitus.

S: For readers who are constrained by the data presented from just one whole-class discussion, it is possible to come to a different view in relation to the claim that the "teachers appear to be almost completely absent." Sure, Tammy and Gitte were not seen to be lecturing in this episode, but they each had a very strong and direct influence on the direction of the interactions. Tammy was a peacemaker who also reinforced appropriate discursive practices and later attempted to anchor students' practices to "real-world" phenomena. Tammy frequently interacted with the students during their presentations. While Gitte interacted less frequently than Tammy, her presence (as an expert) was obvious. Without their contributions, I am not confident that the canonical knowledge would have emerged from the discussions.

For example, in line 125, Jeff referred to Gitte's question in line 66 which was reinforced by Tammy's subsequent questioning in lines 77 and 91, suggesting that these teachers did have a significant impact on the unfolding discussions. Also, this is supportive of the comment that teachers need not be physically present to exist in the practices that constitute the classroom culture. So Tammy does appear to be quite active in the reported episodes. I'm not suggesting that there was anything wrong with her interventions, but wish to reiterate that readers don't experience what the researchers do—they can get a different picture. I return to this point later (i.e., in Chapter 5).

M: Ken, I think it is an interesting and important part of this study that the habitus was not there all along. Even the two teachers in this situation learned as they had interacted with each other to foster the community that came about, and with it its habitus.

K: What you are saying is that the habitus evolved over time.

M: Right. And furthermore, their own learning stands in a reflexive relation to children's learning. Becoming aware of children's evolving competencies to co-participate in and contribute to the conversations enhanced their own understanding of teaching. Furthermore, working at each other's elbow also allowed them to appropriate new ways of interacting with children and thereby modify their very teaching practices. Thus, and this is the reflexive point of the story, coteaching and the experience of children's learning provided an occasion for their own learning in the same way as the artifacts and the process of constructing them in collectives served as a vehicle for the children's learning.

S: This has important staffing implications. In Australia, there is an increasing trend for classes to collocate open-planned classroom space, providing opportunities for teachers to coteach. It makes sense then for principals to match teachers with different strengths. Even where there may be some physical separation between classes (e.g., room dividers) neighboring teachers might still benefit from their attempts to co-participate in activities across the classroom boundaries.

Issue 3: Role of the Artifact

M: The artifacts in this chapter are not merely artifacts but are the products and outcome of students' own activities and efforts to bring about design. Now, when these artifacts become the topic of a conversation, they are not mere artifacts but are associated and endowed with a lot of physical and emotional investment. For Jeff and Jon, the bridge therefore is not merely a bridge but the outcome of repeated cycles of testing and further development; it was their answer to the quest for making the strongest bridge possible. Science here is not just in Jeff's understanding of forces operating in the bridge and the static and dynamic relationships between the parts; it also has a strong emotive component.

S: Bridges and other constructions are similar to students' drawings. I am reminded here of David Symington's[10] research on the role of drawing in elementary science classes. He made the point that the drawings do not represent, in themselves, the scientific understanding of the child. Instead, they provide a wonderful starting point and a focus for discussion between teacher and students about the students' ideas.

K: I do think that it is important to stress the value of connecting science with the emotions of people. The values, interests, and habits of mind are important parts of being-in-the-world and to separate them from knowing and coming to know science has been a mistake. I am reminded by the concerns that Japanese educators have about Western modern science and the extent of its failure to connect with the spiritual aspects of Shizen (Ogawa, Kawasaki). The essence of the concern is that approaches to science often were out of accord with concerns about nature and balance with the universe. Relating this to science in Western countries is relatively straightforward. So many potential learners of science are marginalized by the tendency to present school science as a litany of facts, truths about a universe. Too often science is presented as abstractions that are not related to the natural world and that are derived from the work of clever others. The unfortunate endpoint is to push many potential learners to the margins. Poor, ethnic, and linguistic minorities, and females have been excluded from success in school science, and there is a possibility that this would not be the case if schools science were more connected to the affective aspects of being-in-the-world. The examples from this chapter are consistent with the perspective that those who have a passion for what they are learning will engage with passion, thereby making it possible to build a science-like discourse. Barton's (1998) description of K'neesha's failure to succeed in school science and her success in an out-of-school program that focused on environmental concerns is a compelling argument to support what we see in this study. Perhaps success for all can be a reachable goal if more concern is directed toward the identification of springboards that have an engineering and design component that enable the interests of the participants to drive motivation and learning.

S: Because most of the design activities in this book required the use of familiar materials for the purposes of making fun-like or purposeful artifacts, all students could get started and engage passionately in engineering design.

M: Our conversation about passion and emotions reminds me that many of the students in this class, boys and girls alike, brought other artifacts to the class that provided additional motivations and rationales for their design. However, many science educators might reject these additional artifacts as non-scientific because they were toy cars, people, and animals that "decorated" the bridges and towers rather than changing the structural properties of the buildings and the physical properties of the materials. But in my view, these were crucial in the sense that they provided an emotive and purposive context within and for which designing became the passionate activity that we observed in the class and documented in this chapter. Again, these things might have led, in a different classroom and with different teachers, to a conversion of the curriculum into something else. A critic of one of my articles called the result a "truck" curriculum in which "authentic" issues are converted to children-centered but non-scientific ones. Alicia and Nerida in a subsequent chapter also engage in such activities by beginning to think about ways to include their Barbie dolls in the electricity activities.

S: Once again, the "truck" by itself does not inform us about the scientific learning of the children concerned. Instead, it provides teachers a valuable link to the emotions of the child and a common reference to core canonical discourse. The Barbie dolls and other adorning artifacts described in Chapters 5 and 6 were starting points for design. Even though these rarely figured in the products, they were very much a part of the designing process; they marked the children's out-of-school experiences as important resources for developing canonical knowledge.

Notes

1   This unit was developed by the Association for the Promotion and Advancement of Science Education (APASE, 1991), a non-profit organization whose principal mission is to bring an expanded vision of science and technology education to elementary schools.

2   Readers will notice that girls did not get involved in this whole-class session. Only boys commented upon and critiqued Jeff's design, which may in part be a result of the fact that Jeff could make quite snide remarks—although Tammy did her best to quench any attempt at such behavior. Furthermore, despite Tammy and Gitte's intent to provide equal opportunities for boys and girls to engage in all engineering design activities—including the whole-class discussions—and despite Gitte's experience of providing workshops for teachers on how to deal with gender-related issues in science and technology education, the two teachers did not succeed in including girls to a larger extent. They did, however, spend a lot of time with girls during small-group activities; they also organized larger all-girl groups as part of which most girls willingly engaged in discussions. Tammy and Gitte's struggles to include more girls in whole-class conversations have been described and theorized elsewhere in considerable detail (Roth, 1998d).

3   From a phenomenological perspective, there are an infinite number of aspects an artifact can have. That is, there exist an infinite number of observation sentences that could be uttered and that describe aspects that turn "things" (which we encounter in an unmediated way) into "objects" (which we experience during breakdown, and more specifically, as part of rational science).

4   As Tammy explained to the students, "stays" is a term frequently used by sailors referring to a heavy rope or cable, usually of wire, used as a brace or support for a mast or spar; a rope used to steady, guide, or brace; a support or brace.

5   In an interesting plenary presentation at the twenty-first annual meeting of the North American Chapter of the Psychology for Mathematics Association, Paul Cobb and Pat Thompson talked at length about meaning and taken-as-shared meaning from different perspectives. An unsuspecting audience might have assumed that Paul and Pat talked about the same meaning. Only in response to my [Roth] question what their meaning of meaning was did they acknowledge that they had used the same word but in very different ways.

6   Here, Jeff appeared to take the same view of designing as an emergent and heterogeneous process that we describe throughout this book but particularly in Chapter 2.

7   How students learned from each other, that is, came to participate in the circulation of a discourse, has been described and theorized elsewhere (Roth, 1995d, 1996c, 1998a).

8   Between the previous excerpt and this one, about one minute passed during which Tammy explained to students that they would be establishing a glossary of those terms that they found useful in their designs. She also wrote on the chalkboard several terms that students had used in the past.

9   We use the notion "disclose" in the phenomenological tradition of Heidegger (1977). Accordingly, disclosing does not mean to reveal an underlying truth. Rather, human interpretations disclose the "things" of our undifferentiated experience by attributing specific aspects to them and thereby turning them into "objects" that have aspects and properties.

10   See Symington, 1986.

Chapter 4

Thinking with Hands,
Eyes, Ears, and Signs

Throughout this book, we are concerned with shifts in science-related language games as students co-participate in engineering design activities. In this chapter, I focus on the role of conversations (around blackboard drawings of simple machines) in the development of scientific forms of discourse in a Grade 6–7 class.[1] Central to the instructional design in this simple machines unit were the representational devices (ways of representing simple machines) and technologies (e.g., chalkboard, transparencies) that are thought to facilitate the emergence of shared meanings in classroom communities. The similarities in the overall structure of the conversation may arise from the observed similarities of students' and scientists' talk in face-to-face interaction. In face-to-face interactions, talk cannot be reduced to uttered text alone. Rather, meaning emerges from the interaction of multiple modes of communication that includes the coordination of hands, eyes, ears, and signs (words and drawings). Therefore, we have to account for the fundamental interdependence of hands, eyes, ears, and signs in order to understand "conceptual" talk and thinking in science classrooms organized as linguistic communities. I show in this chapter that access to a shared representational device allows (the for scientists characteristic) multi-modal science talk, that is, thinking with hands, eyes, ears, and signs. This integration supports often very elliptic scientific laboratory talk, which is thereby allowed to evolve into full scientific discourse. I claim that forceful scientific argumentation emerges in classrooms if students are enabled to deploy the same discursive resources (hands, eyes, ears, and signs) that scientists routinely use in their laboratory work. I present evidence to show that access to the representational device plays an important role in determining the structure and content of conversations and who controls the conversation. When students have direct access to the chalkboard, their discourse uses the same multi-modal form available to the teacher here and to scientists in their everyday situations. These claims are illustrated with excerpts from a representative classroom episode—a discussion about the outcome of a tug of war that included a pulley system.

Researchers increasingly recognize that signs—including words, marks on whiteboards or paper—cannot be taken as direct evidence of individuals' thoughts but take meaning only from their situated use (Edwards & Potter, 1992; Lave, 1993). People, especially scientists, do not communicate by language alone, but simultaneously draw on an array of resources: linguistic, pictorial, gestural, musical, choreographic, and actional (Lemke, 1998). Phenomenologists recognized some time ago that thinking can therefore not be relegated exclusively to mind: thinking is handwork. Hearing and seeing—because they always already involve interpretation—are ways of thinking (Heidegger, 1977, 1991). Ethnomethodological studies of scientific and non-scientific work have taken up Heidegger's concerns by emphasizing the integrated nature of communication which includes utterances, gestures, marks on whiteboards, and so on:

> Ethnomethodological studies of lecturing and of mathematicians' work have identified the essential, mutually constitutive relationships between marks and the activity of their use. Rather than analyze whiteboard inscriptions as such, therefore, we are interested in viewing them in relation to activity, through the use of video records. Viewed as free-standing signs left behind in work, we assume that the sense of these marks is largely undecipherable. Viewed in relation to the activity of their production and use, in contrast, they come alive as the material production of "thinking with eyes and hands" that constitutes science as craftwork. (Suchman & Trigg, 1993, p. 153)

In their exclusive focus on mental representation and physical symbol hypothesis, cognitive psychologists and cognitive scientists have overlooked the important contingent aspects of doing intellectual work. The metaphor of information processing has led researchers to conceive of the mind as a container into which knowledge—in the form of declarative and procedural statements—had to be transferred (e.g., Anderson, 1985).

Science teachers have been enculturated into these traditional models of knowing and learning and exclusively focus on declarative and procedural statements as evidence of knowing and learning. Even in the most exceptional traditional classrooms, therefore, discourse contexts are "impoverished" and do not allow students to talk science, let alone integrate talk, diagrams, and other forms of everyday conversation (Lemke, 1990;

Roth, 1996f). But there are no reasons why teachers have to continue using the information-processing paradigm as a referent for their teaching. I show that the simple machines unit on which the present chapter is based was grounded in a different paradigm of knowing and learning and therefore very different in terms of its focus on participation in discursive activities of a community. This simple-machines unit was explicitly designed for participation in a community's discourse practices. Various activity structures allowed students to develop language games for describing and explaining simple machines. Beginning with the language games they were familiar with prior to the unit, students developed new ways of talking more appropriate to constructing arguments along various trajectories of successive evolutionary change. The new language games were constituted by, and made more efficient through, the multimodal nature of the discourse that this curricular unit supported. Before coming to the study itself, I make a brief excursion to the nature of science talk that occurs over and about shared documents on shared paper surfaces, blackboards and whiteboards, or computer screens—inscriptions.

Talking Science

Discourse (in all its modes) is situated action rather than representational abstraction; that is, we use language to get things done in collectivities rather than merely to encode meanings. Language both makes phenomena and expresses them; new phenomena and new experiences co-evolve. In the same way, diagrams are not just representations of concepts but are integral aspects of situated action. When conceptual talk is treated as situated action, discourse analysis provides performance descriptions that must be accounted for by any model of underlying competence (Edwards, 1993). Scientific talk is not just constituted of conceptual text. Like all human communication, it involves the synchronicity of verbal action, inscriptions, pointing and gesturing, body movements, and rhythm (Lemke, 1998). Interruptions of this integration—for example, when conversational participants are no longer in each others' physical presence—become visible as communicative problems. Consequences of such disruptions, as they occur during video-mediated conversation, are interactional asymmetries and "disembodied conduct" in scientific conversation (Heath & Luff, 1993).

Analyses of discourse in scientific laboratories indicate that there is a mutually constitutive relationship of language, inscriptions (representations other than words that are inscribed in some medium), action, and "nature" (Gooding, 1992). Language and inscriptions are not merely representational devices used to understand an independent nature; they constitute it. Scientists' manipulations and gestures depend both on nature and on current language and inscriptions to become meaningful scientific actions. When they talk to each other, scientists use language, marks on paper (graphs, equations, diagrams, images), pointing, gesture, and movement. The process of "seeing" is constituted by a complex of activities that include fingering documents, conversational talk (which involves speaking and hearing), and visual examination; that is, "seeing" is interactively accomplished (Amann & Knorr-Cetina, 1990). When they finally publish their findings in scientific journals, scientists equally co-deploy text and graphs, tables, and images. However, graphs, tables, and images are not merely enhancements of text; they stand with it in a mutually constitutive relationship. They are not simply add-ons or the means to more economically present some information but in fact multiply meaning (Lemke, 1998).

We saw in Chapter 2 that artifacts can be seen and interpreted in multiple ways; that is, they are interpretively flexible.[2] Interpretive flexibility affords changes of meanings that may lead to the emergence of canonical science talk. Artifacts are not only important as objects of conversation (talk about)but also provide a shared background against which students' utterances, gestures, and pointing became meaningful (talk over). Large area display devices that serve as explicit group memories aid face-to-face task groups (Lakin, 1990). In laboratories, meeting rooms and classrooms a common technology for representation is the whiteboard or chalkboard. To get their collective work done, participants use these boards in face-to-face interactions. In the end, these boards are littered with lists, sketches, text, designs, and the like produced by means of collective activities that themselves are not recoverable from these "docile records" (Suchman, 1990). In schools, chalkboards are far more prevalent than whiteboards.

The Grade 6–7 unit on simple machines that provided the data for this chapter supported the transition from science to engineering by interleaving various activities. Designing machines may include constructing plans, marking marks on paper, or using computer video displays. Scientists also use paper and computer displays for modeling purposes. It is through the likeness of these two activities that we can achieve a transition between engineering design and science. Representations of machines and their parts can be based on the simple machines that are used in science for analyzing and showing conceptual components of a Newtonian, mechanistic understanding of the world.

Simple Machines Unit in Grade 6–7

I taught the simple-machines unit in a mixed-grade class of a suburban elementary school in Western Canada. The class consisted of 10 Grade 6 students (five boys, five girls) and 16 Grade 7 students (seven boys, nine girls). There were many aspects of this class that made the learning environment less than ideal. First, this class was taught by seven different teachers, in contrast to other classes in this school (and elsewhere) that are taught by one or two teachers throughout the year. Observations of lessons taught by different teachers revealed that this led to considerable variations in classroom norms and associated differences in student behavior. Furthermore, there were many students with special circumstances that impeded their learning in traditional classrooms. Four students were classified as learning disabled; one boy had muscular dystrophy and had physical and cognitive difficulties that impeded his ability to do the work in his regular classes; two Grade 7 girls experienced difficulties because English was their second language; three Grade 7 students had social and communicative problems; two students refused to submit to the rules of conduct negotiated by the class and teacher; and three students had other problems affecting their academic work.[3]

This unit on simple machines is grounded in the notion of learning as an increasing generation of and participation in discursive practices. I designed it so that students could develop and appropriate language games related to simple machines. Because ways of talking evolve, any language game about simple machines had to develop from the ways of talking students brought to the unit.[4] By choosing appropriate artifacts (levers, pulleys, elastics and springs and the diagrams that represented them), I set the stage for the interactive production, maintenance, and development of new language games that handled the phenomena associated with these artifacts more appropriately.

The simple machines unit consisted of a total of 36 lessons and included two 70-minute and one 55-minute lesson per week. Four types of activities existed that differed in terms of the social configuration (whole class, small group) and the origin of the central, activity-organizing artifact (teacher-designed, student-designed):

- About 25% of the unit consisted of whole-class conversations about simple pulleys, blocks and tackles, equal arm balances (first-class levers), second- and third-class levers, inclined planes, work, and energy. I directed these activities and always included physical devices (lever, pulley, inclined plane, elastic) and transparencies on which these devices were graphically represented according to scientific conventions.

- During 15% of the time, students conducted small-group teacher-designed activities with equal arm balances, second- and third-class levers, or summarized their ideas about specific simple machines on specially designed forms.

- For 30% of the unit, students designed four hand-powered machines in small groups (two or three students). The student engineering designers were invited to submit proposals for hand-operated machines that could (a) lift heavy loads, (b) move loads over a long distance, and (c) move loads by means of self-propelling mechanisms. For their fourth machine, students could specify the purpose on their own, but they were asked to combine a minimum of four processes, two of which had to be based on one of the simple machines discussed in the unit.

- About 30% of the unit consisted of student-directed whole-class conversations. On these occasions, each design group presented a design artifact to the entire class and directed subsequent question and answer.

All four activity structures supported students' participation in talking science and engineering design but with different degrees of teacher input and feedback (McGinn, Roth, Boutonné, & Woszczyna, 1995; Roth & McGinn, 1996; Roth, McGinn, Woszczyna, & Boutonné, 1999):

- During teacher-directed discussions over and about teacher-designed models and drawings, the conversations were most focused on the identification of scientific principles related to simple machines and finding ways to talk about these aspects. However, the whole-class situation limited the number of students who could talk at any one time.

- Small-group investigations involving teacher-designed artifacts and drawings provided opportunities for many students to participate. Students' conversations were constrained by the selection of the artifacts, selected topics, and the language games that described the activity.

- Small-group design of machines again allowed a great deal of active participation in discourse and material design. These activities provided the least constraints so that students could develop their own language games and concerns.

- Whole-class student-directed conversations again limited the number of students who could actively contribute to the design discourse. But the concerns raised and language used were by and large student driven.

Over the course of the unit, the participation of any one individual varied across the same activity structure and between activity structures. The same students who wanted to monopolize some whole-class discussions participated to a lesser degree in small-group activities and some students who contributed little during whole-class conversations participated enthusiastically during small-group work. This is consistent with our interpretation of legitimate peripheral participation (Lave & Wenger, 1991), in which "peripherality" indicates the possibility to participate to different degrees and "legitimacy" indicates the possibility of belonging to our (classroom-bounded) community.

Learning about Pulleys

Throughout the unit, students talked in small-group and whole-class situations over and about drawings and models of simple machines. In this chapter, all excerpts come from one 16-minute conversation. The conversation immediately followed a tug of war between the teacher and students. I rigged the tug of war in my favor by means of a block and tackle attached to the railing around the porch of the classroom's outside door during the children's absence (recess). Figure 4.1 illustrates the block and tackle that gave the teacher, discounting friction, a mechanical advantage of five ($MA = 5$).[5] As a consequence, students lost the tug of war although, their team included 20 members near the end of the competition. My original intent for the conversation was to provide students with an opportunity to participate in a sense-making conversation and to develop and use canonical representations. However, student interest in arguing alternatives was so high that I let the conversation run its course (as happened frequently during this engineering design unit).

In the following paragraphs, I contextualize the conversation in three ways. First, I describe how it is representative of the conversations in this classroom more generally. Second, I situate it in the entire sequence of pulley-related activities. Finally, I provide a summary of students' pulley-related knowing and learning.

Characteristics of Whole-Class Conversations

The conversation was in several respects representative for what happened more generally in this classroom.

side view

Figure 4.1 The configuration of the block and tackle that was used by the teacher to mediate a tug of war. Oblivious to the mediating effect, students had accepted the teacher's challenge. The defeat of the students gave rise to a spirited sense-making conversation over and about a series of blackboard drawings.

- Physical models and two-dimensional representations (inscriptions on chalkboards or transparencies) were always co-present. This co-presence was intended to provide students with an easier transition from the physically experienced machines to the more specialized symbolic representations of them. It was also used to provide students with opportunities for making the transition from engineering design to science.
- Student participation in conversation and material design dominated the unit rather than teacher lectures over and about models and representations. In whole-class conversations, whether they were directed by me or by students, only one speaker was selected at a time, placing an unavoidable limit on how many people could contribute to a conversation.
- Students had a great deal of freedom in deciding whether and to what degree they wanted to participate. In the present conversation, 15 of the 24 students made contributions, although five students talked much more than the others.
- Conversations ran their course; I ended them only when student interest appeared to wane.

Overview of Pulley-Related Activities

This conversation was one of 13 pulley-related activities during the 36-lesson unit. These included whole-class discussions, small-group activities during which students summarized their views of pulley-related whole-class discussions, small-group activities during which students used pulleys for their designs of machines, and written and verbal answers to our pre-test and post-test questions. Because some of the activities were related to our evaluations of student knowing and learning, not every student participated in all 13 activities.

- Day 1. All students answered a paper-and-pencil question about a particular pulley design in an everyday context.
- Day 2. Thirteen students talked about their answers on the paper-and-pencil evaluation with a member of the research team.
- Day 3. One whole-class sense-making conversation over and about two pulley systems and corresponding drawings.
- Days 4–32. Throughout the unit, students designed and built models of machines that sufficed certain conditions (lift a 100-gram object to a height of 15 centimeters; move a 100-gram load over a distance of 2 meters; have a mechanical advantage). In the course of designing their machines, students made use of pulleys and other wheel-and-axle arrangements so that they had opportunities to learn about them. About 37% of all student-designed machines included at least one pulley.
- Day 4–32. There were whole-class conversations over and about the student-designed artifacts. During these conversations, students and teacher raised questions about pulleys whenever a group had used them.
- Day 8. A second whole-class sense-making conversation about pulleys and corresponding drawings. Drawings of the model pulley were projected onto a screen above the model.
- Day 9. Small-group activity during which students summarized their understandings of the pulleys discussed on the previous day. The worksheets included copies of the transparencies used during the whole-class discussion.
- Day 17. A tug of war between teacher and students by means of a block and tackle attached to a banister (with accompanying drawings on blackboards).
- Day 28. A review of pulley systems using drawings on transparencies.
- Day 33. Students provide written answers about the forces on a moving pulley using teacher-provided drawings as a resource.
- Days 34–35. Students talked in pairs (or in threes) about their answers on the written test; students were encouraged to convince each other of their respective answers.

- Day 34–35. Same groups as under the previous bullet were asked how they would use a pulley if they had to lift a heavy load. A set of diverse materials (more than students needed) was provided as resources.
- Day 36. Final, whole-class debriefing on all simple machines, including pulleys.

Students' Competencies Related to Pulleys

In the course of these activities, students' talk about pulleys and answers to pulley-related problems changed considerably.[6] Before instruction, all students maintained that a fixed pulley attached to a ceiling (as in Figure 4.2a) made it easier to pull a load. But they also held that a moveable pulley on a rope attached to a ceiling on one end and held by a person on the other (as in Figure 4.2b) increased the effort. Most students explained that it was easier to pull down in the first situation but harder to pull up in the second. Using their experiences with pulling as resources to construct explanations, students systematically provided answers that were incompatible with a scientific explanation. Throughout the unit, this belief that pulling down on something is easier than pulling up interfered with some students' appropriation of a new, more scientific, language, despite their observations that some pulley setups decreased the effort to

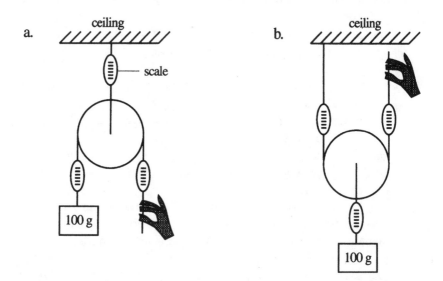

Figure 4.2 Two pulley configurations that were part of the curriculum of the simple machines unit. One item of the unit test asked students to identify the forces in the system by indicating the readings each of the scales would indicate.

one-half. These students argued that even if the effort were to be decreased to one-half of the load, "it [would be] easier on the back to pull down than to pull up."

On the post-test, students were asked to identify the forces in several pulley configurations (Figure 4.2). Twelve students correctly identified the size of all forces in a system involving a moveable pulley (Figure 4.2b); 11 students correctly recognized the symmetry of pairs of forces, but incorrectly identified the magnitudes (four said it was too small, seven said it was too large); and the remaining two students identified other forces (e.g., they included the same friction-related measurement differences that had occurred during demonstrations and class discussions). During the post-test conversations, many students demonstrated a remarkably competent pulley-related language. They argued their cases and, in some instances, changed their answers. The following excerpt from a post-test conversation—in which Alain and Shaun, two Grade 7 students, talked about a pulley system similar to Figure 4.2b—illustrates this competence.

01 Alain: This [ceiling] takes half and this [hand] takes half, so I got 55 grams, I
02   didn't measure the scale, I forgot about the scale, I put ahm, 10 grams for
03   the pulley and a 100 grams for the weight, so I got a 100 and 10 and like,
04   there is 2 scales, so I divided by 2 and I got 55.
05 Shaun: And I got a 120, I just add them all 'cause it would take the same, he is not
06   asking what they both hold at the same time pulley, he wasn't saying
07   like if you pull them both at once, what, ahm, what they would both come
08   to, like, if you were pulling one of them and just holding the other like
09   that, then that's what the scale would come to.
10 Alain: OK, what I have to say is, see how it's tipped to the ceiling?
11 Shaun: The ceiling is taking half of the weight.
12 Alain: Exactly and it shows on Scale 1, so Scale 1, gets half of it and this gets half
13   of it, it doesn't, I understand what you're saying but I think that if
14   this wasn't connected to the ceiling, then I will agree with you that it would
15   be 100 and whatever you said but.

Here, Alain and Shaun argued about whether the scales in a diagram should read 55 or 60 grams. Alain explained that the total weight needed to be distributed over the two strings, one held by the ceiling, the other by the person (lines 01–04). But he had forgotten to account for the weight of the pulley itself (line 02). Shaun described the situation differently, suggesting that one needed to account for the weight of the entire system (lines 07–09). Alain began to elaborate on his description when Shaun suggested that the ceiling was taking half of the weight (line 11), which, as Alain reiterated, was just what he had claimed (line 12). He then provided an explanation under which condition one would measure the weight that

Shaun had indicated: the person would have to hold the entire system (line 14). The two boys maintained this conversation with turns of considerable length and without prompting, which attests to their discursive competence.

In the third part of the post-test, each group was given a range of materials including a 100-gram load, string, and pulley, and was asked how they would lift the load while minimizing their effort. Here, eight groups suggested a situation similar to that in Figure 4.2b, whereas six groups proposed a pulley fixed to a ceiling (support) (Figure 4.2a). These six groups argued that for a moveable pulley system to work, the person had to stand above the pulley on a roof (or an equivalent mechanism). They held that it was easier to pull a rope down (using the person's own weight), although the effort was almost twice that in the other possible situation. Overall, then, students showed a competency in talking about, setting up, analyzing, and representing pulleys that exceeds accomplishments of older students in regular and traditional programs. This achievement is particularly noteworthy given the problems students in this class as a whole faced in terms of their learning. The simple-machines unit and its metaphor of participation for learning (rather than the metaphor of mind as a container) certainly fostered the development of the students' competencies.

We want to understand the relationship between three aspects of the simple-machines unit: (a) the interactions in a science classroom that were organized around engineering design activities; (b) the collective production of the interactions; and (c) the role of the chalkboard as a representational and conversational resource in the production of quality science talk.

Arguing about a Tug of War

After students had returned from their recess, I invited eight of them to a tug of war that, in addition to the normal rope, included a huge block and tackle (Figure 4.1). The rope was attached to a railing (banister) of the back porch of the class. Students did not realize that the block and tackle was set up in my favor (it was geared down 5:1). After the tug of war began, more and more students eagerly joined in until about 20 pulled the rope. To the students' surprise, they lost the tug of war. After they had crossed the line, I announced a sense-making conversation by asking, "OK, what happened here?" During the first five minutes of the conversation, students and I constructed an explanation of why I had won the tug of war. Then, in a major shift of the conversation, the students proposed alternative designs for setting up the pulley so that the outcome would change. Because these proposals were presented in opposition to those I presented, the conversation shared similarities with scientific laboratory talk in which adversarial stances are used to construct better understandings of inscriptions.

Constructing an Explanation

After being invited to respond to my question "What happened here?" students began to provide initial explanations. Their responses included, "The pulley was stronger than half the class" (Amy) and "You were pulling the pulley and I think that gave you the advantage" (Kevin). Shaun elaborated his answer at length:

> You were pulling your own string, though, one end of the string was tied to tha tha end thing, and you were pulling it, and the pulley was attached to the [banister]. So when you pull, the whole pulley moves, and everyone on the string moves with you. The other side we were trying to pull. If we had let go, you would be off somewhere.

In this situation, students described key features of the system, the pulley and banister. However, their explanations did not make explicit why any of these features should have helped the teacher and not the class. My intention was to get students to elaborate a theoretical description of the system (teacher, students, pulleys, rope, and banister) as far as they could. That is, I wanted students to describe and explain the system in scientifically correct terms without getting into telling mode. To move the conversation onward, I drew one of the pulley configurations that had served as a conversational topic in earlier activities (Figure 4.3a). At first, I asked students to relate the simple diagram to the complex situation they had experienced earlier. That is, I wanted to make sure that the classroom community shared an understanding of how the diagram (representation) mapped onto the block and tackle of the earlier tug of war. Such a move is significant, because teachers often take as self-evident how some diagram maps onto a situation in the world. Because all sign forms are more or less arbitrary, experience and familiarity are required to appropriately map one onto the other.

After establishing where the class and I had pulled, students answered the question, "Who or what supported the teacher?" Again, students' answers included the pulley (Matt, Randy, Amy) and railing (Claire). But now, the students talked about the diagram on the chalkboard, pointed to it as they talked, and referred to participants' positions as "A" and "B."

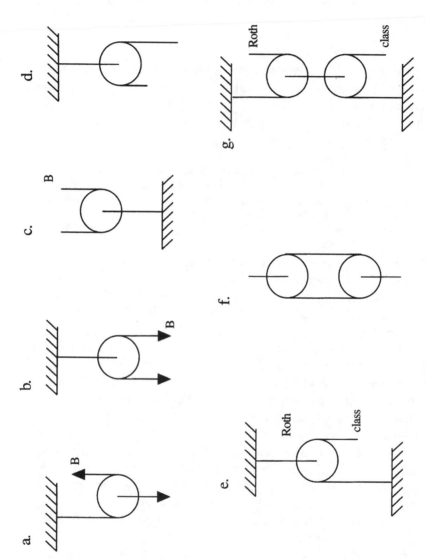

Figure 4.3 The marks left behind on the blackboard after the sense-making conversation. Without the associated videotapes and ethnographic data, the sense of these marks is largely undecipherable.

Rather than having a rather complex experience as the conversational topic—the tug of war with its tangle of ropes, block and tackle, screaming children, and a challenging teacher—the conversation now revolved around the simple diagram. This move from the richness of lived experience to the stillness of line drawings is a form of reduction to which scientists have been encultured over their years of training and experience. This move, which I had carefully orchestrated in this situation, was to allow students to experience authentic scientific practices. Such moves from everyday phenomena to various sign systems should not be taken for granted by teachers; rather, such moves should be part of carefully orchestrated lessons that assist students in appropriating representing practices by participating in situations in which they naturally occur and which are relevant to them. This is important for drawings which, like all representations, pick out and therefore foreground certain aspects of phenomena while leaving other ways of seeing and conceptualizing them in the background.

Moving the conversational topic from the block and tackle situated at the back of the class to the drawing was significant because it allowed a change in discourse and an associated change in the shared discourse. This shift corresponds to the equivalent move by scientists from "raw" phenomena, which present themselves often in complex and messy ways, to inscriptions that outline only key features. In the sciences, this cleaning up of original data, photographs, X-rays, etc. is a central scientific practice because in the rhetoric of scientific publications, the cleaned-up versions are much more convincing. Part of scientific argumentation consists in establishing the equivalence between the two forms data. This conversation between myself and the students was no longer about the messy tangle of pulleys and rope, but about a single drawing in which the block and tackle was reduced to one circle, representing the pulleys, and three lines, representing the rope. This teaching move also corresponded with the ethnographical observations made and interviews conducted throughout the study: students preferred to talk over and about the line drawings rather than the original phenomena because of the smaller degree of ambiguity of referents to utterances.[7] This became clear especially during the discussions over simple machines for which I had made available both a physical machine and a line drawing on a transparency projected against a screen behind the phenomenon. Students' talk brought to the foreground characteristic features of the drawing rather than of the physical device itself. For example, they talked about the ceiling to which the pulley was attached in the drawing rather than the ring stand to which the physical model was attached.

I then drew another pulley configuration (Figure 4.3b) next to the first and asked, "What would have happened in this case?" My intent was to help students make connections between the present conversation and earlier conversations on the topic of pulleys and to further their competencies by talking about a contrasting situation. This new drawing also provided further opportunities for students to participate in pulley talk and thereby extend their competency with respect to the relevant scientific language. In answer to my question, Julia suggested: "It would have been easier for the class to pull you, because there is nothing helping you, only you." Subsequently, various students added further alternative solutions such as, "Let's switch sides" (Randy) or "But you would have lost if there was a thousand people on there" (Alain). Other explanations focused on particular features of students' actions as major aspect of the outcome. For example, Jon suggested that I won the tug of war "because you were pulling on the little rope attached to the pulley, and we were just going in a circle." Shaun proposed that students had pulled on the rope that was attached directly to the banister ("we were just pulling the banister string . . . but the pulley was attached to the banister"), whereas David suggested that students "were pulling where the pulley is." As part of these answers, students also elaborated a description that had not yet occurred during the conversation, the balancing aspect of the force exerted by the students. Jon described students' pull as "support." Other students later returned to this theme by stating, "You had your support, if all of us had let go, you would have been in Kelowna (a distant city)" (Shaun) and "The class was your strong support, we were holding it" (Jon).

Sharon: Well if the other rope is held on to there, then we wouldn't be pulling anything, 'cause it's it's stuck onto there, so
David: No, it was going around something °so he was pulling°

Sharon still described the pulley as attached to the railing, but David disputed this description. He suggested that the rope was "going around something" and that I was in fact pulling rather than holding onto a rope that was attached to the banister behind my back. After about six minutes (one-third of the entire conversation), I summarized what had been achieved so far in the conversation:

The pulley (points to Figure 4.3a) sort of helped me to make use of the railing, and I have you pull at the open end. In this case (points to Figure 4.3b), when you

have a pulley fixed somewhere, and I pull on one open end, and the class pulls
the other open end, I don't stand a chance.

At this point, many classroom conversations might have ended. I had
intended to use the tug of war as another situation in which students
could see a pulley in action, provide observational descriptions of phenomena drawing on their present language, and elaborate the best theoretical description their linguistic resources allowed up to this point. During the six minutes of conversation, students had described several
significant features including the railing (banister) and I—who opposed
students' combined forces—and the mediation of the forces provided by
the pulley. The two drawings were intended to integrate this discussion
with those that had occurred earlier on in the class and thereby create
another example of the recurrent conversations that are characteristic of
knowledge-producing communities.

In this instance, the conversation did not end. Students' interest appeared high so that I decided not to interrupt the flow of arguments
coming from the students. Their interest provided enough momentum to
take the conversation into a new dimension and thereby to provide another opportunity for science to emerge. In this second part of the conversation, students designed and elaborated several alternative configurations that should have altered the outcome of the tug of war. As readers
will see in the subsequent section, it became clear during this second part
of the conversation that the fluency of the interactions were crucially
dependent on the access speakers had to the representational medium,
the blackboard.

Designing New Configurations
The conversation then took a major shift. Rather than remaining with
and concentrating on one explanation of what had happened, students
began to design alternative situations. These alternative situations were
based on the same basic elements (pulley, rope, and banister), but students attempted to design the new configurations such that they not have
been disadvantageous to the student team in the tug of war. Shaun opened
the discussion by suggesting the first alternative configuration. The
adversarial form of his argument likely emerged from the adversarial nature of the tug of war. This was fortunate, for it produced similarities with
the organization of scientists' interactions over and about the data from
their research and during which they did much of the construction and
"fixation" (i.e., in the form of the data collected) work that brings about
evidence in scientific laboratories.

01 Shaun: You can have the banister, if that, if that

02   pulley there, the pulley there, if that was

03   on our side then, ahm.

04 WMR: This was, this <u>was</u> on your side, because

05   the class was pulling here

06   and I was pulling here.

07 Shaun: No, but if that, switch it around=

08 Sharon: =You were B.

09 Jon: ⌈If you were B⌉

10 Shaun: ⌊Switch the   ⌋whole thing around, like

11   say, we were pulling.

12 Sharon: ⌈If we were B⌉

13 Jon: ⌊If we were B⌋and you A

14 Shaun: No, if we were B but you had the

15   banister on your side.

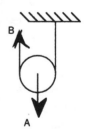

16   (1.0 s)

17 Jon: Ha?

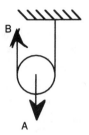

18 Shaun: Like if the banister was on that side (.)

19   OK, just say there was a banister on that

20   side.

In this episode, Jon, Sharon, and Shaun collectively produced the first verbal description of an alternative configuration of the pulleys, ropes, and banister that should have led to a victory for the class. This configuration differed from the one actually used during the tug of war. But it also differed from the students' previous suggestion of simply changing positions ("Change sides") or adding a large number of participants on the students' side ("You would have lost if there was a thousand people"). At the same time, it appeared as if Shaun intended to show with his configuration that it was not the banister that provided me with the advantage ("You can have the banister" and "If we were B but you had the banister on your side").[8] Jon, Sharon, and Shaun were (literally) not in a position to construct their idea in diagrammatic form and had to collaborate to bring about a verbal description of the situation. As I elaborate in the next section, this interfered considerably with the conversation and the possibility of making sense of the events to be explained. It is important to note, however, that the repetitions in lines 07 to 15 can be read as part of the work that is necessary to achieve discursively mutual alignment, stabilization of new and yet unfamiliar ways of talking, and a collective product (Roth, 1995a, 1995b, 1996e, 1999, 2000). These repetitions bear striking similarities with those observed in the collaborative construction of graphs and rhetorical claims that we observed in a Grade 8 science classroom (Roth, 1995b).

In the same way, the Grade 6–7 students proposed several alternative designs. At first, I remained next to the chalkboard and drew diagrams according to students' instructions. It became quite clear that the arguments themselves developed only slowly because a lot of the conversation was spent in producing the drawings. Later, I invited students to draw their own diagrams or invited students to act as intermediaries and draw for other students. All the designs proposed after the initial, explanatory phase were proposed in an opposite manner. That is, their purpose was no longer mere explanation but, reflecting the competitive tug of war, in opposition to my claim that the pulley and banister helped me to win.[9] Several students appeared to argue that there are designs in which I would lose even if the banister was on my side. Frequent use of "but," objections against the proposals made by others or arguing about and negotiating candidate accounts, are further evidence for the adversarial pattern of this conversation. In these features, the present conversation paralleled typical laboratory talk.

Evaluating "free-standing signs left behind . . ."

In the end, the students and I had described and considered seven designs (Figure 4.3). I offered two designs (Figures 4.3a, b) and drew two further designs based on the instructions by individual students (Alain for Figure 4.3f) or groups of students (Figure 4.3c). Students drew the remaining three designs. Alain proposed his configuration (Figure 4.3f) explicitly for the purpose of making the class and the teacher equal; in a similar way, Dave drew his pulley configuration (Figure 4.3g) to equalize the stakes. Both Shaun's and Alain's configurations included two "banisters" previously proposed by Krista. In conclusion, I provided a summary of the conversation:

> In this case (Figure 4.3g), both sides are the same. In this case (Figure 4.3b) and in this case (Figure 4.3f), I don't have a chance. This one to me (Figure 4.3e), it looks to me, someone is cheating himself, because I hold on with the wall, and you stand no chance, you don't move me a bit, and when you're tired then I start. . . . I made use of the pulley in a way that is similar to this (Figure 4.3a) and remember this, for B it's easier than for A, for the class, and in fact, the way I rigged up the pulley, it made it five times easier. Here (Figure 4.3a) you only get half; the way I set it, you get about 5 times.

With the hindsight of the analysis we can ascertain that the overall structure of this conversation shared similarities with those among scientists in their laboratories. The conversation taken as a whole established not only an explanation of the tug of war lost by the students but also generated alternative versions of a tug of war that would have led to different outcomes. The material evidence of this conversation (marks on a chalkboard) was constructed from resources distributed in the community. For example, three students collectively produced a description. Most of the drawings were collective achievements of several members of the classroom community. Through this conversation, therefore, these resources were "pulled together" and found simultaneous expression on the shared representational device (blackboard). On the blackboard, where they were available to all members of the community, the drawings were resources available for inspection and argumentation. In the end, I summarized the various parts of the conversation referencing each of the drawings (records) that the communicative work had left behind.

In its entirety, this conversation also brought together issues that belong to both science and engineering design. On the one hand, the design of machines that mediate forces is an activity from the domain of mechanical engineering. (The fact that the design of pulley systems has a long history does not diminish our claim.) On the other hand, the relationship of the forces applied by two agents (class and teacher), mediated by some device, was clearly an issue in which physicists had been interested. That is, the conversations about technology and engineering design allowed major scientific ideas related to pulleys to emerge.

Communicating with Hands, Eyes, Ears, and Signs

In the previous section, I illustrated the macro-structure of this sense-making conversation. At first, it was concerned with description and explanation of what happened. Then, by means of an opposite device, alternative configurations of pulleys, banisters, and ropes were proposed that would have changed the competition's outcome. The phenomenon under consideration was described by the actual configuration, in contrast to other possible configurations that would have led to different outcomes. This macro-level development of the sense-making process appeared to be facilitated by a concomitant change at the micro level. Here, students increasingly participated in the construction of the diagrams on the chalkboard. Together, students and I drew diagrams of pulley configurations; as a consequence, they brought together and exhibited in material form socially distributed knowledge of pulleys. Finally, this knowledge was simultaneously (in space and time) represented on the chalkboard (Figure 4.3).

In the previous section, I hinted at the fact that the conversation was limited as long as the teacher alone had access to the chalkboard. In this section, I illustrate that the nature of the conversation differed according to the level of access to the representations that were not only visually available but were also constructed by students. My central point is that when students have direct access to the chalkboard, their discourse uses the same multi-modal form available to the teacher in the classroom and to scientists in their everyday situation. In a different way, access can also be viewed from a perspective of power and control. Once individual students obtained control over the representational device, they had more ways to communicate.

For heuristic purposes, I provide three examples that differ in terms of the levels of access to producing diagrams on the chalkboard. First, there are no diagrams to be talked about, only a tangle of ropes and pulleys. Then a mediator rather than the speaker draws the diagram. In the final episode, speakers argue with and over the diagrams. In the course of these episodes, the increased reliance on hands, eyes, and ears in the co-registration of participants becomes evident; furthermore, the speakers have increased opportunities to shape the inscriptions on the chalkboard. In the last episode, a student's full participation in the argument was made possible through equality of access to and power over diagrams on the shared chalkboard.

"What's your point?"

Laboratory talk is replete with utterances and gestures that can only be understood if one also knows the specific context in which the utterances and gestures were produced. That is, laboratory talk is highly indexical.[10] In the presence of referents, the meaning of indexical can be made clear; in their absence, ambiguity makes conceptual science talk difficult if not impossible. That is, although participants' eyes and ears are active during the communication, the physical distance between speakers and referents of their talk excludes the hands as important contributors in communicative acts. Because of this distance, listeners could not understand the particular details of drawings on the chalkboard with enough clarity, even when a gesture was used to draw particular attention to that detail. Talk alone was insufficient to show or "make the point." Students therefore repeatedly asked, "What's your point?" The following episode shows how problematic it is to conduct a conversation when the referents of talk (here, the drawings) are not within reach of the speaker.

In this episode, I was the only member of the classroom community within reach of the block and tackle; I was the only participant who could directly point to the parts of the system—rope, two pulleys, and the attachments. (In a sense, I was in control of the artifact that was the topic of the conversation and therefore of the conversation itself. In such situations, cultural reproduction is much more in the foreground of students' learning experience than cultural production.) My utterances and gestures not only indicated where students pulled but also that I was not clear about what the two previous speakers had said.

21 Shaun: If we pulled the hardest, then the banister would fly.

22 David: We were pulling where the pulley is.

23 WMR: You guys were pulling on this

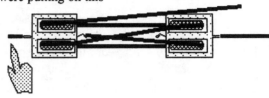

24   one here.

25 Jon: *That's* a strong⌈support.⌉

26 Alain: ⌊But you⌋would have lost if there was a

27   thousand people on⌈ there. ⌉

28 Sharon: ⌊It would⌋n't have moved because I think

29   it is attached.

30 Alain: ⌈Yeah, exactly.⌉

31 Shaun: ⌊See, he is, ⌋actually it does -

32 WMR: It is attached to that

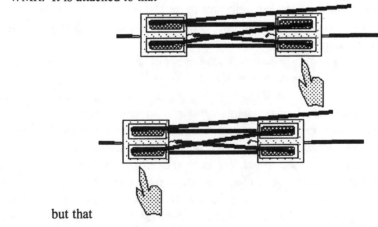

33   but that

34   pulley isn't ⌈attached. ⌉

35 Shaun: ⌊No, but it's⌋attached to the banister.

Students' talk did not provide an unambiguous description, for the referents for students' indexical terms were not clear. That is, in the absence of gestural references to the block and tackle, there was no indication within the talk that would have elaborated the meanings of "where," "that," or "it" ("where the pulley is," "that's a strong support," "It wouldn't have moved," "it is attached," "actually it does"). Shaun (lines 21 and 35), Sharon (lines 28–29), and Alain (line 30) appeared to assert that the students' rope was attached to the pulley, which in turn was attached to the banister. Standing over the block and tackle, I used conversational resources not available to the students. That is, I could point to a particular rope (line 23) so that, together with "this one here," it was evident where students had pulled. I first pointed to the pulley attached to the banister (line 32) and then to the free moving one (line 33) so that the meaning of the repeated "that pulley" remained ambiguous. Although the indexical "that" was the same in both situations, its referent was different. Despite this difference, other participants could clearly see the referent and therefore understand the meaning of "that." The fact that the pulley was not attached to the banister was only implicit in my pointing (line 23). I made this explicit, however by (literally) pointing out that "that pulley isn't attached" (line 33). This utterance was accompanied by my gesture that pointed to the moveable pulley. Thus, although all discourse participants employed indexical terms, those I used were made clear through unequivocal reference. Students' indexicals, however, remained equivocal in this episode.

Here, I found support by virtue of being near the representations. I did not have to make explicit in words many of the ideas that my communication nevertheless made explicit in my gestures and deictic references (pointing). I enacted forces, pointed to parts, and described processes in a multi-modal form that was not accessible to the students. This episode occurred while I stood next to the block and tackle. Thus, in this situation, the conversation was not over and about the design drawings. But even in the presence of diagrams, there were problems of co-registration when participants did not have access to the diagrams. In the first episode, I illustrated the problems in conversations in which not all the participants have access to the panoply of conversational resources. Shaun, Sharon, and Jon attempted to describe an alternative pulley configuration. Because they lacked access to the drawing or the chalkboard as a medium to make a multi-model presentation, they were left with verbal descriptions. Then, I did not understand Shaun's descriptions (lines 01–03, 07, 10–11, 14–15, 18–20). This lack of understanding was indicated by the utterances, "Does anyone understand what Shaun is asking me?" and "I still can't imagine what you are trying to say."[11] Jon's and Sharon's utterances added to confusing the situation because it had been established before (Jon was one of the students) that the teacher had pulled on the end labeled "B." But all three students, Jon, Sharon, and Shaun shifted to suggest that the class should be "B" in conjunction with Shaun's comment that the banister should be on the teacher's side. To overcome this confusion, I asked whether any member of the community had understood Shaun. Many students answered "no," and Jon had already indicated that he did not understand (line 17). Only two students appeared to have followed Shaun's argument. On the other hand, my position next to the chalkboard made available more discursive resources. I used even more indexical terms than the students including "this," "here," and "your side." But each of these terms was accompanied by a gesture that referred to a very specific item. By placing my hand over a drawing or the ropes (e.g., lines 05, 06, 23, 32, and 33), I could be certain that his indexical references were made clear.

We saw in this episode that lack of access to the object of talk introduces a high degree of ambiguity into the conversation and makes it virtually impossible to proceed with any efficacy. Scientists and engineers are aware of such communicative problems and therefore do their utmost to bring drawings and artifacts to their meetings or create rapid facsimiles thereof to make a conversation more efficient. However, the presence of the mediational device is not sufficient when another person mediates access to it. If one person draws for another, much effort must still be spent in producing a drawing rather than in proceeding with the argument. This effort is illustrated in the following episode.

"Is that what you mean?"

When speakers have only indirect access to a joint representational device, much work has to be spent in finding out what the distant person means and in completing the diagrams rather than the elaborating the scientific argument about the effect of the block and tackle on the tug of war. Producing the diagrams can then be regarded as side sequences to the actual conversation about conceptual issues. In this conversation about the tug of war, there were repeated situations in which one member (student or teacher) drew a diagram based on another member's instructions. Prior to the following episode, I declined Shaun's offer to draw the situation he attempted to describe and began to produce a drawing following my and other students' instructions.[12]

36 WMR: The banister is over here? (1.8 s)
37 Shaun: Yeah, the banister is over ⌈here⌉

38 WMR: ⌊And⌋ who is
39   here?

40 Julie: Us.
41 Kevin: Us.
42 WMR: The class?
43 Andre: The class is, against you.
44 WMR: And like this?
45   (3.4 s)

46   Is that what you mean?

47 Julie: Yeah.
48 Shaun: Yeah.

49 WMR: How is that

50   different from ⌈this one? ⌉

A   B

51 Shaun: ⌊No, no, it's⌋ like that, but

52   you have a banister on your side.

53 Krista: Like both have banisters.

Here, I attempted to create a drawing from my hearing of students'
utterances including those just prior to the represented episode. As before, I used the label "A" for the location of the class. In each step, I
ascertained whether my drawing corresponded to students' descriptions
(lines 36, 44, and 46) or where I should put a particular item (lines 38–39
and 42). As indicated by Julie's (line 47) and Shaun's confirmation (line
48), the drawing was finally made to the students' satisfaction. That is, it
corresponded to the students' earlier descriptions. The entire sequence
from line 36 to line 48 was necessary to bring about the diagram; but it
had not advanced the argument. After this sequence, and with the students' configuration available for inspection, I could question its status as
a new contribution (lines 49–50) and make students accountable for their
design. When it was embodied in the diagram, the students' case had
become inspectable and arguable. When I asked students how the new
diagram differed from a previous one, Shaun retracted his agreement and
suggested a modification (lines 51–52); Krista further supported Shaun
in proposing a modification (line 53).

The same situation occurred when I drew a design according to Alain's
instruction or when I selected one of the students (Jon) to do the drawing
corresponding to several students' verbal description. In the next episode, Jon agreed to explain his understanding of Shaun's argument.

Again, Jon (as I had before him) had to seek feedback on whether his
drawing corresponded to the one the student in the audience wanted him
to draw. Jon began to draw the design that Shaun appeared to have
described (lines 54–58). However, he was not certain and requested confirmation from Shaun (line 59). Despite the confirmation, Jon eventually

54 Jon: Well, ok, if you had the (.) banister

55   thing, the railing goes like that⌈then⌉

56 WMR: ⌊yeah⌋

57 Jon: this is the string

58   and then there would be a pulley.

59   ⌈Am I doing this right to you?⌉
60   ⌊[turns to face Shaun]   ⌋

61 Shaun: yeah

62 Jon: And then this would

63   I don't think, come out there.

asked Shaun to come up to the blackboard (line 63). Drawing for his peer appeared to be so difficult that he abandoned his attempt to construct Shaun's design and prepared the way for Shaun to complete it on his own.

Rather than allowing for a multi-modal presentation in which Shaun or another student could elaborate a description, my reluctance to leave the stage forced a separation of talk and gesture (drawing). Students therefore not only had to argue their case but also had to provide a verbal description of something that could be much better expressed by a drawing or gesture. This, then, required repeated instructions and feedback between the person making the argument and the person making the drawing. But from a discourse perspective, the instructions for completing the drawing must be considered side sequences because they only established the drawing rather than proceeding with the argument. "Doing" scientific talk requires that the person making the argument is in control not only of the verbal mode but also of the representational device. Presenters can then focus all their actions and "doing" on the argument rather than engaging in side sequences to get the drawings right. Such integration of the two activities (talking and drawing) leads to a different form of discourse, as the next episode will show.

"You can pull on here . . ."
When all parties in the argument have access to the representational device, here the chalkboard, efficient communication occurs. The production of marks and coordination of hands, eyes, talk, and ears happens all at once, integrated into multi-modal development of arguments in a way that is characteristic of talk in scientific laboratories. This was also the case in the present episode, in which Shaun and I were the major players. Shaun, invited by Jon, came to the board to argue for his design in which the teacher could still have the banister but the two sides in the first diagrams were reversed. I, intuitively realizing that the conversation would proceed efficiently only if Shaun could make his argument while in control of the representational device, no longer tried to restrict the student's access to the chalkboard.

Here, Shaun's argument was constituted by drawing, gesturing, pointing, writing, and talking. His dramatic performance, which was greeted with applause at the end (line 91), underscored his presentation as part of the overall argument of how to use banister and pulley in such a way as to guarantee the class's victory even if there was a banister on my side. (The dramatic performance and the subsequent applause further foregrounded the competitive aspect of the conversation.) Both participants in the argument had immediate access to the drawing that they took as shared space for their interaction. The drawing afforded efficient communication in allowing the participants to point to and unmistakably identify locations and directions. Although Shaun did not talk about a rope explicitly ("this thing," line 66) or that it was positioned around the pulley ("over this," line 67), drawing and gestures together made evident that he was talking about the rope's placement over the pulley. He then proceeded to concede the banister to me ("you can still have that," line 68), and may have been about to indicate the class's position (line 69) when I interrupted him. Up to this point (lines 64–69), Shaun's drawing and talk had not contained hints about where the class and I were positioned in the

64 Shaun: ⎡ OK (2.5 s)
65   ⎣ [Looks at previous diagrams] ⎦

66   And then this thing

67   over this

68   You can, you can still have that

69   but if we=
70 WMR: =Where do I pull? Which end do I pull?

71 Shaun: You can pull on here.
72   [Starts new diagram]

73   With the, OK (3.8 s) this is a banister.

74 WMR: But we have the banister here.
75 Andre: Oh God

76 Shaun: (5.2 s)

77   [Erases diagram, begins new one]

78   <u>Banister</u>

79 WMR: OK

80 Shaun: <u>Long string</u>

81 WMR: OK, pulley.

82 Shaun: <u>Roth</u>

83   pull <u>here</u>

84 WMR: OK.

85 Shaun: Then there is a pulley.

86 WMR: And where do you pull?

87   (1.7 s)

88 Shaun: And then there is another banister

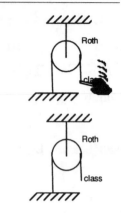

89   and then we pull (.) here

90 Several unidentifiable students: Ah, yeah

91   (4.2 s) [Many students applause]

92 WMR: OK, thank you very much, can you?

93   [Signals Shaun to sit down]

94 Alain: But then Mister, Doctor Roth doesn't

95   have anything to pull at!

design. My question, "Where do I pull? Which end do I pull?" (line 70) indicated that I did not understand where the string was attached or who was pulling at that end. Until then, Shaun had only attributed one rope, the one for the teacher (line 68). If the class was to be at the other end (e.g., that indicated in line 69), it would leave one end of the rope loose. In a sweeping gesture (line 71), Shaun then attributed to me the rope that attached the pulley to the banister.

It is interesting to note at this point that the sweeping gesture not only pointed out where I would be pulling but also the direction of the forces. Gestures can animate the drawings and exhibit dynamic in addition to declarative aspects of the drawings at hand. Thus, talking in the presence of the diagram allowed the participants to express important topological features of the situation, including forces and their direction, that the topological nature of talk cannot easily express.

Visibly disconcerted that I did not understand, Shaun started a new diagram (line 72), but I stopped him short by pointing out that there already was a banister (line 74).[13] That is, I held Shaun accountable to the earlier drawing that already included a banister. By means of theatrical emphases, Shaun aligned me and his peers to the key elements of his design and their placement (lines 76–91). Through his emphases in the uttered words and the accompanying pointing gestures, he rendered unequivocal the placements of exactly those elements that had been ambiguous during his earlier verbal presentations (though some of his peers apparently understood him even then). Shaun completed his drawing. Unlike his verbal presentation, which was difficult to understand, his description on the form of a drawing was much less ambiguous. Furthermore, his design now existed in material form and was available for a critique that made him accountable. This critique was immediately instantiated. It came both in the form of Alain's observation that I did not have to pull at all (lines 94–95) and in my subsequent applause which celebrated Alain's comment. Alain's comment had furthermore underscored a concern that had been voiced earlier in the conversation. Sharon had pointed out that the pulley was attached in such a way that the class was pulling on the banister rather than competing against me.

This final episode clearly illustrates that access by both speakers to the representational device provided multi-modal forms of communication. To communicate, Shaun was drawing on such resources as gestures, hand placement, and signs (written text, spoken words, and graphic symbols). His gestures referred to specific places in the diagram which disambiguated his indexicals "this thing," "this," "that," and "here." To understand, other students and I not only needed to hear Shaun speak but also needed to "see." Shaun indicated the rope and its placement over the pulley both visually (by drawing it) and verbally ("this thing over this") (lines 66–67). Although "this" referred to two different objects, the different position of his hand made clear that the first occurrence referred to the rope while the second evoked the pulley. His gesture, which was co-deployed with "you can have that" (line 68), unmistakably attributed the banister to the teacher. In his second diagram, some of the previously existing ambiguities were clarified by adding graphical and textual features. First, Shaun added "another banister" (line 88) then he not only attributed the different sides to the two competing parties in the tug of war, but he also wrote "Roth" and "class" next to the corresponding ropes. At this point then, Shaun's ideas had become inspectable and arguable. While students and I had found it difficult to understand Shaun's verbal descriptions during earlier attempts, Alain's critique (lines 94–95) and my implied agreement (applause) became possible after Shaun had completed his multi-modal presentation.

However, I was not just a listener in this situation. I actively contributed to the construction of the emergent argument in several ways. First, to clarify the ambiguities of Shaun's diagrams, I asked about the location of the participants (lines 70 and 86). In a sense, these questions already held Shaun accountable and initiated additional sequences of talk. These sequences were necessary for the establishment of common ground (or intersubjectivity) and therefore the construction of shared understanding of Shaun's argument. Only then could Shaun truly be held accountable for his argument and be critiqued in a legitimate way. Later, with a movement of his hand that ended over the existing banister (line 74), I redirected Shaun's attention from beginning a new diagram to the already existing one.[14] Through these interactions, the entire presentation was collaboratively achieved. "Drawing together" can then be understood in a double sense: Shaun and I brought together all the communicative resources necessary (written and spoken signs, hands, ears, and eyes) and therefore co-constructed the diagram.

Conversing toward Competence

This study focused on the multi-modality of classroom conversations rather than being limited to the spoken text. By integrating drawings, utterances, gestures, and ears and eyes of the listeners, the conversation made possible the integration of science and engineering design. In written scientific and technological communication, various inscriptions (graphs, tables, and equations) that interact to give rise to multi-modal communications often accompany text. In the face-to-face talk of laboratories and design studies, new modes of communication become available. Science educators and researchers of workplace competencies alike have long overlooked the importance of these modes of communication. These issues became the focus of attention only recently, especially when sociologists, anthropologists, and ethnomethodologists began to experiment with technology that could mediate the collaboration over distance. The illustrative and iconic elements of the speakers' and listeners' gestures, that is, the declarative and dynamic aspects of their multi-model presentations, lost their performative impact as they were mediated over distance. Although it has been recognized that representational technologies are an integral part of collective thinking, many teachers have not yet accommodated this aspect as part of their science. We believe that these technologies, because of their relationship with engineering design, facilitate science learning by means of engineering design activities. My research program is fundamentally concerned with the role of representational technologies in collective sense-making, the emergence of shared knowledge in classroom communities, and the mediation of different language games. In this chapter, I described the benefits and constraints of whole-class science conversations in a Grade 6–7 classroom around chalkboard inscriptions.

This chapter proceeded in two steps. First, I documented that the classroom conversation as a whole shared structural similarities with scientific laboratory talk. Beginning with the construction of a first explanation for a discrepant event, members of the community began to elaborate pulley configurations by means of an opposite device. In the end, the chalkboard was littered with pulley diagrams, the material productions of this activity. These diagrams provided insights to the functioning not only of the particular block and tackle but also of pulley systems more generally. Because they were produced as "material" evidence, these diagrams had become inspectable, scrutinizable, and arguable. Students had become accountable for their linguistic and material productions. We groped to understand each other when we were only speaking to each other; many representations of simple machines (as with the pulley in this case) can be displayed and discussed much more easily when they are visible to all (here with the chalkboard). In fact, the interactions over and about drawings on the blackboard constituted the material drawings as shared objects. Everyone with visual access to the chalkboard could assume "sameness" of the object that they were looking at. Similar features were observed during the same unit in small-group conversations when students designed their own machines. Again, little ground appeared to be covered as long as students merely talked, supported by some gestures. As soon as students drew diagrams or provided a material basis to their discussions in other ways (e.g., the things they constructed from wood and other materials), their design efforts made progress. The co-deployment of materials, tools, diagrams, gestures, and talk facilitated students' interactions.

In the classroom conversation, participants used graphemes—basic graphical elements representing ropes, the pulley, and a stable support—in various combinations to make their arguments, present ideas, or design alternative configurations. For this to work, the graphical formalism needed to be shared by the members of the community. In this Grade 6–7 class (as is evident from the earlier provided list of pulley-related activities), graphemes were used in a consistent way throughout the course. They appeared on my transparencies, in student worksheets, and in material evidence of classroom discussions "published" on the bulletin board (copies of the transparencies with all marks produced during the whole-class conversations). By the time of this conversation, a set of graphical conventions was already shared so that participants could use them to construct the setting of their work. That is, the graphemes the participants in the conversations had used drew meaning from their intersituational reference to other conversations. Here, I understand this intersituational reference as the conversation-related equivalence of intertextuality. All participants used the same formalism provided by previous meetings. That is, this conversation was situated in a historical context that helped participants to make sense of utterances and graphemes although, in some situations the particular referent of specific graphemes was not constant. For example, marks representing the "banister" in the situation I describe here were previously used to represent the iron ring of a ring stand and a "ceiling." The circle that was previously used to represent a single pulley now stood in for the block and tackle. The lines had changed their meaning from string in earlier sessions to rope in the current conversation. In each situation, however, the grapheme stood for a fixed support. That is, using the drawings of pulleys in different situations and for different purposes provided a type abstraction so that the same graphical units could refer to different things depending on the situation. I note that it cannot be presumed that all students understood the grapheme in the same way and that this has to be determined through an investigation.[15]

On the chalkboard, participants expressed the relationship between the elements (pulley, support, and ropes). These elements (and their names) are the typological features of the drawings. That is, typological features express knowledge in the form of "this is" or "there is/are." However, the typological features do not in themselves constitute the main feature of a scientific understanding of pulley systems. Rather, it is in the relationship among these elements that the "conceptual" (i.e., science) is embedded. In addition to the relationship between the elements, the topological understandings are rendered through gestures that animated the drawing by showing (and recreating) the forces acting in the system. In this way, drawings are subject to a phenomenon similar to language, in which conceptual understanding is expressed through the relationships between words, not in the words themselves. For the present conversation to work at all, relationships between individual elements in a drawing and a physical device had to be specified, and the relationships of elements within each of the two had to be clarified.

In the early part of this conversation, interactional work needed to be done to assure that participants understood how the graphical objects related to the physical device (block and tackle). Initially, I had taken these relationships as unproblematic and proceeded with using formalism in talk. Early in the discussion, however, I realized that this assumption was not warranted. As part of the second episode, I returned to the block and tackle that stood for the common experience of a phenomenon. Here, I pointed out the relation of the individual parts of the system, the ropes pulled by students and me, the "banister," and the pulley. Once the correspondence between device and its representation as diagram had been established, the diagrams substituted for the actual devices as objects of conversation over and about. The drawing can then be thought of as superimposed over the actual device. Talk over and about the drawing can stand for talking about the physical device. The participants' language expresses this substitution. Referring to lines on the diagram, participants used talk such as "you can pull on here . . . and then we pull here" (Shaun); "but then Mister, Doctor Roth doesn't have anything to pull at" (Alain); and "you guys were pulling on this one here" (I, over device). Talk over and about physical devices and drawings that represent them become indistinguishable.

But at the same time, engineering design and science become indistinguishable. The complex block and tackle was from the domain of engineering design. Artifacts of this nature are still employed in many workplaces such as farms, machine shops, logging sites, and garages. On the other hand, the reductionist drawings express relationships and dynamics similar to those in which scientists are interested. Scientists are no longer interested in the specific implementation of a particular machine; they are interested in its "abstract" properties. That is, scientists are interested in the fact that a pulley system changes the relationship between load and effort, but (with few exceptions) in the actual implementation of the conceptions as a functioning machine. The conversation analyzed here shows an important way that lessons organized around engineering design can lead to scientific understandings among participants.

It has been suggested that talk over and about visual displays[16] democratizes discourse (Lakin, 1990). The orientation of group meetings around a visual stimulus changes the control of discourse. Rather than being dominated by verbally (or politically) dominant individuals, it encourages increased participation from the entire group in the generation of ideas, evaluations, and descriptions. The present study shows that this is not generally true. As the sequence of episodes illustrated, such democratization in classroom discourse may be a function of access (which itself is related to the local construction of power). Only when students had free access to the chalkboard (equaling that of the teacher) could we observe interactions resembling those in scientific laboratories.

Talking with eyes and hands, communicating with inscriptions, and mediating talk constitutes a considerable part of technological and scientific practice. It is in this sense that the conversational activity here was "authentic." That some of the models considered by the students did not achieve what they were supposed to (student has "misconception") is not the important issue here; the fact that students employed the graphemes in their overall argument is. From my perspective on discourse it did not matter that students' designs could have been rejected by core members of the physics community on the basis that they are not workable (Figures 4.3d, e) or are equivalent to previous designs (Figures 4.3b, c, f, g). The point is that students here could elaborate through argumentation alternative configurations of the basic elements. When they had direct access to and control over the chalkboard, their discourse used the same multi-modal form available to me here and to scientists in their everyday situation.

Understanding Representational Technologies

In this study, the chalkboard was a shared interactional space to which participants were oriented perceptually, discursively, and physically (body orientations). Speakers integrated various modes of communication (talk, gesture, drawing) to describe and explain alternative designs; they bridged the separation between modes of expression, a separation which is the result of schooling and is ontogenetically posterior to expressional unity (Lemke, 1998). When a lack of shared understanding was apparent, it could be remediated immediately and without verbal description. With access to and control over the chalkboard, speakers had opportunities to employ the multi-modal talk common in scientific laboratories. Thus, the chalkboard became a medium for the construction of shared conceptual objects—various designs constituted by the different arrangements of the graphemes (various versions of the three basic building blocks, "banister," pulley," and "rope"). These diagrams were "configurable." Diagrams expressed relationships that are said to exist in the corresponding elements of the physical device. They are also visible marks that can be pointed to, can serve as reference to a gesture, can be erased, and can be reproduced in different configurations. Over the course of the conversations, topics of talk were visually constituted, and, in turn, brought about change in the talk. Different designs of the tug of war were proposed, considered, changed, and reconsidered.

But access to the chalkboard allowed more than simply the integration of talking, drawing, and writing: through the speakers' gestures, the drawings were also animated. For example, with a sweeping motion of the

hand Shaun and I animated the diagrams, indicating not only the existence of forces but, equally important, the direction in which these forces
acted within the system (see gesture in lines 06, 71, and 89). Furthermore, with the diagram almost completed, Shaun placed the rope to be
pulled by the class, and in the movement of his hand while drawing the
rope, indicated the direction of the force ("and then we pull here," line
89). In this animation of the diagrams, science concepts exhibited their
full nature as "semiotic hybrids, simultaneously verbal-typological and math-
ematical-graphical-operational-topological" (Lemke, 1998). Through
Shaun's hand movement, the diagrams retained the dynamic character of
the earlier tug of war. In his presentation, he not only configured his own
design from the basic graphemes (whose presence was underscored by
his verbal emphases). He also animated them with his gestures and
pointing.

Multi-modal practices such as those described here are not supported
by other modes of interacting with students. For example, I illustrated
how hard it is to communicate when students try to contribute to a whole-
class discussion without access to a representational device that everyone
can see. These problems were remediated when students such as Jon,
Dave, or Shaun used the chalkboard as part of their talk. But even in the
presence of a representational device such as a computer, the interaction
of its size with the social configuration may prohibit the integration of
multiple modes of communication. For example, when more than two or
three students sit in front of a computer, the orientation toward the small
screen and input devices prevents other people from interacting with
others over the images; they no longer have access to one of the modes
(Roth, Woszczyna, & Smith, 1996). Furthermore, I illustrated that mediated access to the chalkboard also leads to inefficient talk. The trouble in
conversations in which one participant draws for another arises from the
potential that both do not refer to the same objects. To facilitate this
situation, the participants have to engage in many cycles of action and
feedback to produce the drawing rather than discuss the "conceptual"
issue to be expressed by the drawing. That is, they have to engage in the
auxiliary activity of constructing the pulley drawing as object rather than
fluidly incorporating its construction in the course of the argument.

This chapter can provide some insights into why some students have
difficulties learning from lectures (e.g., Bowen & Roth, 1998; Roth &
Bowen, 1999a, 1999b; Roth & Tobin, 1996; Roth, Tobin, & Shaw, 1997).
As in the situation I describe here, lecturers engage in a multi-modal

presentation. They talk, draw, write, gesture, and point. What students usually end up with, however, are copies of the marks and traces left by the multi-modal presentation. Moreover, students do not know what to keep invariant when reducing the multi-modal presentation to a representation in their notebooks. What their notes do contain are all the other aspects of the lecturer's presentation. Readers may have had the experience that although they have in their notebooks everything the teacher or professor wrote on the blackboard, the meaning of these marks is gone. They are decontextualized, no longer part of the lecturer's rhetorical practices deployed to enroll listeners into their own ways of seeing the world.

The chalkboard was the setting for constructing alternative designs of tug of war and simultaneously served as a recording device that allowed references between various designs. These diagrams became available in subsequent conversational activity (comparison of Figures 4.3b and 4.3c) and summary. Items entered became records—only Figure 4.3d was erased in the end and unavailable for the summary—during (Shaun studied previous drawings in his turn at the chalkboard) and at the end of the lesson. Utterances of spoken discourse were soon lost in the temporal succession of other talk. In contrast, diagrams could be inspected, analyzed, and re-analyzed at later points or be compared with other diagrams. They became "fixed points" for the discussions. In this, they became inspectable and arguable. However, in contrast to the other inscription devices (transparencies, students' designs in notebooks) used in this class, chalkboard drawings were no longer available during the next class, and for the present analyses they were only recoverable through the video records. Unless someone actually copied the contents of the blackboard, the accomplished work was lost after the next teacher or the janitor erased the information from the blackboard. For this reason, some whiteboards allow their contents to be printed before they are erased; others are electronic and can have their contents saved on computers for further processing and change. In the present situation, the chalkboard had an advantage over the transparencies used in this class in that all of the designs were present simultaneously. It also presented a space that could easily be shared by multiple participants. The space on transparencies is limited, and multiple designs have to be viewed in succession rather than simultaneously. On the other hand, transparencies are easily carried from one situation to another so that they are available for future reference. They are records that could be posted, or projected again: they are immutable mobiles.

Metalogue

Issue 1: Democratization of the Discourse, Evolving Conversation

S: Let's not underestimate the significance of the tug-of-war game here. I asked myself, Why did someone like Shaun (the "troublemaker") bother to participate in the conversation at the chalkboard? I think that the students committed themselves to the design task and associated conversation only after the competition with their teacher. This activity authenticated their design and contextualized the conversation.

M: A central aspect of the conversation, and in fact across the different kinds of interactions that occur as this conversation unfolds, is the type of access to the representational technology, here the chalkboard. In the absence of the chalkboard and in those situations where someone else than the present speaker (designer) makes an argument, much of the conversation is spent in the production of the design itself. On the other hand, when the speaker is also producing (or speakers are co-producing) the inscription, the conversation is about the purpose and functioning of the design, including the direction and size of the forces acting in the systems.

S: This all started when the students were prepared to advance ideas to explain the teacher's success in their own language games.

K: What struck me so much about this chapter is the importance of an individual being able to produce her own inscriptions. It only makes sense for the organizational structure of the classroom to support this practice. Consider what is happening. A person re/constructs what she has learned from an investigation and begins to consider how to modify the design of the pulleys and blocks. The idea in the head has to be communicated to others in the group and it seems obvious that the best person to build an inscription device is the person with the idea. As the person begins to produce the inscription there is established a reflexivity between the idea, the inscription, and associated verbal interaction. It seems intuitive that the best way to get a viable representation of what the person is considering is to allow that person to construct the inscription.

M: I wonder if it makes sense to speak about an idea in the head prior to an articulation? It may be that the idea itself forms in the very moment of articulating what may be a more or less vague image.

K: That's true, but what I wanted to say is that as a person begins to lay out a design others can co-participate in the production of an inscription either on the chalkboard, on paper, or on the screen of a micro-computer. The discussions over the inscription, it seems could enhance learning in a number of ways. To begin with, the inscription in this case is a design that is to address a problem. The pulleys and rigs are to be set up so that the students can defeat their teacher in a soon-to-be-held return match. Thus, the design is to address a problem, and its features need to be such that the end result will be the teacher being dragged over the line. In a sense a thought experiment is conducted in relation to the design. Here the science begins to emerge in the discourse of the students. Just how does this design lead to a different end result? An analysis of the forces in terms of the positioning of the pulley, string, banister, and people provides evidence of a scientific discourse. What seems important to me is that teachers realize in the assignment of roles to students in groups that all students need to be provided with opportunities to create inscription devices and speak to others about them. In this chapter it is clear that the inscriptions, as representations of what students know, were vehicles for the understanding of the science associated with a gaming task. It would have been so easy for the discussions to have avoided the science. However, this did not happen. The habitus of the classroom supported science, and the mediational effects of the teacher constrained the actions of the students. The roles of the students in groups and the ways in which the teacher interacted with groups facilitated the emergence of a scientific discourse.

M: There is also a sense of democratization of the discourse. Students are not just called to provide an answer, and they are not only invited to contribute a sentence or two to the conversations, but the current speaker is in control of different media for expression, including the production of the visual representation and gestures that occur over (enacting/animating the system) and about (pointing to parts) the diagram.

K: At issue here is the extent of the interest the students had in figuring out a viable system to meet a goal. They were engaged and used their autonomy with responsibility. Of course, the teacher in this chapter showed great wisdom in knowing when to step forward to interfere in student activity and when to fade into the background to allow the students to generate their own ideas, inscriptions and associated discourse. It is very clear here that the inscriptions are an important part of knowledge production and representation.

S: After my student teachers have tried out innovative teaching strategies or activities, many have complained "But it didn't work." Regrettably, some of these student teachers revert to the safety of more traditional practices. An important point to make in this chapter (as well as the ones that follow) is that the teacher had developed wisdom that came from practice over many years of reflective teaching. Merely replicating the same sequence of activities and ideas might not lead to the emergence of a scientific discourse. Patience and perseverance will be required before many novice teachers will be able to orchestrate the motivational introductory activities with the follow-up conversations to the same level of success.

Issue 2: Role of Inscriptions in the Conversation

M: The inscriptions, as well as the process of producing them, are occasions for the production of science far beyond the specification of a system and the identification of the forces and the dynamics of the system. They are part of the interaction by providing an arena for the interactions while at the same time being the topic of the talk.

K: It is hard to imagine how a group could progress far with a problem such as this without having some way to share their ideas with one another. Because a new arrangement had to be produced it was useful to be able to represent the ideas in terms of alternative designs and put them to the test in a thought experiment. Thus the inscription assumed the role of a test arena for an idea of how to set up pulleys, string, and banister rail. The inscriptions were vehicles for facilitating tests of hypotheses.

M: The inscriptions have an important function between the worldly block and tackle, the physical experience of pulling on the ropes, feeling the tension in the muscle, the exertion, and the representation of this experience in a variety of forms—discourse, diagrams—in addition to the verbal means. The inscriptions take an intermediate position between the purely typological nature of discourse and the purely topological nature of things in the world (of which the individual is but one). On the one hand, the inscriptions bring to the foreground, through the lines, individual and bounded objects that take specific names—pulley, string, banister. The gestures—which animate the drawing as students enacted the pulling on the system that has occurred before or could have occurred afterward to test the actual outcomes of the tug of war with different constellations and pulley configurations—provide the link between the typological aspects of discourse and the topological aspects of worldly experience.

K: Teachers can learn from this study of the importance of getting students to create inscriptions to serve an intermediate role in learning science. The availability of inscriptions makes it possible to interact with peers and a teacher in a variety of ways and to check the inscription against the images created from a particular experience such as a tug of war. In the absence of the inscriptions it is easy to see how a scientific discourse may not have occurred.

S: Students with language difficulties come to mind here. I agree with the recommendation that teachers should encourage each child to construct personal inscriptions. These inscriptions can then become crutches that might facilitate learning. This isn't restricted to children with limited access to linguistic resources. I have noticed that shy children (e.g., those from culturally different backgrounds) sometimes become more comfortable conversing in social settings when they can make reference to inscriptive devices. Deflecting attention to the inscriptions reduces their self-consciousness. In so doing, the children are more likely to focus on the substantive issues under discussion for the benefit of all participants.

M: There is an additional component about which we have not talked so far. As the conversation unfolds, there is a possibility that the inscriptions begin to accumulate. Thus, in the case of that particular conversation, the chalkboard was littered with drawings that also, upon recapturing, provided the members of the community with a recorded historical trace of the argument as a whole. There was no need to take additional notes, for the conversation itself left the drawings as a record of the work accomplished for everyone to see and appreciate.

S: I think that this is why teachers should encourage children to maintain records of their personal inscriptions. These inscriptions can then act as markers of their personal trajectories of understanding.

Issue 3: Teacher Presence and Cultural Reproduction

M: Much more so than in the previous chapter, we see the teacher's actions and intentions in an overt way in the account. We see a teacher who has planned a lesson, organized a particular set of artifacts (block and tackle), set it up, and arranged for a competition. After the predictable outcome of the tug of war (though the actual participation was originally planned to include 8 students to guarantee the teacher's victory; the sheer number of 20 students who lost was an even more fortuitous circumstance that let the conversation unfold as it did), the stage was set for a planned sense-making conversation about the outcome of this competition. We also see me as a flexible individual who, when the first student began to argue for a different design that would change the outcome, senses the opportunity for design and thought experiments, and therefore for the children's authentic experience of science in action, to emerge. We see a conversation that unfolds, unforeseeable in its specific details, not chaotic but always constrained, as a function of the situational choices of an experienced and knowledgeable (content) teacher.

K: Your actions in planning and enacting the curriculum were highly appropriate. You were wise to select an activity with game-like features that were likely to be well received by the students. Then, as the lesson progressed your flexibility enabled students to participate appropriately. You were co-participating with students in a way that facilitated their learning.

S: What strikes me most about you in this chapter is that you seem to get the right balance between cultural reproduction and cultural production. This was a fluid relationship because there were times when cultural reproduction was in the foreground, as in Episode 4.2, and other times when students such as Shaun took control of the conversation, as in Episode 4.5. Even here your questions kept Shaun accountable for his previously constructed inscriptions. Clearly, you have an active role to play in the process of developing students' canonical language games.

M I am also present in a different way, embodied in the ways of arguing, in the habitus that drives the practices of engaging in scientific argument. I am not just physically present, but—as an instigator of forms of argument and discourse, choice of representational devices and tasks—I am present in the ways of enacting science in this culture by all its participants.

K: Just how can teachers establish and maintain a habitus that supports the learning of science? Here we have some examples of how this can be done but I am sure the readers will want to see even more. It is easy to imagine that activities of the type described here can fail to show any evidence of a scientific discourse. What is it about a habitus that supports science? I want to suggest that roles such as the following are highly appropriate: listening, watching, suggesting ideas, finding evidence to support and refute such ideas, searching for alternative designs, and adapting inscriptions. In making this list, I began to think of what we called the process skills and began to imagine teachers reinventing the process approach to science. But that is not what I am thinking of at all. The types of participation that permeate what is considered to be an ideal learning environment to support scientific discourse are likely to vary from activity to activity and community to community. What is clear to me though, is that the activities described in this chapter were supported by a habitus that was in many respects ideal for the learning of science. You and the students played active roles, and there is ample evidence to suggest that at various times all participants in this community were both learners and teachers.

S: Checklists such as this are sometimes handy when experienced teachers sense that things are not going too well; they can help the teacher to focus on important aspects of classroom practice. Yet it is a very different story for a beginning teacher. Recipes and lists of good ideas don't seem to work. Most of the other chapters illustrate the practices of experienced elementary teachers, some of whom do not have specialist scientific backgrounds. We hope that inexperienced teachers who read these chapters will be able to relate these practices to their own classroom contexts and identify new possibilities for action.

M: It was interesting to note how much students interacted during the design activities, how those with expertise in the use of some tools both instructed and helped others to use them, and thereby contributed to the re/production of cultural knowledge more generally. For example, a particular boy knew how to use electrical saws and drills. He instructed others in the use of these tools that are not normally part of school activities. Students therefore also appropriated (especially material) practices that they normally would only encounter outside of schools.

Notes

1   This chapter elaborates on conceptualizations and data initially published as Roth (1996f). The voice is that of Michael Roth who taught the curriculum on simple machines featured in this chapter.

2   For example, bridges can be interpreted in multiple ways. Usually, they are considered as technologies that allow people to cross another street, a river, or a valley. But they can also be considered political artifacts. For example, Winner (1980) considers the bridges in New York with low clearance as a tool by the architect (working for the rich) to keep buses, and therefore the poor, from going to the beaches. Here, the two interpretations are such that they are commensurable. In other situations, however, alternative interpretations may not be commensurable.

3   It is typical to associate learning problems with individuals rather than the community or some other aspect of the setting. The problems listed here were those identified by the regular classroom teachers. Mehan (1993) describes the social aspects of constructing learning disabilities by attributing differential weights to participants in a decision-making meeting (teacher, parents, nurses, psychologists, and principal).

4   If we think of learning as the modification of language, it becomes implausible attempting to bring about radical conceptual change in understanding (radical change in talking science). However, knowing as continuous, evolutionary change in talking about a particular domain is what I have observed in other studies (e.g. Roth, 1996e).

5   The mechanical advantage is a concept in physics that describes the relationship between the amount of force that would have to be applied to move an object without machine and with machine. The greater the mechanical advantage of a machine, the easier it is to lift an object with it. For example, if a hoist has a mechanical advantage of 10, it is 10 times easier to lift a car with the hoist than it would be to lift it with bare hands.

6   Detailed accounts of learning and cognition in this classroom can be found elsewhere (McGinn & Roth, 1998; McGinn, Roth, Boutonné, & Woszczyna, 1995; Roth, 1996f, 1996g, 1998a, 1998b, 1998c; Roth & McGinn, 1996; Roth, McGinn, Woszczyna, & Boutonné, 1999; Welzel & Roth, 1998).

7   It is important to note that talk in the presence of a drawing, for example, can be both about this representation (so that it is the topic of the talk) and over the representation (so that it is the background against which the communication achieves its meaning).

8   Recall that I treat language as a form of action. Whether people have intentions and what form they take can never be determined because of the elusive nature of mental states. However, utterances that are used to bring about actions can be

interpreted as if they were due to underlying intentions. In this way, others (especially the teacher) heard Shaun's utterance as an expression of specific intention, which is, for members present, all that counts.

9   One of my past studies provided some evidence that female students may not appreciate the competitive aspects of argumentation (Roth, 1994). In a Grade 11 physics course, some students had indicated that they liked "shooting down other students' arguments." By means of a questionnaire, I found out that male students predominantly (strongly) agreed with such a statement, whereas the female students (strongly) disagreed with the statement.

10   In fact, Garfinkel (1967) argued that all talk is indexical and can be understood only because we are already familiar with the context of the talk. He illustrated his argument by showing that any text (uttered or written) never contains enough information to communicate some information or the information necessary to understand the information as the intended information. Any attempt to make a text completely self-explanatory is therefore doomed to failure. The mathematician Gödel showed that any formal system of representation has this property of being incomplete (Hofstadter, 1979).

11   Again, I take talk as one form of situated action. Questions such as "Does anyone understand what Shaun is asking me?" therefore not only ask for an explanation of what Shaun asked but also indicate that I had not understood. Such questions therefore achieve several things. First, they indicate that the listener had not understood. Second, they ask for clarification.

12   The issue, of course, was one of control. Shaun was a "troublemaker" who often attempted to engage peers and teachers in discussions for the sake of arguing and liked to draw all attention to himself and upstage others (peers and teachers). Concerned with the progress of the conversation and with the learning of the community as a whole, I did not want to give Shaun control over the chalkboard and therefore control over this aspect of the conversation.

13   Again, the utterance as a situated action not only indicated that there already was a drawing with a banister but also suggested that the speaker should make his argument by referring to it rather than by producing a new one.

14   The "continuer" (Schegloff, 1982) "OK" merely signaled that I followed Shaun's presentation and attended to the same features and that I conceded to Shaun a possible next turn.

15   There is evidence that agreement on an observation of the "same" event or on a word (even when introduced by students) is not self evident (Roth, 1995a; Roth, McRobbie, Lucas, & Boutonné, 1997a; Duit, Roth, Komorek, & Wilbers, in press). In our experience, more often than not there will be disagreements about what was seen in a demonstration or what a word means.

16   In a series of studies, we showed how the Latourian (1987) notion of "inscriptions" and the associated notion of "boundary object" (Star, 1989) assist in the social organization of students' collectivities and in the collaborative production and reproduction of knowledge in school science (e.g., Roth, 1996e; Roth & Roychoudhury, 1992, 1993).

Chapter 5

Learn as You Build: Integrating Science in Innovative Design[1]

Designing is a non-linear and situated activity that attempts to bring order to messy situations (Chapter 2). However, some curriculum writers (inappropriately) convey to students and teachers the message that the process of producing an original artifact follows some sort of predetermined highly structured and universal recipe. For example, the Australian Academy of Science's (1994) set of elementary school science materials, called *Primary Investigations,* includes a section on design in the Grade 6 book. Lesson 13 states the following objective: "In this lesson your team will actually make something—a toy car. You will imagine it, draw the plan and make a working model. You will then test the car to see how well it works" (p. 46). The lesson then proceeds to describe five steps for the students to follow in order to complete the task of making a toy car. The next lesson ("Back to the Drawing Board") poses the additional problem of making the car travel farther. At the end of this lesson, a summary box describes the design-make-appraise technological process as if it was a step-by-step orderly process that can be iterated repeatedly to improve the artifact (Figure 5.1).

The first step (i.e., design) involves several decisions about the purpose of the artifact and materials required.[2] These decisions lead to the brainstorming of ideas and the development of a plan or drawing of the artifact. Step 2 is listed as "make your device," but only after the children think their plan will work—suggesting that planning is the crucial first step, in which if you get it right, the rest will follow. The third and final step is to appraise or test the artifact. Although it is possible, children are

Summary of the design-make-appraise process

from *Primary Investigations*

There were several steps involved in making the final model. These steps are the same whatever you are trying to make.

1. Design what you want to make.

- Decide what the problem is you want to solve.

- Decide what output you want from your invention.

- Decide what energy you can put into the device.

- Decide what materials you can use to make your model.

- Plan how you will build your device. Planning includes brainstorming, discussing possible ideas and drawing your device.

2. Make your device when you think your design will work.

3. Appraise your model. To appraise something means to test it. Although it might work perfectly, you are likely to find that it doesn't work. You might re-design your model. You might then build it and appraise your new model. You might have to go through this design-make-appraise process several times.

Figure 5.1 Summary of the design-make-appraise process from *Primary Investigations*.

told to get it right the first time and that, presuming the plan was a good one, the outcome of the test is likely to lead to modifications or redesign. At this stage, the children are encouraged to work through the same steps in the same sequence until the artifact eventually satisfies the test. This routinized cyclic process is what Faulkner (1994) means by "normal design." Normal engineering design lacks the excitement of innovation; it is characterized by its well-established paradigmatic nature of canonical knowledge. In contrast, we advocate revolutionary or "innovative design" (Faulkner, 1994) activities for children. In these activities, children's design artifacts integrate over their own history, by which previously tentative design moves become facts that in turn shape future design moves. In this way designing becomes the unfolding conversation in which the designer interacts with the materials and the materials and emerging artifact continuously "talk back" (Roth, 1998a).

Engineering design activities, as we showed in Chapter 2, have a lot of potential to teach science in elementary school classrooms. However, not any engineering activity will assist children in learning science. During innovative design activities children learn not only engineering or science but also about the two domains. While we applaud the inclusion of design activities in the science curriculum as described in *Primary Investigations* (Australian Academy of Science, 1994), the representation of technological development the design-make-appraise sequence suggests is highly simplistic and problematic. To reiterate our position, linear and cyclical processes poorly model the design of new artifacts.

In this chapter we illustrate the dynamic nature of the design process with reference to an Australian Grade 6 class. In part, this dynamic is translated into the bodily understandings of the children we identify in the children's classroom discourse. Although the class teacher selected particular lessons from the book described above, the students were not restricted by the design-make-appraise sequence. Instead, we first show how the sub-tasks of planning, building, and testing were interrelated during the design of simple machines. Although some groups of students in this class valued planning, all groups were able to refine and modify their artifacts during construction. Second, and most important, we show that experience gained while constructing the artifact helped to improve the product and also gave students the opportunity to develop canonical scientific knowledge through their design projects. We start this chapter with a description of a typical design lesson to contextualize the discussion of these two issues.

Purposeful Design: The Marble Machine

Soon after the Grade 6 students entered the room, their teacher, Mr. Hammett, outlined the task for the lesson: the construction of a marble machine with a purpose. He explained that students could use ideas from their previous science activities on energy and their 10-second marble machines. Previously, students had completed a series of lessons from *Primary Investigations* on energy. These lessons focused on such concepts as types of energy (e.g., stored, position [potential], movement, sound, light) and energy transfer. Although the students had prior design experience with projects on structures and bridges, the most recent design project was completed in the preceding science and technology lesson (i.e., the previous week), in which the students constructed 10-second marble machines. In this project, the machines were expected to keep a falling marble moving for 10 seconds. This project was completed in just one 90-minute lesson. Mr. Hammett usually scheduled at least one lesson per week for science and technology lessons. Any unfinished projects were completed in free time and during lunch breaks.

The function of the marble machine with a purpose was to apply the energy of a falling marble to fulfil a particular purpose, which could be to feed a cat or water a plant. As classroom space was limited Mr. Hammett advised the students that each machine had to be restricted to a square base with a side of about 50 centimeters. Mr. Hammett, who made available cardboard bases with the appropriate dimensions, controlled this aspect of the activity. The project was more complicated than the 10-second marble machine and had fewer imposed constraints. Mr. Hammett therefore had set aside about three weeks for this design project.

After describing the design brief for the machine, Mr. Hammett invited students to identify as many ideas as they could to fit the brief. Mr. Hammett recorded even the most playful ideas from individual students on the chalkboard to form a web-like structure that he later called a mind map. As we found out later during the student interviews, students rarely nominated their most cherished ideas, but instead took joy in announcing creative ideas that seemed remotely related and possibly impractical for classroom-based projects. Mr. Hammett then emphasized that during the group tasks the students needed to listen to all ideas and for each group to reach consensus before proceeding to make their machines. The students began this planning task in their established friendship groups.

Mr. Hammett allocated 10 minutes for planning. During this time, Mr. Hammett expected students to canvas possible ideas and to draw a rough plan that represented each group's agreed views. Although this task was similar to the first step in traditional design prior to building a prototype, Mr. Hammett employed it as a strategy to foster equitable participation of students within groups. As Mr. Hammett visited each group he listened to the conversation and sometimes asked questions such as "How did you decide to design this?" and "Did everyone get a chance to put forward their ideas?" as a way of checking the levels of student participation. During the planning segment the noise level increased substantially as students became more excited and animated within their groups. There were noticeable differences between groups in terms of their interaction and leadership styles. In Mitchell's group everybody seemed to promote their own agendas; occasionally, individuals yelled out their ideas as if they were agents on the floor of the stock exchange. In contrast, individuals in Kerrin's group used the planning time for drawing alternative ideas on paper. The silence within the group was broken now and then by Kerrin, who sought clarification of roles and tasks, and then to establish the preferred solution. Alicia's group was still discussing alternatives well after all other groups had commenced building their machines, while Adam's group seemed to start building immediately—without discussing possible alternatives or drawing a plan on paper. As other groups became aware that Adam's group had started the next phase, they too started gathering materials, as if all material resources would soon be claimed. When Mr. Hammett noticed a shift in tasks by several groups, he reminded the class that the present task of planning was still in progress and that no student was to begin either collecting materials or building. Mr. Hammett then spoke to Adam's group to make sure that they had shared possible ideas and had indeed agreed on the nature of their intended design. Shortly after, he advised the class that the manager for each group could now collect the necessary resources.

The students then moved about the classroom collecting cardboard and other resources to be used in the construction of their machines. Although most of the material resources were stored in a central location, it was necessary for individuals to ask other groups for tools, such as Stanley knives, that were in short supply. On these occasions, visiting students exchanged ideas and reacted to progress made by the host groups.[3] Mr. Hammett interrupted the class once to draw their attention to a safety issue (i.e., cutting style); on another occasion, he encouraged interaction between groups by asking one team to advise others on how they could limit their use of masking tape. For some students, this was their first opportunity to use a wood saw. When Mr. Hammett noticed that Eliza (in

Emily's group) was attempting to saw through plywood resting across her lap and that Mitchell slashed carelessly through a plastic milk container with a Stanley knife, he called a halt to proceedings before demonstrating safer practices. Soon after the first whole-class interruption, Mr. Hammett invited the thrifty group to demonstrate their use of masking tape. Following this brief presentation, Mr. Hammett advised the class that it was more economical to cut the masking tape with a pair of scissors than to tear off strips. At the end of this lesson, a volunteer spokesperson (i.e., the speaker) from each group described their group's plan and progress for the benefit of the whole class.

Adam outlined how, in his group's machine, a marble would travel through a descending tube and roll out over a game board before setting off one of several electric buzzers positioned across the board, like a pinball machine. After a slow start, Alicia's group eventually was able to agree to build a good/bad fortune machine. Alicia briefly told the class how they proposed to build a game machine that could indicate whether the player would experience good or bad fortune. A rolling marble was to come to a junction where the main track separated into two tracks. Here, the path taken by the marble would indicate what sort of fortune lay ahead for the player. Because Kerrin's group engaged in the planning exercise diligently, Kerrin was able to describe an elaborate plan for a plant-watering machine. Initially, each member of Kerrin's group prepared individual drawings. Kerrin promoted her plan within her group (Figure 5.2). However, after listening to other students she informed the class of a slightly modified plan, which incorporated at least one other idea, namely a water-filled balloon traveling along a conveyor belt. In this machine, a falling marble was to activate an electric motor that would

Figure 5.2 Kerrin's plan of a plant-watering machine

then drive a conveyor belt. A water-filled balloon was to travel along the conveyor belt until striking a pin directly over a targeted plant. Complications with the conveyor belt forced her group to modify its plan in subsequent lessons.

Emily's group designed the Egg-Cracking Breakfast-Cooking machine. In this machine, a marble was to travel down a vertical zigzag channel, hit another marble, then roll through a long straight tube to hit a large "bungie marble." This marble, inside a plastic bag tied to a long rubber band, was to fall about half a meter onto a suspended raw egg. This collision then would crack the egg open, allowing the yolk to fall into a frying pan.

Gavin's group constructed the Beef-N-Bacon Sausage-Cooker machine. This machine consisted of a raised cardboard and timber platform, which was originally intended to support Gavin's pet rat, a series of zig-zagging thin red tubes (which were supported by cylinder pylons) and an aluminum-lined cardboard box filled with heating coals to cook a suspended sausage on a skewer. A rat was to be trained to move the marble into the tube. This marble would then travel through the tubes, hitting a larger marble, which eventually would collide with a hot coal, knock it into the firebox to ignite the other coals, and so cook the sausage.

During this initial lesson and subsequent lessons, students continued to build and modify their machines. Mr. Hammett gave groups direct assistance during the lessons and provided indirect assistance by modeling the process of design. He constructed a large classroom-sized crazy tennis-ball machine with volunteer students during lunch breaks and after school. This machine was constructed concurrently with the student design projects, incorporating ideas from several of the student projects as well as ideas that the students believed to be too complex for them to build by themselves. As we show later, this machine frequently became a source of ideas for the groups during the design of their marble machines. This development is consistent with earlier claims that both human and material actors contribute to innovative design (i.e., see Chapter 2; Roth, 1998a). The tennis-ball machine involved a circuit of descending tracks, suspended above the students' desks, to slow down the fall of a tennis ball. After completing the circuit, a conveyor belt operated by a geared electric motor carried the ball to the starting position again. Other mechanical and electrical devices, activated by the passing ball, were built along the circuit for entertainment purposes. Unlike the marble machines, the tennis-ball machine was a long-term project—it was begun prior to the first marble-machine lesson and was completed several weeks after the final class presentations of the marble machines.

Planning-Building-Testing

Traditional lore holds that designing is a rational activity based on declarative and procedural knowledge. However, one may ask the question: How can one design in an unfamiliar domain? Designing in an unfamiliar domain is like finding the direct way through a terrain in an unknown country. Even experienced designers familiar with their domain do not always succeed. That is, what they have on paper as a plan does not incorporate essential contingencies that make the design inappropriate. A famous example is the Tacoma Narrows Bridge, which was built in the 1940s. Excited into vibrations by the local winds, the bridge broke apart within days of its completion. As another example, in 1997, the manufacturers Swatch and Mercedes produced a new car. Within days of the first public tests, production of the car had to be halted because it tended to topple in the slightest turns. In a final example, after 18 years of research and prototyping, the French had to abandon their individualized urban rapid transport system ARAMIS because it was riddled with engineering problems that could not be foreseen in the paper versions but that emerged in the process of building and testing. In all of these cases, designing cannot be considered complete, for the design process continued even after the companies thought they had completed the product. For these reasons, it is better to consider the entire process as design.

In this section we demonstrate the interrelatedness of such design sub-tasks as planning, building, and testing. Unlike traditional designing that seems to lead on from planning to building a prototype to testing the prototype before redesign, we show that children adjust plans as they build the artifact. It is as if the developing artifact "talks back" to the students as they build and informs them of subsequent design moves that could not have been made without the experience gained through building. We illustrate this main point through a series of mini–case studies from different design groups or teams. We begin to develop our argument about the dialectical nature of design tasks with reference to Alicia's group. Although we continue to refine this argument through the other case studies, we make several additional points through this discussion. In particular, we reveal that the sub-task of planning helped some groups (e.g., Gavin's group) to generate images of the completed artifact. Although some students found the planning task useful, others soon abandoned their initial plans once they began building and testing. In these groups (e.g., Emily's group) students appeared to benefit from their interaction with the transforming artifact, yet they also reported mental imaging through the design project. We make use of the "thinkering" meta-phor here to describe how thinking and action are inseparable during innovative design activities. The artifact is transformed as students think with the materials available and attempt to convert their mental images into material reality. Finally, we discuss the relationship between the initial plan in Kerrin's group with their partially completed artifact, which was constructed after three lessons.

Dialectical Design Tasks

Alicia's group built one of the two fortune-game machines that were built in the class. The other group (i.e., Mitchell's group) worked adjacent to Alicia's group. Although Mr. Hammett encouraged the sharing of ideas between groups, students from these neighboring groups were somewhat defensive about the origin of the purpose for their marble machines, with both groups denying that they had copied from the other group. Never-theless it was obvious that each group was aware of the other's design (see for example turn 03 below). The students did not seem to be overly concerned that another group had built a different machine with the same purpose, and the machines were sufficiently different to suggest that each group had made a unique contribution to its designs. We have described the diffusion of ideas throughout designing communities elsewhere (e.g., Roth, 1995d).

The good/bad-fortune marble machine designed by Alicia's group was coin operated. After a coin was inserted to start the game, a marble was dislodged from a raised platform. It then rolled down a chute that branched off into two tracks. The critical part of the game was the junction—the point of separation for a pathway that led to either a good or bad fortune. The junction was critical because players would soon tire of a game that was biased towards one or the other pathway. Alicia's group needed to engage in several trials before they could separate the pathways without biasing the path that the marble would take. This meant that the track assembly needed to be level (i.e., viewed from the cross-section, the track needed to be rotated into a horizontal alignment) and the strips of mask-ing tape laid down on the inside track could not channel the marble down one path more frequently than the other. In addition to attending to these aspects of the design, they needed to judge the slope of the chute from the starting platform. A steep slope would cause the marble to travel too fast and jump the tracks entirely, while too gentle a slope would cause the marble to jam on the bulging layers of masking tape. These problems were not foreseen during the 10-minute session allocated to planning at the start of the project. In fact, without a lot of familiarity with these materials in this and similar situations, the problems are virtually unforeseeable. They only emerged during the process of building the tracks. Reducing the bulge of masking tape and leveling the tracks sideways clearly required engineering solutions, but these two tasks were nevertheless dependent on an understanding of basic scientific concepts such as friction and kinematics. Several authors (e.g., Fensham & Gardner, 1994) have suggested that science and technology are interdependent disciplines. Indeed, as we have argued in Chapter 2, attempts to separate science and technology cleanly are probably unproductive. The inseparable (interdependent) nature of science and technology is well illustrated by the nature of the problems Alicia's encountered group during their marble-machine design.

Apart from illustrating the interdependent relationship between science and technology, analysis of transcripts of within-group conversations from Alicia's group emphasizes the interrelatedness of the sub-tasks of planning, building, and testing. The excerpt below was recorded while Alicia's group assembled the tracks for their marble machine and contemplated how to build the receptacle in which the player would deposit a coin to start the marble rolling. Nerida asked:

01 Nerida: How's it [marble] going to fall in [the track]? Or are we just going to push it in?
02 Alicia: Put it in.
03 Juana: [Referring to the actions of a neighboring group; i.e., Mitchell's group] They are.
04 Nerida: Okay, what about the money? Where's the money going to go?
05 Alicia: We have got to make the holes [Alicia answers Nerida's question, which refers to the need to cut a slot for the coin, as she continues to manipulate the tracks for the marble. She releases the marble, elevates one end of the track slightly, pauses and utters:] It works!
06 Nerida: Now we gotta put the legs on [to support the track]. We gotta put the legs on. Put it [track assembly] upside down [so we can put the legs on].

Although the group may have formed an overall image of their operational machine during the planning segment, it was not until they started building the machine that they could decide on the details of their design. Practical issues of whether they would place the marble on the tracks or develop an alternative mechanism were briefly considered in situ (turns 01, 02). Alicia seemed to decide for the group that they should simply put the marble on the track (turn 02). But what about the component to be operated by the coin (turn 04)? Alicia responded to Nerida's question (turn 05) without interrupting her all-consuming task of fine-tuning and testing the tracks. When Nerida realized that the tracks had been successfully built by Alicia she turned her attention to this component of the design by suggesting the need to put legs on the tracks, presumably to support and elevate the track assembly. This would allow the marble to roll down the tracks (turn 06)—yet another engineering problem. Without using the language game (see Chapter 2) of standard science, Alicia's action of raising one end of the track, and her gleeful response (turn 05), suggests that she did understand the relationship between the height to which the marble was elevated and the speed of the released marble at the bottom of the track. So, even without the benefit of probing interview questions, we can see that the design project enabled students to act out their understanding of (but unspoken) canonical science.

The sequence of these sub-tasks was not pre-planned. Instead, the plans seemed to be made in response to the experiences gained in completing previous sub-tasks. For example, when Alicia identified the slope at which the marble reaches the desired speed at the bottom of the track in turn 05, Nerida suggested that they should set this working component by fixing the supporting legs into position (turn 07). The questions and suggestions throughout the excerpt were made during the process of building the machine rather than in the allotted planning segment. Perhaps they could only be made while building, when the students became familiar with the materials in use and the practical issues that confronted them during the building task. Clearly, there was no linear sequence of sub-tasks in use (i.e., planning, building, testing); experience gained in building and testing the tracks influenced subsequent plans of the machine. Success with the elevation of the track (turn 05) informed the group that they needed to set this slope in position. As it was, the developing machine was talking back to them—figuratively telling them the next step. Actor network theory is useful for describing the complex interrelationships between both human and non-human actors in technological projects (Roth, 1998a). Actor networks constitute analytical tools for investigating and understanding the evolution of scientific and technological communities. Actor network approaches view these communities as networks of actors in a seamless web of situated activity without distinguishing between human and non-human actors, between individuals and institutions, or between social or material activity. Viewed from this heterogeneous perspective, there is a dialectical relationship between the transforming artifact and the students, who both initiate and react to this non-human actor. Similarly, the relationship between science and technology (or engineering) problems/learning can be described as a dialectic between actors (see Chapter 2).

Returning finally to the planning-building-testing sub-tasks, we have shown in this mini–case study that without an initial basic plan (drawn or imagined—as we see later), this group would not have even started to build the tracks as they did. Making trials of and testing possible configurations of the tracks helped improve the design as well as suggest a set of follow-up actions to transform the artifact. The transformed artifact also helped to transform the students as they progressively expressed their scientific learning through their technological designing.

Mental Imaging in Design

Emily's group designed the Egg-Cracking Breakfast-Cooking machine. Like Alicia's group, Emily's group encountered engineering problems during the construction of its machine. These problems, as we show below, were not anticipated during the allocated 10-minute planning segment. It was only when they started building to their initial plan that they could identify substantive problems to be solved. Soon after they began building, Emily's group appeared to discard the plan that they had drawn; they no longer made reference to it physically or in their discussions. Emily reinforced this observation during an interview. When asked whether the planning segment was helpful, Emily replied:

07 Emily: No, not really because like we didn't really use it.
08 Interviewer: Didn't use the plan at all?
09 Emily: No, we just thought of an idea and tried that out and tried different ideas. . . . We did get a plan, we did think about it first, but we didn't really. . . . [use it].

In turns 07 and 09, Emily admitted that the product of their planning segment (i.e., a drawn plan) was not particularly helpful or useful for the purposes of designing their machine. Nevertheless, she also admitted that the planning session afforded her group the opportunity to think about the overall concept and explore some preliminary ideas. In Emily's group, plausible ideas that were generated in response to engineering problems were then tested in situ. This designing style created a fun-like atmosphere in their group. The group welcomed contributions from individual members and they put each idea to the test. When an idea worked in practice they appropriated it into their design. For example, when Eliza suggested that they fix their descending tracks to the base or backing board, they tried it. They completed a successful trial of a marble dropping out of the tracks. This component of the track in their design could be seen in their previously completed artifact. However, they did not reject ideas if they did not work the first time. Emily realized that a decision shouldn't be taken from limited data sources, suggesting that she was familiar with the canonical scientific practice of multiple trialing or sampling: "If it doesn't work the first time, you don't just say it doesn't work, you have got to try it again and again."

Although Emily downplayed the usefulness of her group's drawn plan, consideration of ideas generated in situ was essentially a planning task. This planning led to the identification of additional problems and the generation of possible solutions. For example, the initial planning of an egg cracker led to the emergence of several ideas for discussion. In the following interview excerpt, Emily recalled how she was able to draw upon her prior experience to suggest a possible solution. Emily also revealed how ideas suggested within the group activated mental images for her which, in turn, led to worthwhile suggestions. These suggestions seemed to activate images related to prior experiences of other group members, who were then able to articulate new ideas. As the students interacted in this way, the group solution emerged as the product of the collective activity of the group or learning community, sometimes with little apparent discussion within the group. Just prior to this excerpt, Emily acknowledged that Karen had first proposed the idea of a bungie marble—the central feature of their marble machine. As Emily was thinking about the practical difficulties of attaching the rubber bands to the marble she thought of enclosing the marble within a plastic bag. Here, Emily visualized the ideas in action during this planning phase of the design process.

10	Interviewer:	So where did you get that idea from, Emily?
11	Emily:	Well, it was just simple because how was a marble going to stick to elastic bands? And at first I thought at home, I thought of the sock, but we didn't have any odd socks. So I thought how about the end of a plastic bag because that's round, because a plastic bag holds things so you can use the end of a plastic bag because a whole plastic bag would have been too big. I put the marble in it and tied the elastic bands around the marble and then you have it.
12	Eliza:	We had the idea, we still used the idea of the egg and all that but we just thought of ideas when we were chatting.
13	Emily:	You know how you spin sometimes when you put a tennis ball in things and you spin it around, that's what gave me the sock idea, and then I thought, "Well what could be better than just a sock?" And I thought a plastic bag would be good, the end of a plastic bag.

Karen's idea of using a bungie marble to crack open the egg was based upon her prior experience of observing bungie jumps. This idea was relevant to the present situation, the action of the marble falling onto an egg without falling into the frying pan. This idea could have been rejected on the basis of the problem of securing the rubber bands around a marble. However, Emily's experiences of seeing a ball in a sock twirled overhead prompted her to build on Karen's idea (turn 13). This idea, although at first viewed as a problem (turn 11), became a viable and important part of their design. The idea was taken on despite the problems experienced later during testing (i.e., securing the bungie marble to the launch platform). So even though some students may not recognize the usefulness of the allocated pre-building planning sub-task, planning in situ (i.e., as an interrelated component of the design process) did appear to contribute significantly to the final artifact.

In turn 12, Eliza claimed that she thought of ideas while the group was discussing identified problems (e.g., attaching rubber bands to a marble in turn 11) in situ—as they were building their machine. Emily then elaborated how she visualized a possible solution in turn 13. The image of a game involving swinging a ball overhead that is restrained within an elastic capsule (such as a sock) evoked the idea of enclosing their bungie marble with a plastic bag that could then be attached to a rubber band. In the case of the bungie marble, planning involved generating and modifying images of prior experiences. Emily reported that she modified her image as she thought through possible solutions to the problem. This planning did not necessitate drawing the image, possibly because it was sufficiently vivid and relevant to the particular resources available to her in the classroom and could be articulated within the group without reference to a pictorial representation. The final artifact incorporated the bungie marble component as described through Emily's image in turn 13. In this sense, the artifact came about through the children's embodied work in a material world.

Gavin's group plan became an essential component of the construction of their Beef-N-Bacon Sausage-Cooker machine. For this group, the plan was helpful in identifying the materials required and assigning tasks and roles to group members. However, perhaps the most powerful value of drawing a plan, from Gavin's account below, was that he claimed that it helped him to visualize and mentally test the plan prior to construction (i.e., turn 23 below).

14 Interviewer: Was it helpful to plan it out to begin with?
15 Gavin: Yeah otherwise we don't know what anyone else is doing . . .

16 Interviewer: What other parts of the design were helpful in reaching the end
                   product?
17 Gavin: Just having a rough idea of where everything can go, so working from
                   this we will just look at our plan and say, ah, it is somewhere around
                   there. It shows us like where everything will go in relation to each
                   other.
18 Interviewer: Did you adjust your plan as you went?
19 Gavin: Yes.
20 Interviewer: What caused you to change your plan?
21 Gavin: It didn't work. Yeah, because if it doesn't work; like when you are
                   making a plan you can't just see if it will work or not, you have got to
                   think whether it will work and then you have to actually test it and the
                   only way to test it is to build it.
22 Interviewer: So you plan it and you think about it to see if it is going to work.
23 Gavin: Yeah like in your mind you picture the machine when it is finished and
                   you roll the marble down it and like you imagine a marble down it.

In turns 15 and 17, Gavin suggested that his group identified components of their proposed artifact (i.e., firebox and cooker, starting platform, catapult, descending tracks) that they then assigned to each other
for completion. In this way, the pre-building planning phase was perceived to be helpful because group members knew what each other was
doing. Here, two students made adjustments to the fire box or cooking
component (lower right) while another (upper left) assembled the catapult
that was originally intended to project a hot coal into the firebox, where it
would then ignite the other coals. After several attempts to catapult a coal
into the firebox by using the kinetic energy of the descending marble to
set off the loaded catapult, the group eventually decided to abandon this
component. This was one of the components Gavin referred to in turn 08
when he declared that they adjusted their initial plan when "it didn't work."
Gavin's modified rough plan is illustrated in Figure 5.3. This plan shows
the side elevation of the proposed artifact. This sketch was not meant to
be a detailed blueprint but rather to provide "a rough idea where everything can go" (turn 17). The parallel lines represent the starting platform
in the top of the plan. The descending tracks eventually led the marble to
a coal at the end of the track. Here, the marble needed to have gained
sufficient speed to propel the coal into the open firebox and cooker in the
bottom left of the plan. In the original plan, however, the marble was to
have fallen on to the left-hand side of the catapult or effort arm of the
lever. A coal loaded on the other end was to have been catapulted into the
firebox to the left. The unsuccessful trial shows that after the dropped
marble bounces off toward the left of the frame, the loaded coal simply
slides off the rising load arm of the lever in the middle of the frame.

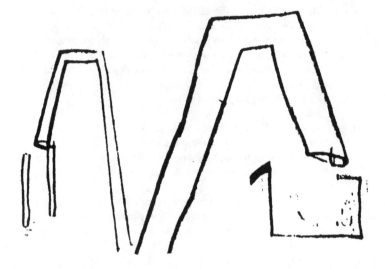

Figure 5.3 A modified rough plan for the Beef-N-Bacon Sausage-Cooker machine.

Although Gavin acknowledged that drawing a plan was helpful for several reasons (turns 15, 17, 23) it was through building the machine that limitations of the original plan were identified. In turn, this experience led to an improved design. Like Emily, Gavin generated some ideas of his machine during planning (turn 23). This was a significant part of Gavin's preparation for building. Here, he tried to imagine how the machine would work prior to building. In this way, he could anticipate design problems and modify his plan accordingly in much the same way as Schön (1987) described designers conversing with their drawings. However, to make his images concrete, Gavin needed to interact physically with the material world—the building resources available to him and his peers. As he admitted in turn 21, the only way that Gavin could bring his ideas into material existence was to build and test these ideas.

During planning, Gavin thought about the materialization of his mental image of the functioning machine but acknowledged that he could not "see" if it would work (turn 21). Although he might have been able to visualize the machine in operation prior to its construction, Gavin could not foresee all building problems. For example, Gavin may have pictured the catapult in operation prior to building, yet his group needed to make several adjustments to the position of the fulcrum in an attempt to get it working. In a sense, Gavin engaged in the process of thinking-in-action with the material resources available or in thinking while he tinkered with the artifact. That is, artifacts such as the catapult promote the integration of "thinking" and "acting" for students engaged in innovative design activities. The metaphor of "thinkering" represents how we view the interrelated tasks of planning, building, and testing. Unlike the traditional view of designing, which separates the generation of ideas from the artifact, children engage in thinkering through innovative design activities. Designing, then, should be viewed as an activity in which thinking and the tools, materials, and the artifact are intricately intertwined. Gavin's group engaged in thinkering as they adjusted their plan in light of the experience and insight gained while building and testing the artifact; the design process involved all three interrelated components (i.e., planning, building, testing) such that each could inform the students about the other sub-tasks.

Transformation of the Design Artifact

Kerrin's initial planning of her plant-watering machine began with a mind map. This was a technique widely used by students in this class to map out their first thoughts or ideas for their designs. Figure 5.4 shows that Kerrin first linked the purpose of the marble machine (i.e., water a plant) with the concept of a water bomb and pin. As Kerrin revealed later within her group, the pin's role was to pierce the water-filled balloon, which would then dispel its contents over a potted plant positioned below it. Next, Kerrin listed several words together below the title of marble machine. These were the various components that were to be connected together to form the artifact. Although it is fairly clear from her plan that the "jump" was related to Component A[4] (perhaps a ski jump or ramp) and the spiral was associated with Component C, it is more difficult to link the obstacle course with the remaining components (i.e., either Component B or D). As we can see from the related transcript below, Kerrin did not attribute a name to her conveyor belt device (Component B) but rather pointed to a similar device in the class-sized tennis ball machine (turn 24). Perhaps this was what Kerrin meant by obstacle course. Alternatively, she could have been referring to the various tracks that linked each of the components (i.e., B to C; C to D).

The following lesson transcript excerpt was recorded during Kerrin's presentation of her plan to her fellow group members. She held her book up and referred to various components of her plan by pointing with her finger.

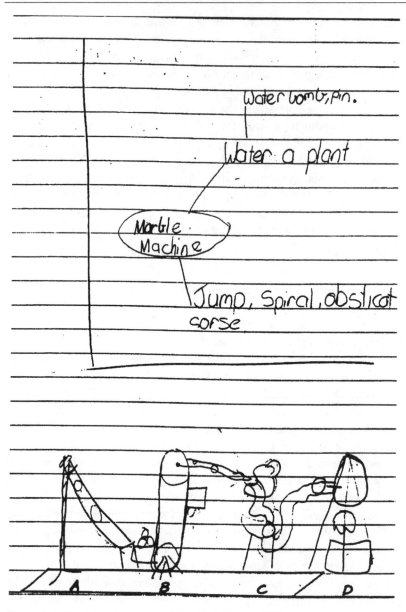

Water bomb, pin.

Water a plant

Marble Machine

Jump, Spiral, obstical corse

Figure 5.4 Kerrin's mind map and (annotated) plan of her plant-warering machine.

24 Kerrin: Okay what I've got is it starts there like the little marble there and the marble rolls down [Component A]. And it rolls down into the container there and you've got one of those things [Component B] like up there [as she points to the conveyor belt device from the class-sized tennis-ball machine]. It's carried straight up, maybe a bit higher. And then it rolls down into Blinky Bill's mouth and out through the toilet [Component C] and then up through the pipe, there's a pin there [Component D].

25 Xanthea: If it's not that high up it won't go down.

26 Kerrin: Yeah I know. That's why it goes up higher but not that high. It will be up high and maybe go down and um and hit the ball and there is another marble and it could hit it and the energy could transfer to the other ball and it cause it to stay there like the pin somehow staying there. It's sticking there like with blue tac or something.

27 Merissa: [Merissa began describing her plan, but her voice was mostly inaudible. She too had incorporated similar components, but the conveyor belt was to function horizontally rather than vertically as Component B in Kerrin's plan—Figure 5.3. This belt was to carry the water-filled balloon toward the fixed pin, where it would burst and drop its load of water onto a seedbed.]

28 Janet: We should make the props things first.

29 Kerrin: I'll get the paddle-pop sticks.

Without deciding which of the two plans in turns 24 and 27 they should adopt (or even a combination of the plans) Janet suggested that they begin by building each of the components (or "props" as she called them in turn 28). Such action would avoid any conflict because the two plans were comprised of essentially the same major components, and it would not distract the group by attending to the details of any perceived differences between the two plans. Kerrin reacted immediately to Janet's suggestion by volunteering to collect the paddle pop sticks, demonstrating an eagerness to start building the components.

They began building Component C. Considerable time (i.e., 30 minutes) was spent trying out different configurations to support Blinky Bill. Blinky Bill was a popular television cartoon character of a koala. Kerrin had brought to class two plastic toy replicas of the character for use in their project. Kerrin's plan showed (in turn 24 above) that a marble was to roll into Blinky Bill's mouth, then pass through a descending spiral that Kerrin likened to an animal's digestive system whose point of exit later was referred to as the "toilet" (turn 24). Eventually, a cardboard cylinder measuring about 50 centimeters long was selected as the pylon upon which Blinky Bill was to sit, as if he was a figurehead on the bow of a yacht. Kerrin cut a hole for a mouth and removed the base so that Blinky Bill could be positioned on top of the pylon.

As soon as Blinky Bill was fixed into position, the group was faced with a new problem; that was, how to fix the spiral inside the pylon so that the marble would roll through as planned. An externally attached spiral was soon tried as an alternative. This trial also was rejected because it was perceived to be too cumbersome in size because the marble descended too far too quickly. The height of Component C was always a concern for the students. In turn 25, Xanthea expressed the view that the tracks needed to be positioned as high as possible. This concern was quickly addressed by Kerrin in turn 26 when she confidently acknowledged that she knew that the tracks needed to be sufficiently high for the marble to attain enough speed to roll up the path to Component D and transfer energy to the pin.

By the end of the allocated three weeks, the group had advanced considerably. The pylon upon which Blinky Bill was to sit is shown in the center of the frame. Blinky Bill was no longer adorning the pylon, and the original idea of a spiral had been replaced by a more gently descending set of tracks that bordered the base of their machine. At this stage, Component B was still included in the design and was positioned to the right of the pylon. However, the students found it too difficult to control the speed of the motor, which caused them later to abandon this component as well. As Xanthea declared during an interview: "The batteries were going too fast for the conveyor belt we had. We had to keep on turning it off and on otherwise the marble would have been thrown over the other side of the room." Nevertheless, they did demonstrate their intended application of Component B manually for their class presentation. A receptacle for the marble was cut out of an egg carton and attached to an elastic band that was stretched over two pulleys.

It is clear from Kerrin's group that the original plan was substantially modified during the construction of the machine. After three weeks' work, only Components B and C were completed. Moreover, Component C was modified considerably when the group encountered engineering problems during construction. Kerrin's group did not foresee these problems, nor did it forsee the problem of trying to slow down their electric motor in Component B. Given more time, Kerrin's group might have solved the problem of slowing down its motor. In fact, Kerrin, Katrina, and Xanthea continued to work on this problem on their own time (e.g., during lunch breaks) and appeared to have improved this component until Janet and Merissa dismantled the machine without seeking approval from the others. As Kerrin reported: "It was starting to go really well because we had spent so much time on it and it was a bit disappointing just seeing it ripped apart." Even with this additional time, Kerrin's group was unable to finish component D and did not start Component A. Their initial plan was far too ambitious in that they were not able to identify many of the design problems until they encountered them during construction. It seems then, that teachers should emphasize that the main role of any pre-building planning time is for generating possible ideas for designing. During designing of the artifact students should expect that they will need to solve engineering problems, the nature of which they do not yet know.

The distinct difference between the initial plan and the final artifact was not confined to those groups that might not have displayed a highly developed set of material practices (i.e., students in Kerrin's group admitted to having limited experience with the practices required to complete several tasks). In Gavin's group, for example, the students were able to build a catapult only to find that it did not serve the intended purpose, which led them to abandon it. During the student interviews with other groups, all students admitted that their final artifacts varied considerably from their original plans. The students in Mitchell's group reached the decision to build a machine that they thought was "doable"[5] during their pre-building planning segment. It was only while trying to build their toaster machine (note: this machine became the second fortune-telling machine) that the group realized the need for a modified plan: "Later on we found it [the toaster machine] a bit awkward, so we changed it" (interview with Jackson). Mitchell's group also refined its design during the building task. When Adam was asked how closely his group's finished artifact of a pinball machine resembled the plan, he replied: "Nothing like it. I suppose we just built it as we went." The same point was made by George (another member of Adam's group) in a separate interview: "We sort of knew that we had to go up high because then you can have more track and we just sort of built it as we go, just made it as we go." In summary, all plans were modified considerably throughout the design of the machines. As the groups encountered unforeseen engineering problems, they adjusted their transforming artifacts until they were satisfied with the machines' functioning. Planning was continuous throughout the design and was interrelated with building and testing the artifacts.

Learning Science from Building

The mini–case studies described above illustrate the interrelatedness of the planning, building, and testing sub-tasks in the designing process. They also illustrate that students encountered engineering problems that needed to be addressed and hint at the possibility that students developed canonical scientific knowledge through building the artifacts. In this section we highlight just a few cases in which students appropriated relevant scientific language games through designing their marble machines. This argument is developed further in Chapter 6 when we turn to a different set of designing experiences.

As we have seen in Chapter 2, members of a design team need to communicate with each other during the design process and with future users of the artifacts on completion. In this sense designing is a deeply social activity. Not surprisingly, when the students were interviewed to ascertain their perceived learning outcomes from the marble-machine design activity, they typically identified social outcomes, such as skills in cooperating with fellow students. Rarely did they nominate canonical scientific knowledge as an outcome of their endeavors except in answer to a direct question about science learning in general or a specific concept that was related to their artifacts. For example, when Kerrin was asked what science she thought she might have learned during the marble machine activities, she replied: "We didn't learn anything about the electricity thing. We just hooked up the wires and turned it on." There was little in this statement to demonstrate that the design activity had led to a better understanding of related scientific concepts. However, without any intervention from the interviewer, Kerrin continued:

> I am just trying to think when we were often trying to hold up things. It was like better if we had, because we were having it on one stick of like holding it up by one stick, but then we saw the video cameras had been held up and so we started to make tripods and it started to hold up better.

Here, Kerrin recalled that her group confronted the engineering problem of increasing the stability of its structure only because it arose during the building sub-task. The tripod supporting one of the video cameras in the room motivated them to try out the idea of using the tripod structure in their own marble machine. After maneuvering self-made tripods into position they quickly recognized the stable features of such a structure. Increasing the stability of the tracks by replacing the unstable sticks with tripods was an effective engineering solution to the problem. Although Kerrin did not initially recognize this episode as one that was related to either technology or scientific concepts, upon reflection the not-so-obvious technological benefits of this design activity were realized.

There were several other occasions when Kerrin's group engaged in discourse that demonstrated that members had appropriated the language game of canonical science. During the excerpt from the previous section, Xanthea and Kerrin (turns 25 and 26) were talking about the motion of the marble as it rolled from Component B into Component C and up to Component D. They realized that the height of the tracks was directly related to the speed acquired by a falling marble. Furthermore, Kerrin then appeared to understand the dynamics of an elastic collision when she revealed that the rolling marble would transfer its (kinetic) energy to the pin (which would then pierce the balloon) and remain stationary after the collision (turn 26). Here, Kerrin had realized that if a marble collides with a stationary marble of the same mass, then the first marble would become stationary while the second will bounce off (with the same velocity) after the (elastic) collision. In this case, Kerrin's drawing (Figure 5.4) and qualified statements about the need to raise the height of Component C to ensure the marble would reach Component D matched. When this occurs (i.e., when there is congruence between actions and language games) teachers can place greater confidence in inferences about learning outcomes than they could if they were based on one or the other source alone. It would seem that inferences based on data from interviews that rely solely on students' recollections of events are less reliable. In this case, Kerrin did not immediately recall that she used or developed scientific knowledge through the design activity when she was interviewed. However, the combination of her drawing and associated language game provided corroborating evidence of the acquisition of the canonical scientific concept of energy transfer.

The application of the concept of energy transfer was not restricted to Kerrin's group. Emily demonstrated her understanding of energy transfer during a conversation with Mr. Hammett. Shortly after the successful trial of the tracks component of their Egg-Cracking Breakfast-Cooking machine, the group decided to build a stand to support the backboard. Eliza and Myles began searching for a piece of cardboard they could affix to the backboard while Emily held the board in the same position that produced the successful trial. As Mr. Hammett approached Emily, he asked:

30 Mr. Hammett: Are you going to hold that up forever?
31 Emily: No, they [Eliza, Myles] are making a stand.
32 Mr. Hammett: How is it [the marble] going to get started?
33 Emily: We will. We are energy. We get energy from food, into our muscles so we can lift the marble and drop it. And then it rolls down the ramp and breaks the egg.
34 Mr. Hammett: Then you can eat the egg.
35 Emily: Right. We can get some of the energy back when we eat it.

During this conversation, Emily's talk about energy was read as an attempt to impress Mr. Hammett. She demonstrated her general understanding of the principle of energy conservation by humorously identifying tenuous links between the marble's energy transition and her possible energy gain from consuming the fried egg (turns 33 and 35). Emily knew that she would need to expend energy in order to lift the marble into position; the work done by Emily as she raised the ball would be transferred in the form of gravitational potential energy before the marble was dropped. Also in turn 33, Emily explained that the (potential) energy of the marble would then change as the marble gained speed as it rolled down the tracks (kinetic energy). Even though the energy obtained from consuming the egg was not related at all to the energy Emily used to raise the marble, in the context of the conversation, the comment suggests that Emily appreciated that the energy stored within the egg would replace the energy previously used in the process of lifting the marble. In this case, the machine provided a context for Emily's conversation with Mr. Hammett. Emily articulated her learning outcomes from this design activity, by making appropriate links between canonical scientific concepts (e.g., energy) and the various actors (e.g., egg, marble, Emily).

In the previous section we introduced the metaphor of thinkering to describe the relationship between students' thinking and their actions during the construction of the Beef-N-Bacon Sausage-Cooker machine in Gavin's group. Thinkering was particularly obvious as Gavin adjusted the position of the fulcrum of his catapult. The students in Gavin's group thought of new positions for the fulcrum as they interacted with the materials and tried out each new position. The reasons for their design decisions were particularly interesting because they were based on previous experiences, thinkering, and their developing notion of projectile motion. When Gavin was asked about his exploration of the seesaw or catapult, he recalled how he decided it was necessary to change the position of the fulcrum.

> Yeah, we changed that [the fulcrum] to. . . . Well it [the marble] was going too high [Gavin moves his hand upward to show the vertical path of the projectile] and that made the marble go really high [vertical height] but not too far [range] so we made it [the effort arm] lower [shorter] so the marble wouldn't get too high and then go over [Gavin transcribes an arc-like shape in the air with his finger as if to show the effect of the fulcrum's shift on the range of the projectile].

At this point, Gavin articulated his understanding of the relationship between the position of the fulcrum and the range of the projectile. Gavin also seemed to understand that changing the position of the fulcrum actually affected the relative lengths of the load and effort arms, which in turn affected the range of the projectile. Although he had not acquired the language games for the canonical science associated with this experience, his recollections of his practices were consistent with the canonical version of projectile motion. This would be the ideal time for a teacher to introduce Gavin to appropriate scientific language games. Nevertheless, even without this language, Gavin's scientific learning was evident from his language game and actions.

Gavin's interview revealed his more general perceptions of thinkering and the learning potential associated with the task of building his machine. In the next excerpt, Gavin compared his learning from such contrasting practices as reading and building.

> When you read a book, you actually can read and understand it but you don't really understand it until you have actually done it and seen why it happens. They understand what it does, but you don't really understand it as how to make it work and all that. Because when you are building it is hands on and you get to understand, ah, if that's how it works and all that, instead of just reading a text.

Here Gavin suggested that he acquired a deeper level of understanding from building the machines and that this same level of understanding would not have been reached through other means such as reading or teacher demonstration alone. In particular, he argued that he did not really understand the impact of his catapult until he tried it in practice. Building and thinking about the transforming artifact (or thinkering) was a powerful way for Gavin to learn about science.

Gavin addressed an important issue often overlooked by science teachers and educators. Scientific representations pick out particular aspects of a phenomenon and reconstitute systems in discrete sign systems (drawings, words, fleeting ideas). However, the relationship between parts of these sign systems are not the same as the relationships in the world: In the former, relationships have to be built into the system as discrete rules, whereas the world functions dynamically and irrespective of the rules humans invent to describe and explain it. Because of the ontological gap between sign systems (representations) and the world, translations between them are not self-evident but have to be learned through experience. Even scientists have to traverse uncounted cycles of representing and experiencing the world before they can consistently map the one onto the other (Roth & Bowen, 1999a). To learn science, it is therefore insufficient to know the words and partial concepts that teachers often require students to put together into complex systems without prior experience (as in exams). Rather, students need to move through the dialectic circle of seeing and experiencing objects and processes in the world and representing them in some sign system.

Building their Beef-N-Bacon Sausage-Cooker allowed Gavin's group to explore such concepts as levers, motion, force, momentum, kinetic and potential energy, and heat. We have previously illustrated the application of such concepts as levers and energy transfer in the construction of Gavin's group machine. During the interviews Gavin did use such terms as energy transfer and fulcrum, suggesting that he had appropriated the canonical use of these language games. The assertion that the design activities provided students the opportunity to learn science can be reinforced further with reference to the concept of momentum—usually a concept not introduced formally into the science curriculum until late in the middle or junior high school years. Before Gavin's group tried to catapult a coal into the firebox, they used a large marble as a substitute for the coal. Initially a smaller marble was released and allowed to roll down through the tracks until it eventually collided with the larger marble. When Colin (a member of Gavin's group) was asked what he had learnt through building the machine, he replied:

> The little marble comes down and it hits the big marble. Because the big marble has a lot of weight, we had to get the little marble at a decent speed, just hit it and it starts rolling down.

Without formal instruction about the concept of momentum, Colin's experience with the materials of his machine led him to conclude that a smaller mass would need to acquire a large speed before effectively propelling a larger mass through a collision between the two marbles. Although Colin did not use the language game associated with momentum, he articulated a view that was consistent with the principle of the conservation of momentum. This learning outcome should prepare Colin well for formal instruction, should that instruction build on his prior experience; the product of the mass and velocity for each of the marbles throughout the collision should take on greater meaning in view of his qualitative experience. Thus, design activities help students learn canonical science and provide significant and relevant experiences from which students can relate more formal associated language games that might be introduced later in the school curriculum.

As well as exploring various physics concepts, the children gained greater insight into the principles of structural design (e.g., strengthening, bonding, and supporting) and had the opportunity to develop skills in cutting and joining materials such as wood and plastic. Several groups realized that excessive use of masking tape to join tracks together slowed down the passage of the marble through the machine. Although some students did not use the term friction to explain this phenomenon, they were able to make the connection between the speed of the marble and the quality of the joints. This was one example of a direct relationship between a structural or engineering feature of the machines and a scientific concept. Another example where students learned first hand about engineering tasks which had scientific implications was the "stickability" of certain materials. Not all groups used masking tape alone to join their tracks. Gavin's group tried both glue and masking tape. Gavin later declared that he learned more about his marble machine. When invited to explain his use of the term "bonding," he replied:

> Like sticky tape and glue. They don't go together very well. Sticky tape just slides off it and you can't get it to stay there and so we have to wait until it starts to dry and then put it on really tight otherwise it will come off. And we learnt that the sticky tape and wood don't go that well together, don't like each other too well.

The incompatible physical properties of glue and tape prevented a lasting bond between these two materials. However, Colin also noted that the chemical properties of the materials might have created problems when he added to Gavin's statement above, as follows: "You have to put the sticky tape on semi-dry otherwise the glue makes the tape form a liquid kind of thing." Once again, he did not use the language game of canonical science but suggested that there was some sort of reaction between the liquid glue and the tape (or at least its dry glue) to form a liquid mulch that did not bond. These examples demonstrate further the point we made earlier about the interrelatedness of science and technology. In the next chapter we elaborate our claim that design activities promote science learning with reference to the design of an electric toy.

Implications for Teachers

We have shown in this chapter that when student design teams interact with material resources during a design activity they engage in the sub-tasks of planning, building, and testing with no particular regard to sequencing or prioritizing these tasks. Instead, these sub-tasks appear to be interdependent in that each sub-task informs and depends on each of the other sub-tasks. But Mr. Hammett did allocate time at the start of each project so that students could begin to plan their machines. By routinely sequencing a planning segment for each design activity it might be possible for less experienced teachers, who observe Mr. Hammett in practice, to think of designing in terms of the design-make-appraise sequence as presented in *Primary Investigations* (Australian Academy of Science, 1994) and other curriculum documents such as *A Statement on Technology for Australian Schools* (Australian Education Council, 1994). The students themselves, however, did not seem to emerge from these activities with an unrealistic perspective of design. In many ways, Mr. Hammett's practice of scheduling planning segments, contributed to the development of social and organizational skills necessary for effective design teams (see Ritchie & Hampson, 1996). Herein lies a tension that needs to be worked through by practitioners. Does one represent design as a linear or cyclic design-make-appraise process where emphasis is placed on building a prototype that is modified or refined in response to subsequent tests? This would appear to be a simple way to introduce elementary students to progressively more complex design briefs and it would align well with the emphasis taken in available resources. Alternatively, should one abandon their students after setting the design brief without providing any guiding principles? Although this latter approach is likely to be too chaotic for novice designers and fail to help them develop a sense of responsible social behavior, the experience might resemble the actions of professional designers. We recommend neither position. In fact, Mr. Hammett's practice probably falls between the two extremes and could serve as a model for a balanced approach that seems to be needed. When Mr. Hammett was questioned about why he scheduled the planning sessions prior to building he reasoned:

> It lets them [the students] get some ideas. It gives them a chance to think the problem through, like a warm-up exercise. They get tuned in to the stuff [i.e., brief, resources, ideas, and roles] and use some of the ideas they share. What I have learned is that it is not always necessary to schedule planning sessions, because what happens later when they are building is probably more concrete, as they are planning and testing at the same time.

In the next chapter we describe Mr. Hammett's practice in more detail. However, it was clear from the range of machines built over the design project that Mr. Hammett encouraged students to interpret the design briefs flexibly. For example, Kerrin's group positioned their tracks around the border of the base. In contrast, Emily's group used the same base, but re-positioned the base on its side and then positioned their frying pan on the floor below the table. This meant that this group was able to start their rolling marble much higher than other groups, taking full advantage of their bungie marble component. Mr. Hammett was faced with a dilemma here. Should he treat such an interpretation as a violation of the original design brief or should he encourage such a creative interpretation? Mr. Hammett took the latter decision because he believed that innovative design activities should promote interpretive flexibility of the design briefs (cf. Roth, 1996a). In so doing, Mr. Hammett fostered a creative learning environment that allowed children to frame problems in different ways from those conceived by him.

We also view design differently from the Australian curriculum materials. Throughout this book we have represented design as an integrated process involving a package of interrelated sub-tasks such as planning, building, and testing. So design is much more than planning. Yet in the design-make-appraise sequence described in Primary Investigations the word design could be interchanged with planning without seemingly affecting the intended meaning. The unfortunate consequence of this is that both teachers and students do interchange the words (e.g., Ritchie & Hampson, 1996) and, in doing so, can lose sight of the practice of professional designers. Ramsay, Ryan, and Beck (1995) provide a more detailed description of design and the design process that shifts the *Primary Investigations,* interpretation a step closer to our position. They represent design in terms of two sub-tasks, namely investigating issues and needs and devising proposals and alternatives. However, to be fair to the authors, they do not make this claim. Instead, they describe designing-making-appraising as an "integrated process where students will be involved in tasks demonstrating the interaction of: investigating issues and needs, devising proposals and products, producing processes and products and evaluating consequences and outcomes" (p. 35). We agree that design is an integrated approach involving the interaction between such interdependent sub-tasks as investigating, devising, producing, and evaluating. But "producing" means much the same as making and "evaluating" means much the same as appraising. It seems not too much of a shortcut then to simply interchange planning and design. Clearly, the nomenclature adopted by the *Technology Statement* (Australian Education Council, 1994) and Primary Investigations is confusing. It would be better to describe the design process either in terms of the interrelated tasks of investigating, devising, producing, and evaluating or, better still, as planning, building, and testing. We prefer the latter because they are relatively unambiguous words in common use, unlike the more "scientific" word of investigating and the less commonly used words of devising and evaluating.

In our view, curriculum documents and texts should not separate design from the sub-tasks of building and testing. Instead, teachers should be presented with more accurate accounts of the design process (see Chapter 2) so that they can model designing as the interaction of such interdependent sub-tasks of planning, building, and testing. Scheduling planning sessions prior to classroom design activities would serve novice design teams best if teachers stressed the need for participants to share ideas, clarify roles, consider the availability of resources, and generate proposals and alternatives ahead of the production of an unrealistic blueprint. These sessions could be reduced as the students' design experience grew. However, apart from modeling design projects with their students (cf. Mr. Hammett's crazy tennis-ball machine), the way in which the teacher interacts with their students during design activities would appear to be crucial in developing a realistic perspective of design. Apart from influencing the progress of each design team, teachers have the potential of helping students develop a better understanding of design and of canonical scientific knowledge. We illustrate this point in the next chapter.

Metalogue

Issue 1: What Is the Role of the Devices Children Build?

M: In contrast to the earlier chapters, many conversations in this chapter do not seem to draw much on scientific discourse, that is to say, what science educators would qualify as canonical science. Rather, most of the conversation is about evolving the design, getting the work done, dealing with the problems at hand. We hear Alicia talking about the holes they need to make in their marble-shoot machine or Nerida proposing the addition of supports to the artifact as it stands before them. Thus, at this point, the issues at hand are quite different from those that Jeff and his classmates raised, such as the nature of the forces acting in the structure or questions about the relative strength of alternative configurations. In the same way, Shaun and his classmates argued with me about the nature of a pulley configuration that would not have disadvantaged them. They enacted the forces over the design making clear who pulled where and which aspects of the design were important to winning or losing the competition.

K: Just what is the purpose of activities like these? There certainly was a context for establishing an increasingly scientific discourse. However it is apparent that the actions of the teacher do not constrain the actions of students such that they participated in science-like language games. Of course there were some notable exceptions to this, but even then there was little effort to build on these seeds or to ensure that all students had opportunities to access the emerging discourse. In some respects I found the activities reminiscent of the approaches of many who were buoyed by the curriculum development efforts of the 1960s and implemented hands-on science in a somewhat mindless way. I do acknowledge that the activities were fun and may even have evoked the passion we spoke about in the previous metalogues. I also recognize that the students were active and had to solve problems and test them out. Hence there were efforts to coordinate claims about the models with data. When the activities are described in this way they do sound like an embryonic form of science.

S: The activities I saw in Mr. Hammett's class were very different from the hands-on minds-off activities of an earlier period. The design briefs were always linked to conceptual areas under consideration, which were in turn linked to other curriculum areas. The lead-in activities simply were not described in this chapter. This is one of the difficulties in reporting classroom research. We tend to present snapshots of what we have seen to illustrate the issues we have identified for discussion. In doing so, we never fully capture the student and teacher practices. There is another point here that relates to student discourse. In an integrated classroom such as this, where the traditional curriculum or discipline boundaries are blurred, children are less likely to use canonical discourse within their groups because they don't necessarily label their activities as science or technology. Children will use the discourse with which they feel more comfortable. So when the teacher does not label or set the scene for a particular type of lesson, in this case science, the children will employ a more natural discourse, as if employing a sort of default mechanism. This does not mean that they can't or don't use canonical discourse. Nevertheless, the points you raised are valid—teachers should be encouraging children to use canonical language games, and the design activities do provide excellent opportunities for children to begin to develop more confidence in their use.

M: These activities then appear to me to be providing the children with opportunities to build a rich tapestry of experiences to ground a more formal discourse about related issues. Furthermore, it seems that especially when children identify something as problematic, there emerge potential occasions that lend themselves, in the hands of an experienced teacher, to changing the topic of the unfolding conversation to issues that are of concern in science. So when Gavin identified a problem with the marble shoot in that the marble went too high, a teacher such as Gitte might have asked him, "Is there a relationship between the steepness of the shoot and the reach of the marble?" Here, both the question about a possible relationship and the foregrounding of the terms "shoot" and "reach" would be good attempts in making salient what the issues are that a scientist or engineer might raise.

S: This suggestion makes a lot of sense to me and, as a former physics teacher, is what I would have been inclined to ask in this case. Mr. Hammett too asked questions like this, but they were not always recorded.

K: I feel that the teacher could have done more to mediate in the construction of a discourse that was science-like. The context was ripe. I liked the way that there were opportunities for between-group and within-group collaboration. This opens the way for students to disseminate what they have learned and to learn from one another's disparate activities. However, there was no formal mechanism for ensuring that this happened or that students knew what to do when others were reporting to them. How might the teacher have enacted his roles differently so as to be facilitative of language games pertaining to a scientific discourse? Perhaps his own approach to asking questions could have changed and so too might the roles of students within their groups.

S: There is always more that can be done. However, I think we also need to look at the broader picture. Mr. Hammett had multiple goals for the enacted activities—science learning was one of them, language development (or English) was another. As science educators, it is natural for us to focus on science and even identify lost opportunities for science learning. The suggestions we make should prove helpful for teachers wishing to improve science learning in their classes.

Issue 2: Teacher as Co-Investigator

M: In this chapter, it was interesting and in many ways unusual how Mr. Hammett engaged in activities not unlike the children, though his machine was much larger than those of his students. There are a number of points one might raise. On the one hand, one could see Mr. Hammett as constituting himself as a member of a design community. Because of his experience, he might be recognized as someone who plays a particularly central role because of his practical experience and understanding of principles that he embodies. In the community-of-practice model that Lave and Wenger[6] developed, he would therefore play a particular role in the enculturation of newcomers into the design community. On the other hand, some students might also perceive what he creates as so unattainable that it stifles their own creativity and interest.

K: In some respects I think one of the most important things to model in a classroom are the habits of mind: to be curious, persistent, to be calm about unexpected happenings, to a good listener, to show respect, and to have interest. I was pleased to see Mr. Hammett involved in his own project because it is a sign that he "walks the walk." In the earlier chapters I found myself wondering "What kind of community is this?" "What are the characteristics of the underlying fabric, the habitus that gives shape to the types of participation that usually occur?" The building of his own model is just one way that Mr. Hammett places his stamp on this community. It is to be hoped that, by working at their teacher's elbows, the students in this class will begin to participate in ways that are analogous to those of Mr. Hammett.

S: The tennis-ball machine was a larger-than-life artifact produced by the classroom community rather than Mr. Hammett by himself. The children spoke of it as "our" machine and were always keen to demonstrate its operation for visitors. In his interactions with students, Mr. Hammett didn't dominate discussions nor did he dismiss the children's ideas. Instead, they all created the machine together. Without Mr. Hammett-the-craftsperson, many of the structural features could not have been undertaken. But without the children's ideas and labor, the machine would not have taken on its appearance or function. So Mr. Hammett was clearly a member of this design community, and I suspect that those children who worked alongside him benefited in much the same way that Lave and Wenger had envisaged in their model.

M: There are other models of teacher as co-participator. For example, when I taught high school physics, students often asked questions and designed experiments to which I did not have any answers. This provided an ideal context for exploring issues together when students got stuck. Thus, rather than giving the impression of an all-knowing teacher, or eschewing the issues so not to be embarrassed, I engaged in brainstorming activities and testing of equipment and theories together with students. Here, the role of teacher as co-investigator appears to be more credible because students and teacher engage in the same issues with the same materials, and with similar ignorance, rather than engaging in a task that, though challenging in its own right, by far surpasses those that the students face.

K: You make a good point here. I regard co-participation as the critical component of an appropriate learning environment. If students and the teacher can access and appropriate a shared-as-negotiated discourse then learning can be optimized. The discourse should continue to evolve through co-participation in activities that are like those described in this chapter and yet extend beyond them in ways that are linked to a goal of building a science-like discourse.

Issue 3: Talking and Gesturing: But Is It Science?

M: Some readers may seriously question whether students actually "articulate" their understanding if they gesture without actually describing pertinent issues in words. I have in mind particularly the episode with Gavin where he explains how he had to modify the shoot in order to get the marble do what he wanted it to do. One could argue that all Gavin did was describe the outcome of his manipulations that ultimately led to the right position of the shoot. But this in itself does not constitute understanding of the scientific discourse that is used to explain why the shoot has to be positioned in the way it is. Let me use another example. When I ask a quarterback or a golfer how they get the ball to or near a particular spot whatever the weather conditions, they can most likely provide explanations. They might talk of overthrowing a little because of the wind or shooting into the wind to make the ball come out where they want it. But these explanations, while sensible in everyday conversations, would not be acceptable to a physicist in his work where an entire conceptual machinery including vectors, forces, wind and ball velocities, friction, and angles is put into action in order to derive a formal answer to the question. While Gavin showed the interviewer what he did and how the ball went too high/far when the shoot was positioned otherwise, he did not use the discursive machinery a student of physics would. The question therefore is whether we can make the claim that Gavin showed an understanding of the phenomenon.

K: I have absolutely no problem in looking at your examples from an epistemological standpoint and coming to a conclusion that Gavin, the quarterback, and the golfer all have knowledge that allows them to solve problems. The knowledge is of the genre that scientists must use in many aspects of their lives as scientists. The doing of science requires much more than being able to speak and write science. To me, the knowledge of building a model and being able to explain how it operates to solve the problems you were addressing in the building of the model is impressive and clearly involves knowledge that is distributed through the body and associated interactions with the artifact.

S: I know a golfer who has read just about every golf book available. He is a good partner because he can advise on almost any shot under any condition. When he addresses the ball, you can almost see him mentally checking everything he has read—a bit like a flight-deck check before takeoff. Regrettably, whatever he does, he still manages to slice or hook or even worse. Each time, he can tell you what went wrong and then he tells himself what he should do next time. On the other hand, we all know of stars who can't explain their actions in a way that would assist less-than-ordinary players such as myself improve their game. The point here is that there is a difference between talk and a physical act. Despite Gavin's limited use of canonical language games in this example he convinced me, through his actions and my historical knowledge of his discursive practices, that he understood the phenomena. Teachers routinely make these judgments about their students every day with fewer cues.

M: But such a view, as I pointed out, does not sit well with many of our colleagues.

K: You are absolutely right in stating that many of our colleagues would not regard the knowledge associated with the situations you describe as scientific. Rather than get into a debate about whether or not it is scientific, I would ask what could be done to make it more scientific. Making the issue dynamic forces me to identify what it is about a learning community that enables scientific ideas to flourish. Later we address this with Ms. Mack, a teacher who changed her teaching roles and transformed the learning environments in her class so as to promote the learning of science. The ingredients of her changed environment, on which I will dwell for a moment, were active listening, oral reporting by all students on what was learned and the questions that remained to be answered, presentations in which knowledge claims were to be supported by evidence, and book-length reports on what was done and learned. If Mr. Hammett had engaged students such as Gavin in activities such as these, I am sure that the knowledge they had could have extended to be more science-like.

S: In isolation, Gavin's gestures are not particularly convincing. He was communicating his ideas in a rather natural way, for him, which I matched with possible canonical explanations. I made this match, as one does in any conversation, by following on from what I had recently heard and seen, as well as what I knew of Gavin—something that outsiders, or those who weren't there, may not ever accept.

M: It also occurred to me that the interview situations themselves do not call up students' knowledge but rather are new occasions for students to construct discourse in the situation, by drawing on all the available resources. Among the resources, we might include their past experiences, but we have to account especially for the resources provided by and through the interviewer's questions.

K: One point I would like to address is the issue of power. I was struck while reading about the initial design vignette by what I consider to have been an example of inappropriate use of power by the teacher to constrain the activities of students. Of course, Mr. Hammett could rationalize what he did in many ways and I am not criticizing what he did. I just use it as an example of a broader set of issues. I like to see participation in activities being aligned with what students know and can do. The idea that a whole class should and can proceed at one pace does not make all that much sense to me. When Adam's group began to immediately build a model rather than plan, I thought it was highly appropriate for them to engage in this way and a good example of Mr. Hammett's understanding of the need for students to exercise autonomy and responsibility. However, when he stopped their building and suggested they return to planning tasks I began to think about the problems that many teachers have in managing science activities. Because the use of materials is involved in many science lessons, it is not unusual for teachers to experience difficulties in the distribution and use of materials throughout a lesson. Here I think it is imperative to have a system that maximizes autonomy for students and responsible action by them. As the chapter progressed there is much more evidence that Mr. Hammett did just this.

M: I also thought about that vignette and how I would have acted differently in the same situation had it come up in my Grade 6–7 class that builds simple machines. Because of my research on designing, and because I know the constraints on what we can do in a domain with which we are not familiar, I think of planning, prototyping, and building as integral aspects of designing rather than as separate stages. I therefore saw the students as engaging in an exploration to get a feel for the domain, a crucial aspect of being successful. Out of this personal experience with teaching and thinking about designing, I viewed Mr. Hammett's teaching as constraining in a more negative sense. Your point about an entire class moving in lock step is also important. This in fact seems to be the standard approach. But in a recent conversation with a teacher who had, as I have, worked with multi-grade classrooms, it occurred to me that this experience actually allowed me from the beginning of my career to choose a different option. Rather than having students work in lock step, at the same rate, and in whole-class activities, students work at their own rate. However, there are other structures in the enacted curriculum that bring small groups and the whole class together for the purpose of exchange, learning, teaching, negotiating, and so forth.

S: Mr. Hammett insisted that groups should first produce a plan because there was an important equity issue here to address: all group members should have the opportunity to make a contribution before proceeding. After this identifiable planning segment, there was very little structure to the remaining lessons. Sure, there were regular progress reports, but in an integrated curriculum that claims to contribute to language development, I wouldn't expect anything less.

K: This relates to my final point, about the way students were encouraged to share what was learned across groups. In my own science teaching this is a characteristic of what happens routinely. I see it as very important for students to share what they have learned, describe the evidence for what they have learned, and indicate what they want to pursue next. If artifacts have been built they also can demonstrate their salient features to the other groups. I like to see this happen in a routine and planned way and do not like to see it happening only occasionally. An effective learning environment will allow knowledge distribution to occur seamlessly throughout a community.

M: The reason some teachers may not use opportunities for "sharing" may lie in the perception that such an activity takes away from the "real" learning that occurs. Also, the very notion of "sharing" may be misleading when it is thought of as a show-and-tell activity. If we construe "sharing" as a learning opportunity for listeners, then engaging with other groups in conversation about the central issues of the tasks is of crucial importance. I believe that your account of Ms. Mack's classroom, where children also are co-listeners who take notes when a peer speaks, is the kind of image we want for useful "sharing" sessions.

Notes

1 This chapter draws on the research conducted by Ritchie with Mr. Hammett, the teacher whose Grade 6 class is featured throughout (see, for example, Ritchie, 1998). All student names are pseudonyms.

2 As we argued in Chapter 2, design really should be thought of as a process that includes brainstorming, drawing, building, prototyping, and refining.

3 Learning in such situations where students have to share tools and interact while they meet when looking for materials is a central process in the establishment and maintenance of knowledge-building communities (McGinn, Roth, Boutonné, & Woszczyna, 1995; Roth, 1995d, 1996c, 1998a). This is one example of ethnographic descriptions and explanations that are viably transportable to different contexts.

4 These components have been labeled for the reader's convenience. Kerrin did not label them in her drawn plan.

5 Fujimura (1992) and Knorr-Cetina (1981) showed how scientists' work is driven, to a large extent, by "doable" problems, that is, research problems that lead to success, publications, further funding, and so forth. Here, the children were also concerned with engaging in a design that they were reasonably certain would work.

6 See Lave and Wenger (1991).

Chapter 6

Learning Science in Design Communities

In the last chapter, we showed that it was possible for children to develop canonical scientific knowledge through marble machine design activities. In particular, we highlighted several cases in which students appropriated relevant scientific language games involving energy transfer. We also showed how design activities provide students with the opportunity to develop an understanding of such scientific concepts as momentum and projectile motion without exposure to canonical scientific language games. Instead, students used their own language games to describe their first-hand experience with these phenomena. This argument is extended in the present chapter. Students used self-generated analogies to constitute their understandings of physical phenomena encountered during design activities. These student language games proved to be successful in helping other students articulate their understanding of the same experiences. We present evidence to show that students can elaborate ideas and analogies generated by other students within their design teams. We use this evidence to assert that students do indeed learn science from each other while they are engaged in design activities. Apart from describing how students learn from each other, we emphasize the significant role of the teacher in fostering an effective learning community and introducing students to canonical scientific language games. We argue that the teacher is an integral member of each design team whose input can help students learn science. Before presenting our main assertions, we contextualize our discussion by describing the design activities from which our data are drawn.

Electrifying Experiences

The design activities in Mr. Hammett's class were integrated through the science curriculum. This means that the design activities were scheduled so that the children could map discourse to experience and further develop related conceptual discourse. For example, the marble-machine activity followed lessons that focused on energy transfer and, as we show in this chapter, science activities on electric circuits preceded the electric-toy design activity. Thus, scientific learning outcomes cannot be attributed solely to the design activities in Mr. Hammett's class. For this reason, we extend the context of our discussion in this chapter to include those lessons that were planned specifically to support the development of a design discourse.

The project that followed the marble machine was the design of an electric toy. This design, too, fell into the energy unit. This was the third activity to be undertaken by the children within the lesson called "Electrifying Experiences" from *Primary Investigations* (Australian Academy of Science, 1994). Mr. Hammett alerted the children to the design activity well ahead of schedule. Mr. Hammett announced the "Electrifying Experiences" unit so that the children knew about their next design activity even before they started the unit on electrical circuits. Some students had even discussed possible ideas for their design and collected materials to be used prior to the start of this unit. Not surprisingly, one group (i.e., Alicia's) was so preoccupied with the impending electric toy design that they began their design project in class when they should have started with the first activity from "Electrifying Experiences" (i.e., connecting a simple circuit to light a torch bulb), as the following excerpt shows.

01	Alicia:	I thought we were doing a solar-powered Barbie Ferrari, so my Barbies could sit in it.
02	Nerida:	I have got Barbies too. I've got three (2)
03	Alicia:	Well, do you want to start?
04	Nerida:	Come on.
05	Alicia:	We're going to put a light in a car.

This excerpt shows that these children had quite different concerns than their teacher. For this group, the idea of designing a toy was the significant activity to be addressed, and they appeared to have made an early decision about the nature of their design. In contrast, Mr. Hammett had scheduled a number of activities that he thought would have provided helpful background experiences upon which students could draw for the purposes of their design activity. Alicia suggested that a prior agreement had been reached with Nerida, at least, concerning the nature of their design well before the first lesson from "Electrifying Experiences" (turn

01). Their electric toy was to be a solar-powered car with lights. Alicia and Nerida decided to begin the toy project (turns 04 and 05) before attending to the activities scheduled by their teacher. It should not come as a surprise that one group had started their design activity ahead of schedule. Various teaching approaches have been designed to take advantage of the motivational power of student-initiated problems and questions. For example, *The Interactive Approach to Teaching Science* (Biddulph & Osborne, 1984) was centered on elementary students' self-generated investigative questions. Secondary students who have opportunities to generate their own problems for investigation remain motivated throughout their projects (e.g., Roth, 1995).

Both the students and their teacher recognized the central role of the electric toy design activity. The design activities (e.g., marble machines, an electric toy) became the integrative devices that provided the skeletal structure for the science curriculum. The supporting science activities (e.g., building a simple electric circuit) added a substantive emphasis. In relation to the electrical energy topic the intended (and eventually enacted) sequence of activities or lessons required students to explore a simple electrical circuit (with a switch), explore conductors and insulators, design an electric toy, and listen to a haunted house story. The last lesson departed from the *Primary Investigations* activities; it involved an unfinished fictional story told by Mr. Hammett about a group of children who sought shelter in an abandoned house during a storm. The children were then asked to discuss in their teams possible endings to the story that explained why the lights in the house failed. The activities for this unit were completed over a four-week period. They provided the context for discussion of the scientific knowledge developed by the children through their interactions with each other and their teacher.

In the previous chapter, we referred to actor network theory to explain how both human and non-human actors influenced each other in design activities. More specifically, we argued that the students transformed their artifacts as they manipulated the material resources in situ and that the transforming artifacts appeared to "talk back" to the students by informing the designers of subsequent design moves. We now turn our attention to the interactions between the human actors of the design teams. There were two types of human networking within the design teams. These were the interactions between the students and the interactions between the students and their teacher. Our discussion first centers on how Mr. Hammett's students helped each other in learning canonical science through the electric toy design activity.

Learning Science: With a Little Help
from Your Friends

By the end of the four-week unit on electrical energy, the design teams had engaged in a variety of activities and presented a wide range of electrical toys. Some of the toys included a lighthouse, a boat, a camera with a flashbulb, and games such as mini-golf and basketball shooting. In the basketball-shooting game, for example, a successful shot was identified by a buzzer and lights that were activated when the ball passed through the ring. To illustrate how students helped each other in constructing canonical science through design activities we focus on the team that designed the basketball-shooting game. During this project, Joshua invented two analogies to help explain his understanding of the phenomena under investigation for the benefit of his fellow team members. The first analogy (i.e., Thomas the Tank Engine) was invented to explain the operation of a simple electric circuit. Kerrin and Katrina made sense of electric circuits with this analogy and demonstrated an understanding of electric current by elaborating parts of the analogy during their team discussions. The second analogy (i.e., strawberry yogurt) proved to be viable in terms of the students' observations of electrolysis even though it was inconsistent with canonical science. This created a dilemma for the teacher. Should he intervene by introducing students to the language games of canonical science? In this way, he potentially would contribute to the cultural reproduction of science. But it is well known that if science becomes too teacher-centered, students quickly lose interest. Should he let children continue their activities? In that case, children would engage in cultural production and developed their own interests and discourses. But it is also well known that in such a situation, students would have little reason to re/produce canonical science (Roth & McGinn, 1996; Roth, McGinn, Woszczyna, & Boutonné, 1999). In this classroom, both situations were observed. We also note that the students were not restricted to the elaboration of self-generated analogies. With reference to the within-group discourse of another team (i.e., Emily's team) during the final lesson from the electrical energy unit, we show that students learn science together by elaborating on ideas generated during design activities.

The Thomas the Tank Engine Analogy

Joshua generated the analogy of Thomas the Tank Engine in response to Kerrin's persistent requests for the boys on her design team to explain what they knew about electric circuits. During his description of the transforming analogy, both Kerrin and Katrina demonstrated the discursive power of the analogy by elaborating on parts of it that related more closely to their own experiences. Apart from showing the effectiveness of this discursive device we provide further evidence for an earlier claim that the activity of designing an electric toy was an integrative device that provided students with a framework for their science learning.

At the end of the third lesson of the unit each group was asked to describe the progress of their design to the whole class. The self-appointed speaker of the team that designed the basketball-shooting game, Kerrin, described her group's design to the class:

> Okay, yeah, it's a basketball ring. And when someone shoots they stand there [a position on the floor about one meter away from the ring] and when someone shoots it goes down there [the path the ball would take through a return chute if the shot was successful]. And when we are ready, it [the ball] will hit a buzzer and go beep and there are going to be lights up here [above the ring] and the lights will light up if you get it in.

At this stage of construction, the backboard and ring were in place, the return chute was assembled, and the circuits were connected except for the buzzer (which was yet to be acquired) and the batteries. The children completed building their project on their own time (e.g., on lunch breaks) over the next two weeks. Joshua and Jackson worked principally on the backboard and ring while Kerrin and Katrina connected the circuits. Even though there appeared to be a division of labor based on gendered friendship dyads, there was considerable exchange of ideas between dyads throughout the project.

The children in this group were well aware of the design project at the start of the unit; they exchanged possible ideas during the first activities on constructing simple circuits and testing the conductivity of different materials. (The decision to design this particular game was a complex one and is not pertinent to the present discussion.) In the following excerpt the children were nearing completion of a task that required them to classify tested materials as conductors or insulators.

06	Katrina:	Water is an insulator.
07	Kerrin:	Hang on. What have you got?
08	Katrina:	I've got rubber, wooden ruler, paper book, zinc, lead, pen, clip-on lid, shoe leather.
09	Joshua:	What toy do you think we should make?
10	Katrina:	You know that toy I made for my science project, do you reckon we should make one of those?

11	Joshua:	I reckon we should make a lighthouse.
12	Jackson:	Joshua, we could make a Morse code thing. We could make a Morse code thing.
13	Katrina:	I was just saying, 'cause I don't want to make one of those 'cause they are too boring.
14	Joshua	(?)
15	Kerrin:	A what?
16	Katrina:	Yeah.
17	Kerrin:	Hmmm, a smartie.
18	Katrina:	A smartie. We will have to think of something really cool.

Katrina listed the materials that they had classified as insulators (turn 08). But Kerrin (turn 07) questioned Katrina's previous assertion that water was an insulator (turn 06). Interestingly, this particular issue became a major learning opportunity for the group later, even though Joshua at first appeared to treat Kerrin's concern as a mere extension of a routine activity by changing the subject (turn 09). Joshua then initiated diversionary conversation about the nature of their forthcoming design project. All others were drawn into the conversation, with Katrina suggesting a modification of her previous project (turn 10), Joshua nominating a lighthouse (turn 11), and Jackson emphasizing a Morse code device (turn 12). However, the criterion to design a "cool" toy rather than something as "boring" (turn 13) as a Morse code device was established by Katrina (turn 18).

Unlike the friendship groupings that existed during the design of the marble machines described in Chapter 5, Mr. Hammett assigned group membership for the electric-toy design project. Not surprisingly, team members had to negotiate different sets of roles, expectations, and practices. In their previous group, Joshua and Jackson made assumptions about the material practices of his fellow team members that were no longer appropriate in their new team. Kerrin and Katrina needed and demanded the opportunity to develop skills in connecting simple circuits. Although Joshua and Jackson appeared to be competent in stripping wires and connecting simple circuits, Kerrin and Katrina acknowledged their limited competence; they refused to be denied the opportunity to participate in this component of the design. In the next excerpt, Kerrin continued to question the boys about circuits with the expectation that they would help her to reach a similar level of competence. After hearing how Jackson intended to proceed with the first circuit, Kerrin asserted:

19	Kerrin:	But you can't just say this is how you do it. You have got to let us think 'cause Katrina and I don't know what to do—we don't know nothing about it.
20	Jackson:	I don't know a lot about batteries.

21	Kerrin:	Yeah, so Joshua: how do you know which sides of the wire to connect to the battery? (.) To connect the light.
22	Joshua:	You don't need to know.
23	Katrina:	Well the negative goes to the positive (1). No, doesn't the negative go to the positive and the positive go to the negative? Or does negative go to negative and positive go to positive?
24	Kerrin:	No, negative to positive.
25	Joshua:	I don't know.
26	Kerrin:	Well that's not really a good way of learning, is it?
27	Joshua:	That's how I do it.
28	Kerrin:	You just trial and error?
29	Jackson:	Well we know there are only two ways you can do it. 'Cause both ends of the wire have to be connected, you know that. If one way doesn't work.
30	Kerrin:	Both ends of the wire have to be connected?

Jackson and Joshua seemed content with their "thinkering" activities (see Chapter 5). When quizzed about their practices by Kerrin (turn 21), Joshua responded nonchalantly: "You don't need to know" (turn 22). With this response Joshua signaled that he did not need to know the canonical scientific explanation of electric circuits to complete the task. Instead, both Joshua and Jackson looked comfortable as they set about thinkering with the material resources. In contrast, Kerrin expressed discomfort with what she initially perceived to be a differential level of expertise between the boys and girls (turn 19). Kerrin turned to Joshua for help (turn 21), but was not satisfied with his trial-and-error approach (turn 28). She displayed displeasure with the boys' different approaches to the task (turn 26). Kerrin needed to know the "right" way of connecting the circuit before she felt sufficiently comfortable to try it for herself.

Katrina attempted to recall how a series circuit was connected, perhaps from previous school encounters, but then became confused with additional contradictory recollections that she may have associated with parallel circuits (turn 23) or even with her experience with magnets. Eventually, Jackson intervened by rationalizing that there could only be two possible connections and that if one didn't work, the other combination would (turn 29). His response here added to Joshua's earlier claim that one didn't need to know or remember which way was correct (turn 22), suggesting that the proof was in the making; that is, if one continued thinkering after an unsuccessful attempt a workable solution would be achieved. For Joshua, it seemed more important for the product to work than to remember or learn how it was supposed to work. However, when pushed for an explanation, Jackson (and Joshua, as we demonstrate shortly) thought aloud to work through the issues of concern, suggesting that he did understand what happened in a simple electric circuit. When Jackson proposed that both ends of the wire needed to be connected in the circuit (i.e., to complete the circuit, turn 29), Kerrin seemed puzzled or surprised (turn 30). Along with her previous admission (i.e., "We don't know nothing about it," turn 19) this confirmed that, at this stage of the unit, Kerrin (and Katrina) had a limited understanding of electric circuits.

Jackson and Joshua could not avoid justifying their actions to Kerrin; they could not proceed as they had previously—completing tasks as if they assumed their co-learners knew intuitively what they were doing (and why) without discussion. At first, Joshua appeared to be annoyed or bothered by Kerrin's initial questions. Kerrin's persistence eventually caused Joshua to address her concerns seriously. He tried to explain his practices by means of a self-generated analogy, that of Thomas the Tank Engine. This not only demonstrated his own understanding of the related scientific concepts; his strategy of using the analogy also proved successful in enhancing Kerrin's understanding of electric circuits. Prior to the following excerpt, Joshua and Jackson had connected a simple circuit when Kerrin interrupted:

31	Kerrin:	Just wait. Can I have a go because you guys know how to do it, so we need to have a go?
32	Joshua:	First just connect the light bulb to the battery.
33	Kerrin:	Yeah.
34	Katrina:	Yes.
35	Kerrin:	And I want to see.
36	Jackson:	[Connects circuit] One terminal on there.
37	Joshua:	I will explain it easy for you. Just say this [bulb] is a bridge, right? This is where all the cars go across. In order to get one car to another place you have got to open that bridge. So you have got to have like a train track circuit; the train goes from one station to another station and back to the other station again. It's basically the same except all electrics here.
38	Katrina:	Don't connect those [battery terminals] two together.
39	Jackson:	[Connects wire to terminal] And that one goes on there.
40	Joshua:	⎡Yeah so. ⎤
41	Jackson	⎣And they⎦ get connected, that one goes on there.
42	Joshua:	So this [battery] is a station and this [bulb] is a station.
43	Jackson:	And we will see if this is right. Hey, first time! [bulb illuminates]
44	Katrina:	What else do we have to do?
45	Jackson	That's it.
46	Joshua:	That was easy. Just pretend that it's a train station, two train stations. The electricity is the train and the train just goes.
47	Kerrin:	And if you take that [wire] off [the terminal]?
48	Joshua:	It doesn't work.

49	Kerrin:	And if you clip it on there it will flatten the battery [Gestures as if connecting battery terminals].
50	Joshua:	Yeah. So, that's that. You have just got to think of that; it's pretty easy.
51	Kerrin:	Mr. Hammett, we're done!

In response to Kerrin's request to "have a go" (turn 31), Joshua began his explanation (turn 32) while Jackson connected the circuit, occasionally describing his own actions (turns 36, 39, 41). But both Kerrin and Katrina appeared to be more interested in seeing how the circuit should be connected (turns 35 and 38) and hearing Joshua's explanation than in putting the circuit together themselves, as Kerrin had initially requested (turn 31). This supports our earlier assertion that Kerrin wanted to know the correct way before trying it for herself. Joshua's analogy unfolded progressively. It did not seem to be copied from a previously heard description from another teacher, for example, because he clarified possible confusing aspects of the analogy along the way. In particular, he first likened a light bulb to a bridge (turn 37) that needed to be opened to allow cars (presumably the electric current) to "go across." In the next sentence he changed the bridge idea to a train station after using the notion of a train track to explain a closed electric circuit. Then, components such as a bulb became train stations (turn 42) and the train took on the role of electric current (turn 46). As we see in the next excerpt, Joshua refined the analogy further in response to questioning from Mr. Hammett. However, at this stage, the analogy did not differentiate between a battery and a light bulb (turn 32). The group seemed to be pleased that the bulb lit up on their first attempt (turn 43). Once again, Kerrin questioned Joshua about the circuit as if she needed an approval from an authoritative source before doing something (turns 47 and 48). Satisfied with Joshua's explanation and Jackson's efforts, Kerrin attracted Mr. Hammett's attention by exclaiming, "We're done!"

Prior to Joshua's explanation, Kerrin and Katrina were not prepared to connect a simple circuit and acknowledged that they did not know how it worked (e.g., turn 19). When Mr. Hammett visited Kerrin's group shortly after Kerrin called out to him (turn 51), she confidently retold the analogy by referring to Joshua's "story of Thomas the Tank Engine." The next excerpt shows that both Kerrin and Katrina described electric circuits in ways that are consistent with canonical science.

52	Kerrin:	You have got to have a railway circuit.
53	Joshua:	In order for the train to get from one station to another and back again you have got to have a circuit.
54	Katrina:	A circle.

55 Jackson: But at this [points to a point in circuit] Say if this is where the track is
                broken it can't get there, can it? [Mr. Hammett nods]
56 Kerrin: And so the train goes chug a chug a chug down to the station to get
                more petrol and chug a chug a chug back there.
57 Mr. Hammett: What do you mean, gets more petrol here?
58 Katrina: Well, it gets more energy.
59 Kerrin: It gives the energy to there [points to the light bulb].
60 Joshua: Taking coal from a coal mine to a power plant along the train track.

Kerrin and Katrina elaborated on Joshua's analogy, suggesting that they now understood the related scientific concepts (turns 56, 58). Although Joshua did not refer to the battery (station) as supplying energy (petrol) to the electrons (trains) in his circuit analogy, Kerrin's version of the story included a reference to petrol, which was immediately clarified with the substitution of the word energy (for petrol) by Katrina. In subsequent interviews, both Kerrin and Katrina explained simple circuits in ways that were consistent with canonical science. For example, when Katrina was asked what would happen to the brightness of the bulbs in a series circuit if an additional bulb was connected, she replied: "It dims, because you have to share all the energy around." Although Joshua's analogy led the way for Kerrin and Katrina to enhance their understanding of electric circuits, they nevertheless made a contribution to the design team themselves with their elaborations of Joshua's analogy (turns 56, 58, 59). Kerrin summed up the extent to which team members had helped each other's conceptual development when she said during an interview, "I think we all learned a bit off each other, but I'm not sure how much they learned off us, but we learned a lot off them."

The Strawberry Yogurt Analogy
The Thomas the Tank Engine analogy was not the only one Joshua invented to help him explain a scientific phenomenon within the group. Late in the first lesson from "Electrifying Experiences," Kerrin's design team observed bubbles rising from one of the electrodes that was immersed in a saturated solution of salty water. Here they were testing whether salt water was a conductor of electricity. They became excited upon realizing that they might be "sizzling water" (Kerrin). Joshua questioned whether it could be salt. Minutes after close observation, Joshua again announced, "All the salt is coming up to the surface." Still minutes later and after many within-group exchanges, Joshua speculated, "Maybe it has something to do with the electricity and the aluminum foil." Jackson then realized the potential application of this phenomenon when he announced: "Perhaps we've made a major breakthrough. We'll

go down, so now all ships can take something like this. Something like this so they can purify the salt sea water." When Mr. Hammett asked the group to explain what they meant by "purify," Joshua responded with the following analogy, "Like you know when you take the strawberries out of strawberry yogurt you know what I mean? And you have plain yogurt." This analogy also made a significant impact on Kerrin. It was part of her story when she presented her group's report at the end of the lesson to the class. The following excerpt demonstrated that although the group learned something new from its investigation of electrolysis, there was much more that could be done with appropriate teacher intervention.

61 Kerrin: When we were doing—trying to see if salt water was an insulator or a conductor we found that if you connect these like in a circuit and make sure you don't have—we put foil on the ends of the alligator clips so—and when we were doing it because they didn't touch, I don't know why, but—yeah the salt in the water—because we did it with salt water—electricity must be going into the water and it is separating, well Joshua said purifying the salt and the water and so

62   the salt comes up in little bubbles, little swirls come up in a spiral and just makes a layer of salt on the top so Jackson started to taste it and so he stuck his finger down and the stuff on the bottom here, was like almost like normal water—it wasn't very salty and the stuff up

63   the top was very salty because all the salt was up there. [Mr. Hammett appears to mouth a prompt for Kerrin to explain what purify means to the whole class.] No you say it—yeah everyone knows what purifying is.

64 Mr. Hammett: Ask them.

65 Kerrin: Does everyone know what purifying is? All right Joshua said that purifying would be like if you got strawberry yogurt and you took the strawberries out of the yogurt, the yogurt would be purified because there is nothing in it, just yogurt.

66 Mr. Hammett: So it is made more pure. Pure yogurt. No additives.

67 Kerrin: Yeah this is like nearly pure water without the salt, but there is salt in it. And now because it is sizzling if you can listen to it, it is all—like sizzling and air bubbles are coming up and they are all gathering around the sides.

68 Katrina: And it is only happening to one alligator clip which is the one coming from the light bulb and down into there it is not this one. The negative current.

69 Kerrin: You can see that if they touch, if the two things touch, if the alfoil touches, the light bulb lights up and the sizzling stops, but if they are not touching it works.

Kerrin and her friends noticed swirls of "salt" rising to the surface (turn 61) and "air" bubbles at only one terminal (turns 65, 66), they heard the solution "sizzle" and tasted it in an attempt to test their hypothesis that it was the salt that was rising to the surface (turn 61). Kerrin reported to the class that even though she did not know why, her team believed that the electricity separated (or purified) the salt from the water. When coaxed to explain what she meant by "purify," Kerrin called upon Joshua's analogy, in which the salt would be like the strawberries in strawberry yogurt. After a while the strawberries would be completely removed, leaving only the purified yogurt behind (turn 63).

At the time of their whole-class presentation, Kerrin's design team viewed the salt water as a mixture rather than an ionic solution. They did not know about the ionic properties of salt and could not possibly be expected to recognize the bubbles as anything else but air and salt. Their explanation (i.e., separation of a mixture), albeit uninformed about ionic compounds and solutions, was viable in this context. After all, in a supersaturated solution of salty water, some undissolved salt may indeed float to the surface on the bubbles and form a layer as Kerrin described. However, even though the analogy Joshua offered accounted for the frothing layer of salt, it can not account for the bubbles. Only some form of teacher intervention here could have possibly advanced the students' understanding to approach that of canonical science.

Another interesting aspect of this activity was the test Jackson used (turn 61). Jackson dipped his finger into the solution to test his idea that the water was more salty on the surface. Although he believed that the test supported his hunch, he acknowledged during a subsequent interview that it was a very crude test ("Yeah it would have been easier if I had a straw and I could have gone down and put my finger on top and drawn it out"). This reaction suggests that Jackson had tinkered with straws in a similar fashion previously. It also suggests that Jackson, and possibly others in the team, might have developed a more sophisticated and reliable test given some form of teacher intervention. We explore this issue in more detail later.

Elaboration of Shared Ideas

In our presentation of the two student-generated analogies above, we argued that analogies were powerful discursive devices that helped students to appropriate the concepts targeted by the analogies. The Thomas the Tank Engine analogy was so effective that both Katrina and Kerrin elaborated ideas that were expressed initially by Joshua. However, the students were not restricted to elaborating on ideas presented within analogies. The design activities provided the team members with many opportunities to generate ideas and elaborate then during their team discussions. With reference to Emily's design team, we now illustrate how students learned science from each other as they elaborated ideas generated within their design team.

In the final activity for the unit on electrical energy, the design teams were asked to apply their knowledge of electric circuits to a teacher-posed imaginary problem about why the lights might not work in an old deserted house found during a vacation exploration. Emily's group was seated on the floor around a large sheet of poster paper. Susan had taken on the role of recorder. Apart from recording students' ideas in the form of a table (Figure 6.1), she also illustrated the team's preferred scenario(s) in an annotated drawing (Figure 6.2). Figure 6.1 shows that the group generated five possible scenarios ranging from the most obvious scenario (i.e., number 3), that the power company might have disconnected the supply, to a scenario that possibly demonstrated students' alternative concepts about the "reactivity" of gold, possibly located beneath the house (i.e., number 5). It should be noted, however, that Mr. Hammett's fictitious story that contextualized the problem for the design teams was set in an old gold-mining town in North Queensland. For each scenario, the students were asked to propose how they might check or test their predictions or scenarios. For example, the team decided that they would simply telephone the power company to determine whether the house's power supply had been disconnected.

Figure 6.2 shows that the students illustrated two preferred scenarios. First, if the power lines were positioned underground, there could be some form of (electromagnetic) interference between the gold deposits and the electric current. Second, if the power lines were positioned overhead, as is typical in older towns and suburbs, a bat may have caused a "shortage" (i.e., an open circuit) by nibbling through the wires. This representation is particularly interesting because, as shown below in the following excerpt, the team had discussed the effects of mice in the ceiling rather than a bat on the outside wires. It seems that somewhere between the team discussion and the final illustration, Susan exercised some artistic license in modifying the drawing by substituting a bat for the mice. Nevertheless, the same scientific concept (i.e., an open circuit) was represented by both scenarios. Susan's exchange in context may have demonstrated her understanding of the significance of the break in the circuit and the secondary importance of what caused the break. The following excerpt began with Emily's description of what the children might have experienced as they first entered the house.

Reasons	How you would test your prediction
After a while light bulb would blow.	built up pressure and its just a fact that all light bulbs blow when it gets old.
the wires up in the roof could had a mouse chew through the wires which causes a shortage.	Check up in the roof.
Norqueb could have stopped the power.	Ring up Norqueb (In morning or). later
there might be a gold reaction in the ground	Mine the ground.
Something could have stripped the wires and caused a shortage which made all the lights go out.	Check out the whole house.
Ext: 1 a ghost 2 Someone tried to scare them.	Call ghost busters look for someone who made the prank.

Figure 6.1 Completed team chart of possible scenarios and tests for the deserted house problem.

Figure 6.2 Pictorial representation of two preferred scenarios to explain why the lights in the deserted house did not work.

68 Emily: They walked into the house and feel against the wall for a light switch.
              They turn the light switch on and the bulb didn't work . . . So cross out
              that [points to sentence] and its age as well [to Susan].

69 Susan: Is this in the house? [She crosses through sentence—see the scribble
              on the first line of Figure 6.1]

70 Emily: Yeah.

71 Eliza: No Emily. Emily, a light bulb blows, it blows.

72 Emily: Yeah, I guess.

73 Susan: Light bulbs blow when it gets worn out. It is worn out [looks at Emily]
              [Emily shows puzzled look] when it gets old.

74 Emily: Yeah, when it gets, Ah!, Yeah.

75 Eliza: Ahm, like ahm, like you have wires up in the ceiling and something
              like a mouse or something could have like.

76 Emily: Yeah!

77 Susan: Oh yeah!

78 Eliza: Chewed . . . OK!! Um [Lying down on stomach raises head, shoulders
              and throws hands to the floor in a quietly ecstatic response. Susan,
              Emily and Eliza all laugh and giggle for a short period. Meredith smiles
              in recognition.]

79 Eliza: The wires up in. [laughs. Looks at Susan.]

80 Susan: [Laughs] The roof [laughs] [writes scenario, Figure 6.1].

81 Emily: The wires.

82 Eliza: The wires up in the roof a mouse or something could have gotten up
              and chewed through the wires.

83 Emily: Yeah! and chewed [gestures nibbling] the um the conductor and chewed
              the insulator, and then through the conductor.

84 Susan: Chewed through conductor [completes recording second scenario,
              Figure 6.1].

85 Eliza: Chew through it.

86 Emily: And so that. . . .

87 Eliza: So no longer did it work.

88 Emily: It would cut the um circuit to the light.

89 Eliza: We got it [throws down hand, eyes closed, shakes head].

In this excerpt, individual students contributed to the group product by
continually building on each other's suggestions. For example, Emily
emphasized that the age of the house was a factor for consideration (turn
68). In response, Susan suggested that the light bulbs wear out over time
(turn 72), but only after Eliza first reiterated (albeit poorly) a link between
age and the bulb blowing (turn 71). This aging idea later activated Eliza's
image of mice chewing through wires in old houses (turns 75, 78 and
83). Emily further refined the description; she introduced scientific terminology for the first time when she replaced the word "wire" with "insulator" (meaning the plastic coating around the metal wire) and "conductor"
(for metal wire) (turn 83). This provided clear evidence that Emily used a

discourse she had evidently appropriated during the first activity from the "Electrifying Experiences" lesson. Eventually the team's response involved the scenario of rodents chewing through the wires, thus breaking the circuit (turn 88). Concepts such as conductor, insulator, and circuit were introduced into the discussion by Emily and later used by Susan in a different context (turn 84), suggesting that she could use it for her own intentions. Eliza appeared to be delighted as well with what she perceived to be the group's solution (turn 89).

An initial analysis of the conversation from this excerpt (i.e., turns 68–89) might suggest that the team, and each of its members, was now competent in this discursive practice. However, it is difficult to tell for sure, from this excerpt alone, the extent to which individuals use this discourse in different contexts, that is, the extent to which they can be said to understand these concepts. As revealed during an end-of-unit interview, Eliza did not demonstrate a basic understanding of simple circuits, even after several lessons on the topic and completing the electric toy design activity. While Emily and Susan both drew and described the operation of a simple circuit during their interviews, Eliza appeared uncertain about the canonical model of an electric circuit developed in class and, more important, did not demonstrate that she understood what would happen if one of the wires in a circuit was cut (perhaps by the actions of a rodent). Both Emily and Susan fluently explained this last component of the interview task related directly to the scenario developed by their group. Eliza suggested that the light in a circuit before her would come on if one of the wires was to be cut. Although the decontextualized nature of a post-unit interview may have mediated Eliza's attempt to express her understanding, her responses nevertheless did not demonstrate that she had developed the canonical scientific language games for open and closed circuits. This suggests that although students can indeed help each other learn science through design activities, student-student interaction alone is probably not sufficient for developing these language games.

As we argue in the next section, teachers are needed to interact with design teams in ways that help individual students make links between their design experiences and canonical science. As ideas were progressively elaborated by students within the team as the project neared completion, the children freely expressed their ideas for the benefit of the team. By participating in this process they not only helped the team to make progress but also learned from their peers. The students regularly acknowledged the importance of sharing ideas within teams during their interviews. For example, Emily commented during a post-unit interview,

"Well like if you have tried it and it is not really going to work and you have tried and tried and added in new things, you just go find a friend or someone that's interested and they can actually help you to get it and eventually it will work." Here, "get it" meant "understand the concept."

Sharing ideas with respected students outside their immediate design team was one way ideas "diffused" between groups (Ritchie & Hampson, 1996).[1] Peer interaction of this sort appears to be an important component of learning science through design activities in elementary or primary classrooms (cf. Roth, 1996b). However, students in Mr. Hammett's class did not confine their search for ideas to their team members and outside respected peers. Both the teacher and available texts were perceived as valuable sources of new ideas (Ritchie & Hampson, 1996). We now turn to the issue of teacher intervention during design activities.

Learning Science with the Teacher's Help

We illustrate throughout this book that students do not operate in isolation in design classrooms. In fact, the artifacts that result from children's activities can be characterized by a network of things (including materials, people, norms) that shape them (Roth, 1998a). Among these influences are interactions with other students and the teacher. In Mr. Hammett's classroom, teams interacted with other teams both formally and informally. Also, while the teams were engaged in their design activities Mr. Hammett visited each team, not only to supervise material practices and the equitable distribution of material resources but also to interact with students. Although many of these interactions were related to interpersonal issues, several interactive episodes were concerned with helping students to refine their designs or develop a better understanding of the related scientific concepts. On these occasions, Mr. Hammett became a significant member of the design team. Rather than thinking of the within-group interactions in terms of student-student interactions only, we now should consider the contributions that Mr. Hammett made to the design team. In this way, we view Mr. Hammett as an important member of each design team and a contributor to the seamless web of factors that constitutes the emerging artifact. Through the person of the teacher, students' activities were oriented toward the cultural reproduction of science in addition to the children's own cultural productions.

In this section we focus on those teacher-student interactions that were concerned with scientific concepts and design practices. In particular, two contrasting interactive episodes between Mr. Hammett and Kerrin's design team are described. The first episode occurred during the electrolysis of salty water referred to previously. In this episode, Mr. Hammett faced the dilemma of whether to intervene by introducing the language games of canonical science when the students expressed alternative concepts on topics not usually studied in the elementary school science curriculum. The dilemma was multifaceted. At issue here was not only the need to balance the autonomy of a design team's activities with a perceived need for formal instruction but also the consequences of choosing one option over another; that is, to sacrifice the intended curriculum for an interesting but risky diversion with uncertain outcomes. The second episode illustrates a successful teacher intervention. It was recorded two weeks after the first lesson on "Electrifying Experiences." Here, Mr. Hammett intervened as Kerrin and Katrina connected a series circuit of lights for the basketball-shooting game design.

Balancing Student Autonomy and Teacher Intervention: A Teacher's Dilemma

Teachers with constructivist referents often find themselves in a dilemma between student autonomy and intervention. That is, teachers have to balance children's cultural productions of science and their cultural reproduction of canonical science. If teachers intervene too often, the teaching and learning environment becomes too teacher-centered and children are likely to lose interest and find science too difficult. If teachers intervene too little, children are likely to make few advances in developing discourses that have sufficient family resemblance with canonical ones to justify the name "science" (or "technology") for the lessons. That is, intervening too little deprives children of the proven resources the disciplines of science and technology offer them with for solving problems.

As we demonstrated earlier, Kerrin's design team became excited when they thought that they had made a major technological breakthrough by way of a water purifier. At this time they were highly motivated to account for their observations. The strawberry yogurt analogy did account for the separation of the salt from the water in the context of their observations. However, the students themselves were concerned that they did not know why the apparatus "purified" the salty water like the physical separation of strawberries from strawberry yogurt.

Students at this age are normally unfamiliar with language games associated with ions and ionic transport.[2] Furthermore, Mr. Hammett had not specifically targeted a change in children's discourse about these topics. It was therefore not surprising to find that several weeks after this activity the students still did not express the canonical scientific explanation for their observations. For example, Jackson remarked during his end-of-unit interview, "We saw all these things rising to the surface and some were bubbles and the others were salt. . . . That was quite interesting. I don't know how it happened, but it was interesting." Similarly, Joshua admitted: "We don't know how" it happened. But it would be quite unrealistic for students to stumble onto the canonical version without some sort of teacher intervention in this case. At no stage during the lesson did Mr. Hammett refer to the ionic properties of salt in solution, nor did he dissuade students from their separation analogy. It would seem that an opportunity for these highly motivated students to be introduced to the canonical scientific explanation for this phenomenon was lost.

Here, Mr. Hammett faced a dilemma. On the one hand, this was an opportunity to introduce such concepts as ionic compounds, solutions, and electrolysis. But to do so, he would need to engage in a telling mode. This telling would involve a considerable investment of time and also a departure from his usual classroom practices. Furthermore, by digressing from the planned sequence of activities, the original goal of introducing students to the properties of conductors and insulators and simple electric circuits in readiness for the design activity would need to be set back. On the other hand, he could just let the activity run its course and thereby let a great learning opportunity go by. Mr. Hammett partially resolved the issue by waiting till the end of the class. During the whole-class discussion following the activity, he waited to call on Kerrin until after all other groups had presented their reports. Without delving into possible explanations for the observations made by Kerrin's team, Mr. Hammett invited other students to file past Kerrin's apparatus to observe for themselves the "sizzling" salt water. In doing so, the teacher publicly acknowledged the value of their interesting "discovery" without trying to offer an explanation.

Even though Mr. Hammett did not tell Kerrin's group about electrolysis on this occasion he did interact with them in a way that advanced their design practices. For example, when Jackson was describing his salt taste-test, Mr. Hammett's probing questions elicited a sequence of refined improvements to their current practices, as the following excerpt shows.

90   Joshua: I'll just taste the water. [tastes water]
91   Jackson: Tastes like normal water.
92   Mr. Hammett: Down the bottom. Well, how are you going to get your finger to the bottom without touching the top?
93   Katrina: We'll scrape it off.

94   Joshua: You cut a hole in the bottom.
95   Mr. Hammett: You cut a hole in the bottom.
96   Joshua: Yeah. Taste the top then taste the bottom.

Without Mr. Hammett's question (turn 92), the students may not have realized that their procedure would not provide the sought-after result. Katrina then suggested that they could scrape off the layer of salt forming on the surface (turn 93) while Joshua suggested that they could drain the bottom layer by cutting a hole in the container (turn 94). These suggestions represented an improvement in their practice of dipping their fingers into the solution. These improvements served the same purpose as Jackson's idea to draw up samples of the liquid at different depths by manipulating the air pressure in a straw with the use of his thumb. Thus, although Mr. Hammett did not introduce the students to the scientific explanation for their observations, he challenged them by questioning the reliability of their current practices. In this sense, Mr. Hammett's teaching differed considerably from that of some other teachers we have observed. For example, when faced with a similar set of circumstances, Mr. Hook (see Ritchie, Tobin & Hook, 1997) fostered a "try and see" approach to laboratory practices. In doing so, Mr. Hook inadvertently allowed his Grade 8 students to develop observational and theoretical discourse that was incommensurable with canonical physics. Similarly, in the next chapter, Ms. Scott regarded herself as a facilitator and tended to minimize her efforts to mediate the students' constructions of canonical language games.

Mr. Hammett's questions were not restricted to challenging student practices. We already showed that he asked questions that invited students to qualify statements or words (e.g., "purify") both within the design team and for the benefit of other students in the class. In the following excerpt, Mr. Hammett's question encouraged the students to extend their current practices. This excerpt came from a long interactive segment of text related to improving the conductivity of the salt water previously only summarized in this chapter.

97   Mr. Hammett: [approaching Kerrin's team] What was interesting, Joshua?
98   Joshua: Yeah look!
99   Kerrin: It's sizzling, bubbling.
100   Joshua: The water's all sizzled, like sizzling up. All the salt is coming out.
101   Mr. Hammett: Ohhhh.
102   Kerrin: And listen to it. It goes pop, pop, pop.
103   Joshua: Like snap, crackle, and pop.
104   Mr. Hammett: So it is. You've got something happening there, haven't you?
105   Joshua: We don't know what it is.

106	Mr. Hammett:	Good one. Now, does the light light up?
107	Kerrin:	Um, no.
108	Joshua:	No.
109	Kerrin:	Only when the alfoil touches.
110	Mr. Hammett:	If we added more salt, what do you think would happen?
111	Joshua:	Probably.
112	Jackson:	It might.
113	Joshua:	I tasted it. It wasn't very salty.
114	Jackson:	[Kerrin adds more salt into the cup] Stick a lot more in.
115	Joshua:	It's happening again.
116	Katrina:	Kerrin, do you want to put a bit more in?
117	Joshua:	No, don't. Don't, we'll show Mr. Hammett how it is. Mr. Hammett! Look! It's happening!
118	Kerrin:	Mr. Hammett!
119	Jackson:	If you look a lot closer it's happening a lot more, so I think it's the salt.
120	Joshua:	It's the salt.

Mr. Hammett reacted more to children's talk than imposing his own descriptions. In this way, students rarely engaged Mr. Hammett in information- or answer-giving episodes. Instead, they showed him what they themselves had found, thereby illustrating that the team was used to exercising autonomy in their design practices. This was evident from the very first turn in the above excerpt. Responding to the excited voices of team members, Mr. Hammett nominated Joshua to describe the cause of their excitement. As Joshua and Kerrin shared their revelations intermittently (turns 98–103), Mr. Hammett listened pensively, acknowledging their descriptions (i.e., turn 101) momentarily before affirming their observations (turn 104). Joshua admitted that they did not know what was happening but avoided asking a direct question for Mr. Hammett to answer (turn 105). Rather than attempting to provide an explanation for students' observations, Mr. Hammett redirected their attention to the primary purpose of the activity, which was to classify materials as conductors or insulators by asking whether or not the light was glowing (turn 106). Kerrin appeared to suggest that water was not a good conductor (turns 107, 109). Mr. Hammett's next move was a productive question (Harlen, 1985) because it opened a door to children's inquiry to find out "What would happened if . . .?" (turn 110). Interestingly, Mr. Hammett selected the inclusive pronoun "we" in his question, affirming his membership on the team. Earlier Joshua and Jackson had suspected that the salt in the water might be the factor causing these spectacular observations. So when the teacher directed students' attention toward the amount of salt in solution, Joshua and Jackson speculated, not surprisingly, that the light might indeed glow if additional salt was added (turns 111, 112).47 Joshua tried to rationalize his prediction by claiming that when he tasted the water before it was not particularly salty (turn 113), evoking Kerrin's action and Jackson's demand to pour in more salt (turn 114). To their excitement, team members noticed more activity in the cup leading to the conclusion expressed by both Jackson and Joshua that it was the salt that caused the water to sizzle (turns 119 and 120) and the light to glow. So, although the team had suspected that the salt had some role to play in their "discovery," it was Mr. Hammett's question that led them to identify a relationship between the amount of salt in solution and the sizzling activity (and conductivity of the liquid).

Although Mr. Hammett did not enact a telling mode, his carefully selected questions did two things for the team. First, his suggestive question, which invited the team members to predict what would happen to the illumination of the bulb upon adding salt, led the team to identify a relationship between conductivity and the concentration of salt water. Second, Mr. Hammett interacted with the students as if he was a valued member of the team rather than an authoritative source of canonical scientific knowledge. This meant that the power for learning was vested within the team, albeit extended to include Mr. Hammett. This differs from traditional classrooms in which the teacher controls teaching episodes in such a way that student activity is restricted to the rote learning of teacher-ordained propositional statements, forgotten or rejected shortly after the teacher intervention (cf., Ritchie, Tobin, & Hook, 1997). However, Mr. Hammett's interactions on this occasion did not advance the students' understandings of electrolysis. We now examine another teaching episode that did lead to the acquisition of canonical scientific knowledge.

A Successful Teacher Intervention

By the third week of the electrical energy unit, Mr. Hammett's students were nearing completion of the design of their electrical toys. Kerrin's team was busy building their basketball shooting game. While Joshua and Jackson were responsible for the backboard and the return chutes, Kerrin and Katrina had taken on the task of connecting the electrical circuits that were to signal successful shots. Kerrin and Katrina had worked at a table trying to connect three bulbs in a series driven by one power supply when Mr. Hammett first approached. The teacher initiated the conversation by asking, "What are you trying to do?" Kerrin replied, "I am trying to make a circuit. I did that on the battery from top to bottom and they only lit up the tiniest bit." Here Kerrin revealed that she had connected a series circuit of bulbs to the terminals of a power pack only to find that the bulbs illuminated dimly—this was unsatisfactory for the purposes of signaling a successful shot in their basketball-shooting game. Kerrin accounted for the unexpectedly dim lights by suggesting that the terminal connections of the wires had to be swapped. At this stage in the conversation, Kerrin suggested that the brightness of the bulbs might be affected by reversing the polarity of the bulbs component of the series circuit. Mr. Hammett encouraged Kerrin to follow through with her first hunch, to rearrange the terminal connections and check her prediction. Kerrin asserted that she thought that there might be a difference between the two connections but Mr. Hammett intervened by asking a set of more direct and probing questions. These, as shown below, scaffolded Kerrin toward producing an explanation that was consistent with canonical science. Through the following excerpt, Mr. Hammett demonstrated that he was not prepared to allow Kerrin's view (which was at odds with canonical science) to go unchallenged.

121	Mr. Hammett:	So, why are they dimmer?
122	Kerrin:	Um, I don't know.
123	Mr. Hammett:	Katrina, come on you're thinking here too.
124	Kerrin:	Why are they dimmer than they were before?
125	Katrina:	Because they (1) . . .
126	Mr. Hammett:	Like if I took this off here and touched it on here [Mr. Hammett now disconnects two of the three bulbs from the circuit] (3). Why is it brighter?
127	Kerrin:	Because you have got more. They don't have to share out the volts.
128	Katrina:	Yeah.
129	Mr. Hammett:	What do you mean, share out the volts?
130	Katrina:	You have got to have all the same thing.
131	Kerrin:	You've already got two volts and they are two and a half each.
132	Mr. Hammett:	Yeah?
133	Kerrin:	And um, it's got to divide. It's got to, like you can have a circuit with just one bulb and it will be really bright.
134	Mr. Hammett:	Why is it bright?
135	Kerrin:	'Cause it's got it all to itself, two volts to itself.
136	Mr. Hammett:	Two volts to itself; so, what's happening here now?
137	Kerrin:	The other ones have to take some, they have to get some too. So they have to share it out.

Mr. Hammett's initial question and prompt did not elicit a plausible explanation (turns 121–125) as to why the bulbs should be dimmer upon reversing the polarity of the series circuit component (i.e., the bulbs connected to the power pack). He then changed the focus of the original question. Mr. Hammett first disconnected two of the three bulbs and then asked, "Why is it brighter?" (turn 126). This seemed to remind Kerrin of a previous experience where she explained energy distribution in a simple electric circuit drawing on Joshua's Thomas the Tank Engine analogy. Kerrin's response attracted Mr. Hammett's clarifying question (turn 129). Kerrin thought aloud by noting that the power supply was two volts and that each bulb can bring about a drop of up to two and one-half volts (turn 131). Mr. Hammett then encouraged Kerrin to continue her explanation (turn 132). Here, Kerrin articulated that the single bulb was brighter because it no longer shared the available energy from the power source with the two other bulbs (turns 133 and 135). After paraphrasing Kerrin's response, Mr. Hammett then returned to the original problem (turn 136). Kerrin responded successfully, demonstrating that she understood why the series combination should cause a dimming effect.

Building on Kerrin's successful explanation above, Mr. Hammett led Kerrin to a more detailed appreciation of series circuits in the following excerpt.

138   Mr. Hammett: How much do you think each one is getting when we give it four volts? How much do you think they are getting now?
139   Kerrin: Four divided by three.
104   Mr. Hammett: Yeah, all right. What's that? Four divided by three?
141   Kerrin: About one, one and a quarter.
142   Katrina: One point.
143   Kerrin: One and a third.
144   Mr. Hammett: One and a third, all right. So if we went to six, six volts across the three, how much would they be getting then?
145   Kerrin: Two, so that would be even brighter.
146   Mr. Hammett: So that's what it was before when it was on two [turns the power pack up to 6 volts].
147   Kerrin: Yeah.
148   Mr. Hammett: So your theory must be right.
149   Kerrin: 'Cause they are getting two volts each.
150   Mr. Hammett: That's what about two volts looked like.

Mr. Hammett asked Kerrin and Katrina a direct application question (turn 138); it built on Kerrin's understanding that the entire supply of energy (of two volts) would drop across the single bulb but that this same amount would need to be shared by all of the bulbs in any augmented series combination (turn 137). When Mr. Hammett asked what the potential drop would be across each of the three series connected bulbs if the supply was switched up to four volts; Kerrin correctly responded that four should be divided by three (turn 139). Kerrin corrected her first response (turn 141), after Katrina's interjection (in turn 142), when she answered that the drop would be one and one-third volts across each bulb (turn 143). Mr. Hammett ratified her efforts with a low-keyed response before directing another application question in the same mold as before (turn 144). There was no problem this time with the arithmetic, but Kerrin provided the additional unsolicited response that the bulbs would be brighter now—demonstrating a link between potential drop and brightness of the bulbs (turn 146). Mr. Hammett switched the power supply up to six volts to confirm Kerrin's prediction. More important, now that Kerrin had answered the series of questions successfully (i.e., turns 136, 138, 144), Mr. Hammett appeared to accept that a general case or "theory" had been established. This was important for two reasons. First, by scaffolding Kerrin to the generalized description, he implicitly told Kerrin, "Now you can work out any combination." Second, by selecting the words "your theory," Mr. Hammett acknowledged that it was Kerrin and not he who had worked through the issue, albeit with his guidance. Here was additional evidence that the interactive style employed by Mr. Hammett was empowering. This contrasts with an interactive style observed elsewhere (i.e., Ritchie, Tobin, & Hook, 1997), in which the students were told by their teacher what the canonical view was with the expectation that they needed to commit that particular view to memory. Not surprisingly, the latter style was not particularly successful. In contrast, several weeks after the above episode, both Kerrin and Katrina successfully answered a series of interview questions that demonstrated that they knew how energy was distributed in a series circuit. Below, Kerrin responded to the same interview question about the effects of adding an extra bulb to a series circuit. (We have already quoted Katrina's response to an interview question.)

> They would be dimmer, because you had to share out the volts. Because when we did it we only had them on, they were 2.5 volts and we had three lights and we had it on 2 volts and they weren't working because they were getting hardly any volts. So when we turned it up to four they were getting a little bit brighter. . . . The more lightbulbs you've got, and if the voltage stays the same, they are going to get dimmer.

Mr. Hammett provided some scaffolding comments that could move Kerrin and Katrina toward producing a canonical description of energy distribution in a series circuit. But he had not addressed Kerrin's own proposal that switching the polarity of the series circuit might change the light intensity. Mr. Hammett originally intervened because Kerrin proposed that the action of switching terminals accounted for dimming the lights. After their lengthy interaction above, Kerrin then reminded Mr. Hammett of their unfinished business.

151 Kerrin: Hang on Mr. Hammett. Wasn't that because that was the dimmer side? Remember how we had them and then we swapped it and that was dimmer?

152 Mr. Hammett: So, you are saying.

153 Kerrin: If we swap them over they might be . . .

154 Mr. Hammett: Okay, try it.

155 Kerrin: [swaps terminals]

156 Mr. Hammett:: So you swapped them back now?

157 Kerrin: Yeah, they were brighter before. That's two [volts].

158 Mr. Hammett:: Any difference? [Students rearrange the circuit]

159 What do you think?

160 Kerrin: I'm just checking them again to see. They're sort of brighter.

161 Katrina: They look brighter.

162 Mr. Hammett: This way is brighter? Let me check.

163 Katrina: This one is brighter.

164 Mr. Hammett: [swaps terminals, checks]

165 Katrina: That other one that was on at the start is brighter.

166 Kerrin: Yeah, that's the brightest.

167 Mr. Hammett: You reckon?

168 Katrina: Yeah. (1)

169 Kerrin: I'm not sure, I reckon this one is.

170 Mr. Hammett: [swaps terminals] You're saying this way is brighter?

171 Kerrin: Yeah, they're the same. Yeah, they're the same.

172 Mr. Hammett: Katrina, what conclusion can you make about the connection of your wires? About the brightness of your bulbs?

173 Katrina: Well if we swap them then they're the same.

174 Mr. Hammett: Is that what you are saying?

175 Katrina: Yeah.

176 Mr. Hammett: Right, you've found out something that you've investigated. Do you think they are the same, Kerrin?

177 Kerrin: Yeah.

As previously demonstrated, this excerpt shows that Mr. Hammett did not rush in to counter Kerrin's suggestion that the polarity of the bulbs component of the series circuit was a factor in determining the brightness of the bulbs (turn 152). Mr. Hammett sought clarification and urged Kerrin and Katrina to put their idea to the test (turn 154). Unlike traditional teachers' "try it and see" approach, Mr. Hammett had first established that his students could test their idea fairly, this time by simply switching terminals. Second, Mr. Hammett checked back with the team to see what their test revealed (turns 156, 158, 159). But it now appeared that the intuitive everyday non-scientific discourse had merged with their observation description (turns 161, 163, 166).

Because students' everyday non-scientific discourse is the most salient resource in any situation, their observation sentences are unavoidably non-scientific. For example, science graduates maintained their non-scientific theory descriptions despite evidence to the contrary (White & Gunstone, 1992). That is, after having predicted different fall times for different-sized masses when released from the same height (at 2 meters and then at 9.6 meters), they observed the two masses strike the ground at the same time when dropped from 9.6 meters. In a similar way, Australian Grade 12 students conducting open investigations of rolling objects initially observed objects rolling at the same rate. They maintained their observation descriptions of equal velocity although there was subsequently clear evidence that the objects rolled at different rates, something they recognized themselves during a stimulated recall interview (Roth, McRobbie, Lucas, & Boutonné, 1997a). We made similar observations during teacher demonstrations in which students' predictive descriptions actually seemed to drive what students later reported as an observation of the actual event (Roth, McRobbie, Lucas, & Boutonné, 1997b). In all of these cases, perception was mediated by previous descriptions and explanations of what should happen; observational and theoretical descriptions significantly shape future observations.

In the present case, both Katrina and Kerrin claimed that the original circuit arrangement effected a dimmer illumination of the bulbs. Mr. Hammett then took over by reversing the terminals himself (turn 164). Once again, Katrina and Kerrin predicted a difference (turns 165, 166), this time evoking a disbelieving retort from Mr. Hammett (turn 167). Katrina confirmed her prediction after the test (turn 168), but following a brief pause, Kerrin expressed doubt for the first time (turn 169). Once again Mr. Hammett reversed the polarity (turn 170), but Kerrin acknowledged that the illumination was the same in both arrangements (turn 171). Mr. Hammett sought to dispel any lingering doubts by directing his next open-ended question (turn 172) to Katrina, who had not yet affirmed the result. She announced that switching the terminals made no difference to the brightness of the bulbs (turn 173). With this declaration, Mr. Hammett provided positive reinforcement for their investigative efforts (turn 176).

Cultural Production and Reproduction
of Science Discourse

We began this chapter by demonstrating that students within design teams do indeed contribute to each other's development of scientific knowledge.

The evidence presented supports our claim that elementary students can learn science through design activities. Although the previous chapter was concerned exclusively with the within-team discourse associated with the design of marble machines, the present chapter broadened its focus to include those teacher activities that supported the students' design of electric toys. Collectively, these activities provided an effective set of experiences that enhanced the scientific learning of participants. Accordingly, we argued that it was not possible to attribute scientific learning outcomes to either the supplementary activities or the design activity itself. Instead, the design activity should be viewed as an integrative activity that allows students to learn science purposefully—in the context of designing a particular artifact.

Interestingly, in the course of communicating ideas with fellow design team members, one student used analogies to help explain his understanding of the scientific concepts associated with a basketball shooting game. In particular, the Thomas the Tank Engine analogy about electric circuits, first articulated by Joshua, was further developed by both Kerrin and Katrina in such a way that it demonstrated not only an understanding of the canonical science targeted by the analogy but also the effectiveness of the analogy as a discursive tool to communicate meaning between peers. The term "analogy" here has been used in a pragmatic sense by which an unfamiliar phenomenon (such as electric circuits—the target concept) is explained by likening it to a familiar situation (i.e., train track and stations—source) (see Dagher, 1995). Such a definition includes related discursive devices such as metaphors, models, and similes. Although some researchers have argued that analogies underpin the mental modeling essential for learning science (Solomon, 1986), others have reported inconsistent results when the effects of teacher analogies have been investigated in science classrooms (Lin, Shiau, & Lawrenz, 1996). Although we have found that teacher-generated metaphors have been successful in changing teacher practice (Ritchie, 1994; Tobin, 1990), little research has been conducted into the effects of student-generated analogies. Recognizing the learning potential of student-generated analogies, Wong (1993) set out to train university students to use a set of heuristic devices to generate analogies for themselves. This preliminary work suggested that these students improved their explanations and understanding of the target concepts. Although Wong recommended that further studies should focus on implementing this strategy in middle school classrooms, we have shown here that elementary students do benefit from self-generated and peer-elaborated analogies of scientific phenomena. We suggest that there is great potential for future studies to focus on the explanatory power of student-generated analogies in science classrooms.

The Thomas the Tank Engine analogy proved successful in preventing the possible formation of the commonly reported alternative conception that electric current is used up by components in a circuit (Grayson, 1996). By thinking of the battery as if it was a petrol pump at the train station that supplied the energy to the train (electrons), Kerrin and Katrina could explain why the light bulbs in a series circuit were the same brightness and that the electrons needed to move through the circuit in the same direction to renew their supply of energy. Yet they still found difficulty in using this resource to back an argument about the brightness of the bulbs. Here, Mr. Hammett's skilful intervention guided the students to gather compelling empirical evidence to refute possible alternative explanations. In addition to providing the necessary support that enabled Kerrin and Katrina to reach a viable explanation, Mr. Hammett supported their earlier revelation about the energy distribution in the circuit with mathematical representations. By working through a set of problems that required the students to predict, observe, and explain (White & Gunstone, 1992), Mr. Hammett helped these students acquire scientifically desirable practices. These students could now estimate correctly the potential drop across each bulb connected in series, given the power supply.

Mr. Hammett's intervention with Kerrin and Katrina was successful because he did not attempt to "extinguish" his students' extant knowledge. Instead, he guided the students through a set of practices that enabled them to empirically justify their observation that reversing the polarity of the power supply made no difference to the brightness of the bulbs. Similarly, throughout the electrolysis episode, Mr. Hammett did not attempt to replace the strawberry yogurt analogy with another or dissuade the students from their belief that a physical separation was in progress in the cup of salt water. In this case, the analogy did have satisfactory explanatory power in the context of the students' observations; they did see bubbles rising to the surface, and the frothy layer on the surface tasted salty. Many analogies that are now discarded were once effective explanatory resources that clarified a broad range of observations; they were useful and satisfying as long as they were kept within that range (White, 1994). The analogies that follow and replace the initial ones are more sophisticated because they provide resources to explain a wider set of phenomena, but they are also less easy to fit to a common analogy. This possibly offers a partial justification for Mr. Hammett's non-intervention during the electrolysis episode. Mr. Hammett acknowledged the viability of the students' analogy without even hinting that there might be another, more sophisticated explanation. The conceptual change literature offers support for this practice. We can expect successful transitions to a more formal discourse only if (a) students recognize the viability of the initial conceptions and (b) the new explanations provide new possibilities for problem solving (Duit & Confrey, 1996). Mr. Hammett was faced with a dilemma here. Even though he acknowledged that the analogy did provide a satisfactory explanation for the most obvious observations, the unresolved tension was whether or not he should have intervened by introducing the more sophisticated concepts of ionization and electrolysis. If he had told the students about the ionic properties of salt using his authority as a teacher, the students might have accepted this explanation. It is more likely, though, that their current views would have persisted without an attempt to work through the procedural practices the way that Mr. Hammett did with Kerrin and Katrina later during the electric circuit episode. The teacher-as-authority approach would have posed additional problems or dilemmas, the result of which would have taken the focus of the activity away from conductivity and the design of the electric toy. As Duit and Confrey point out, "more elaborate and complex mathematical and scientific ideas must be demonstrated to allow deeper or broader explanations if they are to become viable to the students" (1996, p. 85).

An important condition for conceptual development in the science classroom is the promotion of students' sense of autonomy (Duit & Confrey, 1996). As we have shown throughout this chapter, Mr. Hammett empowered his students in a variety of ways. He acknowledged viable explanations, encouraged student reporting to the whole class, welcomed between-group interactions, challenged students' practices and scientific procedures, discussed improvements to practices and procedures, used inclusive language in order to present himself as a co-learner rather than an external authority, and referred to students' predictions and explanations as valued personal theories. By establishing an effective learning community as he did, Mr. Hammett made it possible for his students to learn scientific concepts and lay the foundations for the future development of more sophisticated concepts. Knowing how to interact, with whom, and for how long, required the execution of many decisions, some of which caused ongoing dilemmas or tensions. Yet Mr. Hammett's actions seemed natural and fluent, as if the decisions were taken without procrastination. The bases for these decisions, along with decisions concerning lesson sequencing and resource distribution, form an essential component of a teacher's personal practical knowledge or theories for teaching, sometimes referred to as craft knowledge (Cooper & McIntyre, 1996). By accessing teachers' theories, researchers and student teachers might benefit from a better understanding of the complexities of classroom life.

In addition to a teacher's practical knowledge, the extent of a teacher's scientific knowledge has important implications for classroom practice. For example, we found that when teachers have an incomplete understanding of prescribed scientific concepts, the authority of available texts can be overused and students' alternative concepts can be unidentified or, worse still, reinforced through uninformed instructional moves (Ritchie, Tobin, & Hook, 1997). Mr. Hammett was familiar with electrical circuits because of his previous background as an electrical fitter prior to becoming a teacher (Ritchie & Hampson, 1996). This confidence and interest in the topic could account for his persistent and extensive efforts to help Kerrin and Katrina during the electric-circuits episode. In contrast, Mr. Hammett admitted later that he was less confident with electrolysis than the electric circuit topic although he had a basic understanding of electrolysis. Perhaps this lack of confidence partially contributed to the dilemma that arose during the electrolysis episode; that is, he did not know whether he should intervene. Accepting that most elementary teachers would have limited understanding of a wide range of scientific concepts, it would be prudent for curriculum developers to provide supplementary readings or background information concerning the scientific concepts associated with design activities. In this respect, *Primary Investigations* has done an admirable job.

Metalogue

Issue 1: The Role of Teachers' Subject Matter Competence and Experience

M: At this point, I think it is interesting to raise the issue of the subject matter background that the teachers had in the studies that we presented thus far. Mr. Hammett had been an electrical fitter before he became a teacher. Gitte had developed and taught the engineering for children curriculum in a Grade 4 class and subsequently further developed it as an employee of a curriculum development organization. There, she had met with many structural engineers and architects and had visited many different sites where structures were built. Also, she had presented more than 40 workshops for teachers who wanted to use the curriculum in their own teaching. Finally, I have graduate degrees in physics and extensive teaching experience in physics and physical science. Thus, it may come as little surprise to many readers that the teachers in these case studies had a lot of embodied knowledge on which they could draw in the planning and implementation of the curricula. However, many readers will immediately recognize that the experience and preparation of these teachers is not the norm for teachers at the elementary level. We therefore need to raise a number of questions. To what extent do these chapters show knowing and learning (of students and teachers) that we want and can achieve in other classrooms? What is the role of the subject matter background in making science emerge from technology and design activities?

S: Several studies of exemplary teachers have shown that these teachers (and their students) experience problems when teaching out of field. Although Mr. Hammett was confident with the activities related to electric circuits, he admitted to lacking confidence with the concepts associated with electrolysis. The good thing about Mr. Hammett's practice here was that he did not try to persuade students that their strawberry yogurt analogy was inappropriate and substitute it with another inaccurate model. All teachers confront gaps in their scientific knowledge base. This is one of the reasons that we might like to de-emphasize teacher exposition in science classes. What we need to do is encourage teachers to communicate with their students in ways that do not always privilege the teacher's ideas. In other words, teachers need to get the balance right between cultural production and cultural reproduction.

K: The next two chapters deal with teachers who have science backgrounds that are more typical of those we might expect to encounter in elementary schools. Ms. Scott is recognized as a wonderful teacher whose strengths are associated with literacy and art. Her classroom was always bustling with learning and was a very pleasant place to be. Ms. Mack also was an expert in the teaching of language arts. For the initial 20 years of her career she avoided the teaching of science. The chapter describes how she educated herself and transformed the classroom to support independent student inquiry in science.

M: This is an important issue that we have to pick up later. Many elementary teachers may be able to identify with Ms. Scott. But they may not see how to move from providing an exciting engineering classroom to providing an exciting engineering classroom in which students not only appropriate canonical scientific discourse but are also enabled to appropriate a scientific habitus.

K: It is not just a case of what teachers know and can do but what they choose to do as they enact the curriculum. As we have seen in the chapters so far, a key ingredient in the learning of science is to co-participate in language games that involve the use of an evolving science discourse. Hence the interactions between students and between the teacher and students are of paramount importance. The teacher's knowledge in action is a critical factor.

S: I think that this is the point I was touching on previously. When teachers work alongside or *with* students they are less likely to invoke their authority as an expert or old-timer. The interactive approach to teaching science is one model that can lead to teacher-student coparticipation.

Issue 2: Student-Student Interactions and Gender

M: An interesting turn of events seemed to be related to Mr. Hammett's decision not to continue with the friendship groups in the earlier marble-machine activity but to assign students to groups. As a consequence, Kerrin and Katrina got into a group with Joshua and Jackson, who seemed to be little interested in collaboration or in assisting their female partners in developing an understanding. The episode is interesting because Kerrin insisted that the boys let them participate and think so that they could develop an understanding. There is much literature on the gender issue. In Gitte and Christina's class there were also problems, in the sense that the whole-class sessions were dominated by the boys and the teachers could not do much about it, despite their awareness, and despite repeated efforts to address the issue. On the other hand, in my Grade 6–7 class, many of the girls were passionately involved in learning about machines and learning to operate tools, and some of them contributed more to the interactions than the boys. Yet such insistence by the girls that they have equal space for action and equal responsibility for design in a collectivity still appears to be too rare.

S: I can understand why the turn of events and Kerrin's discourse led you to identify gender as an important issue. On the one hand, we might read this as another case in which boys dominated girls—reinforcing the literature of the 1980s and early 1990s. But Kerrin refused to be positioned as a meek bystander. She demanded a different working relationship with the two boys. This was a powerful move on her part and some progress was made. Interestingly, in subsequent groups, Kerrin positioned herself as a leader, which caused varying degrees of resistance from group members.

K: An issue that comes up all too frequently is the use of girls to control the rowdy or otherwise inappropriate actions of boys. What often happens is that males who are unable to work cooperatively with others are placed in groups with females to "dilute" their rowdy effects. The effect of using such a grouping strategy is to make it possible to manage the class but to create a less than optimal learning environment for the girls, who may be disrupted from their learning. The literature is replete with other examples of females being disadvantaged in science activities with respect to males. A problem is that the nature and extent of the disadvantage is often invisible and is accepted as part of what is normal for science classes.

M: This is not an easy issue to deal with. I always had the sense that gender was not an issue in the classes that I taught, but I might have an unrealistic perspective. On the other hand, my classes never talked about subject matter alone; issues of epistemology and learning also were important topics of discussion. In these conversations, then, interferences with the learning of individual or groups of students became issues that were discussed, negotiated, and in most cases settled by the class and myself in a mediator role. With girls such as Kerrin and Katrina, potentially crucial interferences are settled before they come to a forum. But this requires a teacher who is sensitive to what is going on in the class as whole.

S: We should remember that equity was a central concern for Mr. Hammett. He initiated strategies to maximize equitable student participation—this does not happen by itself. Nevertheless, social practices have changed since the 1980s. I can't help feeling that the real issue here is broader than gender itself. A closer examination of the power relations between students is required. Some of the most dysfunctional groups I studied involved either single gendered groupings or those in which domination by a female student generated passive resistance from male members of the group. I now need to study the within-group discourse of these groups more closely. Positioning theory[4] might be a useful starting point for this analysis.

Issue 3: But This Is Not Science!

M: Several situations in this chapter struck me in the sense that I expect some science educators to be suspicious and exclaim, But this is not science! For example, Jackson stuck his finger into the solution and tasted the substance that appeared on the surface. More important, Mr. Hammett did not seem to be concerned when Kerrin told him about it. I have met many teacher colleagues in my classroom career who freaked out at the very idea that children tasted anything. Not that there would have been a danger, for it was only salt water; but they would have freaked out because of a belief that children must be told early on that substances can be inspected visually and perhaps by taking in whiffs of odor, but not by tasting them.

S: Safety is an important issue. However, I was more concerned with the children's use of Stanley knives and saws. There was much greater potential for serious injury here, and Mr. Hammett did intervene. I would have gone further by insisting that cutting and sawing be conducted at predetermined bench sites to which access was controlled and where risk to operators and passersby could be minimized. Also, I agree that tasting solutions should be dissuaded. At the same time, there is a danger that we can go overboard. I think that teachers need to exercise common sense and not treat all science-like activities as if they were potentially dangerous—after all we should be attempting to demystify science activities for children. In this respect, we should be comparing some of these activities with those undertaken in the kitchen or workshop rather than a laboratory.

K: Later in Ms. Mack's class she got her students to dress like scientists and wear safety goggles. At the time I was amused by this and thought in terms of stereotyping scientists and the types of pictures that students draw when they are asked to depict a scientist. Then as I thought about it in relation to the creation of a habitus, the whole idea of wearing lab coats and goggles made sense because it might become a characteristic of this science community. Safety must permeate all science activities, and there were examples in earlier chapters where Mr. Hammett had to intervene to remind students about safety. The fact is that students should not taste solutions in a science laboratory. So the fact that Mr. Hammett did not draw attention to safety issues when they arose could be seen as a missed opportunity.

S: I felt very uncomfortable about Ms. Mack's practice. While dressing up certainly might set the scene or create a scientific habitus, it does not seem to be an authentic practice in this case. Sure, one should wear goggles and lab coats in activities with acids and bases, but why would one dress up for an activity on structures or electric circuits? If Mr. Hammett had wanted the children to protect their clothing from the salt water, a kitchen apron would have been a more authentic item than a lab coat. This reasoning can be extended to tasting. In a kitchen, one would expect to add salt to taste, but why would we expect different behavior as soon as we change the name of the lesson to science, especially when the same room is used in all types of activities? Nevertheless, Mr. Hammett did lose the opportunity to impress on his students the need for more cautious practices, such as avoiding tasting unknown substances.

M: The other situation I was thinking about concerns the strawberry yogurt analogy. There may be many teacher colleagues who would have the tendency to tell children "the way it really is," that is, by telling them about ions that are in an aqueous solution.

K: There is nothing inherently wrong with telling. I am not arguing that it is always appropriate for teachers to tell students the right answers. But I do not like to see these rules that imply that it is wrong to tell students right answers or facts about science. Nor is it wrong to tell students whether or not they are right. In fact, one of the most interesting science teachers I had was interesting because of the neat things he could tell me about science. He was always sharing these neat things with me, and it got me curious. I believe it comes down to an issue that there is no one right way to teach. Depending on the teacher involved, it can be quite all right to tell students facts about science, to weave them into motivating stories, and even to present mini-lectures.

M: In academic and educational situations, I frequently find myself in the position where I am opposed to teaching as telling. And yet, I will gratefully listen to my neighbor, an experienced gardener, give me advice—in a telling mode—about how to do this or that and thereby improve the yield of my crop. So I agree, there are situations where the right level of telling is appropriate. It seems like the listener has to be ready to construct meaning with and around that which s/he hears.

K: But, and this is a big but, the telling becomes a problem when it shuts down inquiry or becomes too protracted. Mary Budd Rowe's research in the 1980s on what she called the 10–2 method is salient. She found that lectures were more effective when they did not extent beyond eight minutes without a two-minute break. Her research on the 10–2 method was undertaken in college classes and it related to the extent to which students could get information from a telling mode. By having two minutes for sharing after about eight minutes of lecture students could recall much more of what was being told. There are two points here. It is hard to concentrate for more than about five to eight minutes, and when students pool ideas they contribute to the learning of one another. Later we used the 10–2 method as a way to assist teachers to implement group work in classes that were accustomed to lectures.

M: One of the questions we might want to raise is whether telling is the only option in a situation like that in which Mr. Hammett found himself. Are there other ways in which he could have interacted with the children to provide an occasion for the change and growth in their discourse about solutions?

S: I have racked my brain over this question ever since I observed the episode. If the students had been in Grade 9, I would have felt much more comfortable about foregrounding cultural reproduction through "telling" or at least moving the conversation around to ionic solutions and electrolysis. But these children had not studied acids and bases or ions, and they had just begun to study electric circuits. At the same time, this was clearly a case of heightened interest and motivation—an opportunity not to be lost. I wonder if the students would have appreciated reading a historical account of the discovery of electrolysis? Perhaps such a reading would have established links between their inquiries and emotional experiences and those of Nicholson and Carlisle within the nineteenth-century scientific community. They might then be better prepared for the introduction of the canonical language games associated with electrolysis.

K: If we think about elementary classes it is even more important to vary the activity to maximize co-participation. Hence telling should not be excessive, no matter who is doing the telling. And it is an imperative that active listening be on the learning agenda for everyone in the class. What can you do as a listener to increase the probability that you will learn something from a speaker? Since so much speaking goes on in classes this is a significant question to answer. In Chapter 8, Ms. Mack shows us how she used strategies for her Grade 1 students to become active listeners, strategies I now use with my doctoral students with the same goal in mind.

S: An associated issue relates to students' levels of understanding. Perhaps there are superficial explanations that might satisfy students until they are conceptually ready for a deeper understanding of the phenomena. I know that the various curriculum documents in Australia are starting to describe different outcome levels for particular concepts. Although I think that there is some merit in recognizing that there may be different levels for some concepts, I feel uncomfortable when such a recognition turns into a much more systematic procedure in which all concepts are deconstructed arbitrarily; that is, without empirical evidence to support the hierarchical sequence of levels.

Notes

1 Although resources (facts, materials) can be thought of as literally spreading or diffusing through a community, the processes of how discourses and material practices come to be shared within a community are much more complex and involve actions and embodiment (Roth, 1998a).

2 Readers may be tempted to characterize the topics of ions and ionic transport as abstract. But this would not be appropriate, for to a physical chemist ions and ionic transport are very palpable objects and discursive topics. Thus, ions and ionic transport in themselves are neither abstract nor concrete. Rather, phenomena and concepts appear "abstract" and "concrete" depending on a person's familiarity with them. As a phenomenon becomes a familiar element in one's ontology, it loses the relational quality of abstractness and gains in concreteness, another relational quality.

3 We wrote "not surprisingly" because from phenomenological and discourse perspectives, any part of the conversation makes salient some things in the world. Whatever is currently salient is likely to be incorporated in the discourse productions, either overtly or as taken-for-granted background. Thus, when the children hear their teacher ask, "What happens if we add salt?" both the salt and the addition take on relevance. Neither would have been made salient in the talk if they were not relevant. Therefore, it is not surprising that children would use this salient aspect as a resource in their descriptions and explanations. For this reason, interviews are never neutral, so that "misconceptions" are as much the result of researchers' ways of presenting tasks and asking the questions as they are children's ways of making sense of the world. "Misconceptions" as categories and as children's productions are in a deep way teachers' (co-) constructions.

4 See Harré and van Langenhove, 1999.

Chapter 7

Castles, Castles, Castles: And Where Is the Science?[1]

The teaching and learning of science in elementary schools has its advocates who list many advantages for children of engaging in a carefully structured program that begins early and extends consistently through each of the elementary school grades. However, in some countries such as Singapore, elementary science is not taught in the first three years of school because of a belief that there are more important things to be doing in the initial grades. Since it is not possible to do everything that is important the feeling is that subjects such as science can wait for the fourth grade and perhaps even beyond that. If students can read and write then they can catch up in subjects such as science. As a science educator who has been an advocate of elementary science, this attitude is not acceptable to me. I do believe the advantages of doing science in the elementary grades are as Harlen has described them and that students are not as well educated when teachers do not include science in the curriculum. Of course the irony is that in many elementary schools in the United States of America, Canada, and Australia science is one of the first subjects not be taught when teachers experience a shortage of time. Also, the evidence suggests that when science is taught, students often do not learn and understand scientific concepts such that what they have learned makes a difference to them in their lives.

When I first approached Ms. Scott about participating in a study, she agreed and suggested that building castles would provide a suitable context. Her Grade 2 classroom was in an elementary school in the northern part of Florida and contained students from diverse socioeconomic backgrounds. The ethnic composition of the school was approximately 60 percent Caucasian and 25 percent African American; the remaining 15 percent consisted of Asian American and Hispanic students. Few students in Grade 2 had limited English proficiency.

The decision to focus on castles was based mainly on what the class was going to do anyway. Accordingly, when castles were suggested as a possible topic, it made sense for many reasons. In an era when teachers are encouraged to integrate what they do across many subject areas and when so much of what is done fits under the label of whole language, the selection of castles allowed us to see if students would engage in their activities. I was particularly interested to see if students' engagements were scientific and whether students would learn science though their physical interactions with the materials and associated verbal interactions with peers and the teacher. Ms. Scott and I discussed the importance of students linking evidence to their knowledge claims, but we did not discuss the science concepts (including both conceptual resources and practices) that might reasonably be developed in a unit on structures. The activities lacked coherence and there was not a strong emphasis on learning science concepts. The main goal was to complete the castle rather than build the castle as a way of also constructing conceptual knowledge about the building of structures that are stable, rigid, and self-supporting.

I employed interpretive research methods that accessed multiple data sources and were responsive to my experiences during intensive visits to the grade 2 classroom during a three-week sequence of activities. I provided multiple opportunities for Ms. Scott and her students to discuss their roles in their own language, collected artifacts from the classroom, and undertook intensive analyses of videotapes and 35-mm photographs taken by the teacher. This paper is based on two complementary perspectives, the first incorporated in a narrative from Ms. Scott and the second derived from my analysis and interpretation of data from the study.

Ms. Scott's Perspective: Building Castles

"Once upon a time . . ." there were 27 second-grade students who turned into castle architects. The transformation was part of a multicultural study of fairytales and folk tales that began as my students boarded an imaginary plane, suitcases and passports in hand, and set off for their first destination, Germany. It was in Germany that the students' fascination with castles became apparent.

I like to think of myself as a facilitator rather than a "deliverer" of knowledge. As the children became interested in castles and decided that they would like to study and construct castles, I knew that the first thing I needed to do was to find out what they already knew. We sat together and had a brainstorming session that resulted in a large idea map of their prior knowledge of castles. We focused on the structure of castles, and the children offered ideas such as "Castles have dungeons, halls, and rooms for armor." Soon, the children began asking questions. After activating prior knowledge and witnessing the excitement build, I asked the children to search for books that would give us answers to the questions we formulated. I shared information from books that I read aloud. The children and I made books, with a foldout castle on the cover, in which to store our information. The books contained castle diagrams and idea maps, and they would ultimately contain blueprints and reflective writings.

I wanted children to plan, discuss, and construct a structurally sound resemblance of a castle. In the process, I had hoped for lively discussion in which the children would argue about and support their decisions. I was convinced that it would be a difficult task, but because the curriculum was child driven, I knew the interest level was high. I also knew that this project was a major undertaking that would consume a great deal of time. What I did not know was that I was the one who would learn the real lesson—that these children would work together, building, ripping down, and rebuilding castles to meet their expectations.

The children grouped in threes and began by discussing and creating a "bird's-eye–view" blueprint of their castle. A few groups asked if they could draw the front view of the castle, stating that it would help them in their planning. Together, we brainstormed about building materials: toothpicks and marshmallows; newspaper and tape; straws and paper clips; and, craft sticks and glue.

Construction began and progressed for some groups. However, it was not an easy task. Some groups of children realized that they needed to tear down their walls and rebuild. These decisions seemed painful at times, but they were made by the children. I was simply a facilitator. At times, I was just an audience. The children did not need me—they were making their own decisions based on serious discussions. I truly believe that because the task was intrinsically motivating and child selected, the children were very comfortable with their decisions.

The construction process was videotaped, and I also took photographs so that the children could have a visual record of their progress. The children made records of their own, and, after each building session, they wrote reflections in their castle books.

As I reflect upon this castle experience, I realize many things. In this particular scientific learning experience I was needed as a facilitator, not as a deliverer of knowledge. Because this role is the one in which I am most comfortable, both personally and philosophically, I felt secure. I know that my students are capable, hard-working children. I know that they value their peers' opinions. The children worked together to produce a structure that met their expectations. Any constraints were self-imposed.

There is much to be gained from facilitating learning and empowering children to make decisions about their own learning. When children are empowered to make decisions, they feel free to take risks without fear of failure. This, in turn, builds self-esteem. Allowing children to explore, create, and discuss fosters ownership and independence. The classroom environment in which such empowerment, collaboration, and respect exist proves to be a place where all children can thrive and ". . . live happily ever after."

A Researcher's Perspective: Where Is the Science?

Ms. Scott is a marvelous teacher with seemingly boundless energy and enthusiasm. She is not complacent and I had a sense that she was a curious teacher who wanted to learn by studying her experience. The students were completely at ease with her and her respect for them was obvious. Students were arranged in groups to facilitate discussion. There was no obvious front to the class, and each corner of the classroom was dedicated to different projects. Ms. Scott's love of teaching was reflected throughout the classroom. Nothing about her classroom was sterile. The class was alive! Rabbits, interesting pictures, and lots of student work were attached to the walls and to lines stretched across the classroom.

When the students commenced the castles activity they were spread throughout the classroom in groups. Some worked at desks and others sat on the floor. They were free to move around the classroom and learn from others, but only a few did that. Even when I suggested to some that they might look at what others were doing, they seemed reluctant to move far afield. They appeared much more interested in doing their own work and figuring out their own problems rather than having someone else assist them. It did not seem to occur to the children to copy or learn from someone else.

The Grade 2 students in this class were enthusiastic participants in collaborative activities. The students were arranged in groups of three to five to discuss what their castles might look like, identify what they would include in their models, plan a blueprint, and use selected materials to build a structure. The students enjoyed what they were doing and were intellectually challenged by the problems they encountered. On occasion there were signs of frustration. Since the castles were planned to be large in volume the materials were, in many cases, not optimal for the task. For example, toothpicks and marshmallows have limited strength and are of smaller scale than the dimensions of the castle to be built. The groups using popsicle sticks, glue, toothpicks, and marshmallows had to solve significant engineering problems to get their structures to stand and support their own weight. Furthermore, when either of these groups managed to get their structure to stand, it did not particularly look like a castle. In contrast, the group that used newspapers had initial success because a sheet of newspaper had dimensions that were of the same order as the side of a castle. This group was relatively successful and after one class period made a self-supporting structure that looked like a castle.

As I circulated around the room I was impressed with the cooperation between students. They were interested in the task and were confident about their probable success in meeting their goals. However, as the lesson progressed and few of the groups were able to attain success there was more of a tendency for some students within each group to take a leadership role and for others to follow or sit back and watch. For example, a group building with soda straws had difficulties in securing vertical walls. They were confident that the structure would be rigid when they linked the four walls to one another. Thus, they built the walls and tried to coordinate their efforts to hold them vertical for enough time to connect them. There were two problems. First, the connectors they were using, paper clips, were not holding the straws together as the structure was moved. Thus, there was a tendency for the structure to come apart. Second, the walls were not rigid and collapsed as they were moved. One child knew that the walls could be made rigid by including a triangle within them, but the available materials made this a difficult idea to incorporate into the structure. Had they been available, straight pins could have been used to link straws to one another and thereby create triangles within the rectangular walls.

For the most part, the challenge of building the castle was psychomotor and the inability to build models that resembled their ideas about what the model should look like denied students opportunities to search for patterns associated with rigid, self-supporting structures. Throughout the class, the students were extended to the limit as they endeavored to coordinate their physical actions to build the castle, raise the walls, and hold them together while the walls were secured. Despite many frustrating moments, the students persevered with their plan and worked cooperatively and cordially.

Toward a Scientific Discourse

Science is viewed as a discourse that is a relatively recent activity of humankind, the goal being to make sense of a universe of phenomena in terms of knowledge that is viable. To be accepted as scientific, knowledge must meet several tests. First, it must be coherent with other viable knowledge claims. Second, it must be accepted by members of a scientific community through a process of peer review. Third, it must withstand conceptual and empirical challenges in repeated attempts to refute its viability. Skeptical acceptance of scientific knowledge claims is a part of what is considered as acting scientifically. Thus, even at the earliest of stages, an idea is carefully scrutinized in relation to what else is known and efforts are made to refute claims associated with the knowledge. In the event that knowledge withstands those tests, the activity of gaining acceptance becomes increasingly social as attempts are made to convince others of the acceptability of what is claimed. When viewed in this way, it is apparent that science can be regarded as a form of argument during which ideas are formulated and then argued out in a social forum in which efforts are made to persuade peers to accept a particular point of view. The process necessarily involves the production of evidence and discussions about the extent to which the evidence fits the knowledge claim.

Learning science can be considered as constructing a new way to make sense of experience. Discourse as it is used here refers to a "social activity of making meanings with language and other symbolic systems in some particular kind of situation or setting" (Lemke, 1995, p. 8). In a school science community one might expect to see students engage in ways such that, over a period of time, the discourse of a class would become more science-like. If the essence of science is to examine the coherence of evidence and knowledge claims then one might expect a form of discourse in science classrooms that involves students routinely in arguments about the efficacy of the warrants for knowledge claims. As has been advocated by Kuhn (1993), science can be regarded as a form of argument in which emerging conceptual understandings are related to evidence and the extent of the fit with canonical science. If materials are to be an integral part of science teaching and learning, and I believe that they should be at the elementary school level, then there needs to be more to learning than manipulation and following the steps of an activity. Based on a study of science learning in Grades 6 and 7, Roth concluded that:

"Hands-on" alone can neither be the focus of instruction, nor its replacement "hands-on, minds-on." Rather, educators need to realize the possibilities for learning through design: designing and constructing artifacts produces a good deal of problem solving in ill-structured settings, allows students to construct an experience-based design-related discourse, and facilitates interactions and sharing of knowledge in the classroom. (Roth 1996a, p. 163)

The goals of learners are essential, yet often ignored, components of a learning environment. To what extent are learners committed to engage as intended by a teacher and to pursue the goals a teacher has for them? Roth (1996a) noted that learning through design is integrally related to those aspects of a setting that students construct as important. He identified a tension between the notion of design as open-ended activity and goals being set by teachers. This was not the problem in this study. There was a high level of congruence between the goals of the teacher and the students, goals related to building a castle that was free-standing, self supporting, had the appearance of a castle, and contained features that would be found in castles, such as walls, rooms, and flags. What was problematic to me was a lack of any visible emphasis on goals related to canonical science. How could such activities qualify as science? The following excerpt from a conversation of a student with Ms. Scott reflects the typical concerns of students as they pursued a goal of building authentic castles.

Eric had an idea to put the Popsicles on top of each other, like stacking. We just put three popsicles facing up on the wall for the towers. For the rooms, we just tried to make little boxes. We made flags and a flagpole. We made a church also and Mary just made a cross for the church. We made towers for the keeping room to keep all the king's stuff. We made a treasury room and a place to keep the animals. [Alex]

The knowledge that was evident in the language of students included propositions about rigidity, an understanding of the properties of different materials, the creation of firm joints to connect materials, and the ability to manipulate and coordinate components to form a larger structural entity. Students used their personal language resources at all times during the study, and Ms. Scott imposed few restrictions. The following excerpt from an interaction of Thomas with the teacher is typical of many in which the natural language of students linked design to specific problems experienced while building castles.

> By putting two sticks and putting two marshmallows on each corner. Two sticks and two marshmallows. . . . The only reason it fell was because there was paper on it. It had all the marshmallows and the toothpicks on it and the paper fell. [Thomas]

The groups using marshmallows and toothpicks appeared to make less progress than any other. Even Erin, who seemed less capable than others in her group, could explain what she had done and apply her knowledge to suggest design modifications that would be appropriate for future similar projects. The following interaction between Ms. Scott and Erin occurred in a one-on-one conversation.

Ms. Scott: If you had to build another castle or another building out of marshmallows and toothpicks how would you do it next time?
Erin: I would build a huge tower and I would make a fence and hallways if I had a bigger piece of cardboard and marshmallows and toothpicks.
Ms. Scott: You had no problems? It never fell over? It never caved in?
Erin: A little bit. It caved in some of the time. The first time when we built it. But if you let the marshmallows dry on the toothpicks, you can actually have it standing up that day. If you do it on Monday and skip that day, you can have thick marshmallows and they won't do that. They can stand up.
Ms. Scott: What would you do the next time if you had to build a castle or another building out of the same materials?
Erin: I would take all the things that I did it with and all those things that I've already used to make that thing and I would do it over with that.

Ms. Scott's questions are focused on eliciting information that links what Erin and her group did and what they learned. Erin's responses are linked to the activities in which they engaged and there is nothing much in what she said that reflects knowledge of science. However, her responses may have been seeds for building canonical ideas. For example, after Erin's first response she could have been asked to elaborate on why she would have built a tower and how she would have accomplished the building of a tower. As it was, her responses were not used to build a conversation. It was as if responding to the prompt by the teacher was enough to justify moving to another topic of discussion without fully exploiting the previous student comments. The initial one-sentence response from Erin contained many seeds for an extended conversation that may or may not have been productive in terms of building additional knowledge. How would Erin construct hallways within the castle? Would the hallways be inside the tower? Within the conventions of this classroom community it seems reasonable that Erin and her peers might be expected to elaborate on points made in their initial responses to questions. Finally, the issue of the cardboard is interesting. Why did Erin need cardboard? Was it for a base for her structure to stand on or was it to be incorporated into the structure itself? What did Erin mean by bigger, and why was it preferable to have bigger cardboard? Did her response mean that she wanted bigger marshmallows and bigger toothpicks?

Although the students worked together throughout the activity sequence and appeared to cooperate and collaborate, they did not understand their roles in terms of assisting one another to learn. Neither the teacher nor the students had established conventions to identify problems to be resolved and then to articulate the answers and assemble the evidence for them into a form that could convince others. There appeared to be no joint responsibility within groups for students to learn and identify evidence for what they had learned. The following comment from Alex alludes to a problem he experienced throughout the castle building activity. Alex did not perceive his group members to be helpful to his participation in the activity or his learning. A problem appeared to be lack of clarity about who was in charge and whose goals would be pursued. There did not appear to be a convention for reaching consensus on what to do next. At times Alex showed frustration with his group members who were unable to manipulate the materials to achieve his goals or were unwilling to implement his ideas. His comment suggests that he would like to be in control in his group and there is a hint that lack of success in building a castle may have been frustrating.

> That it takes long time and it's really hard and you need to get who you're building with. You need to tell them right stuff and you need to follow plans. . . . You need to tell them all about building and how to build. [Alex]

A significant part of a scientific discourse community is providing a rationale for claims that are made. What does this look like in a Grade 2 classroom when it happens? The following excerpts from a discussion between Matt and Ms. Scott illustrate that the language is simple and from his everyday register and that Matt coordinates claims about his structure and evidence from the hands-on activity.

> I'll try and build a bigger one, longer, taller and a lot more solid so it won't fall down as easily as the one that we made this time. [Matt]
> Making a lot thicker, getting thicker. Make extra triangles and put two together, then connect them with each two. So it'd stay up more than this one did. [Matt]

Matt appeared to know more about engineering principles than other students in the class. The following excerpt from a conversation between Matt and Ms. Scott contains a description of his prior experiences of building castles and a comment on previously having done a similar activity. The latter remark was the only explicit reference to knowledge being infused into the classroom community from an outside source. Matt shared this knowledge with others in his group as they endeavored to increase the rigidity of the structure through the use of triangular braces.

> I had a problem by getting our straws together and getting them to hold up. So we had to try different things to make our castle and finally we got something. Then it messed up and we kept trying and finally we got something done. . . . We made triangles out of straws with paper clips and three straws together so it'd make the bottom of it so it'd hold up. Then we made the top and we added some things on to it. . . . A long time ago, I made a castle with somebody else, and we did it with triangles and the stuff we made our castle out of. [Matt]

Ritchie and Hampton highlighted the importance of the link between working with materials, empirical validation through trial and error, and the generation of ideas. They regard mistakes as a source of learning. They noted that "all of the children acknowledged that the activity of building and exploring with available resources was important in developing understanding and clarifying their ideas" (Ritchie & Hampton, 1996, p. 21). Similar findings apply to this study. Throughout the sequence of activities, students spontaneously generated ideas and tested them by building castles. Continuous conversations between students were used to coordinate knowledge-in-action with the evidence of whether or not structures were viable. In a sense knowledge was represented in the interactions of the students with their castles. The fact that structures that were not free-standing (i.e., were not rigid or collapsed) or did not meet the standards of the group were disassembled even after hours of painstaking work provides evidence that specific knowledge was not present. The structures provided a context in which knowledge could be put to the test, a necessary ingredient of authentic science.

If students are to learn science as a form of discourse, it seems imperative that they adapt their language as they practice science in settings in which others who know science assist them to learn by engaging activities in which co-participation occurs (Schön, 1985). As it is used here, co-participation implies the presence of a shared (as negotiated) language that can be used by all participants to communicate with one another to promote appropriate practices in the community. Students receive opportunities to practice and observe others practice such that at any time a person might be both a teacher and a learner with respect to others in the community. In a setting in which co-participation occurs, students have the autonomy to ask when they do not understand, and frequently the focus is on what students know and how they can represent what they know. Students should not feel that they cannot understand and that their only recourse is to accept what is said as an article of truth based on faith that other authoritative sources understand the warrants for its viability. Thus, co-participation can involve discussions in which co-participants test one another's understandings and are sensitive to their roles as both teachers and learners.

Going Deeper

In the 1960s, I would have confidently stated that the students' use of psychomotor skills was an important part of building basic process skills and establishing a conceptual framework to provide a foundation for the later development of conceptual knowledge. Although I saw students make and implement plans and test the extent to which resulting models met clearly held specifications, science-like conversations, such as those that related the presence of triangles to rigidity, seldom occurred. In building models students exhibited knowledge-in-action but demonstrated little evidence of canonical science in their talk or inscriptions such as writing and sketches. Even though students talked to one another without restraint and most of the talk was task related, interactions concerning the development of canonical science were essentially absent from the sequence of activities. The essence of science was missing from students' conversations since there were virtually no statements that connected assertions with evidence, justified claims in terms of experience, or evaluated their own knowledge or that of their peers.

The students were denied complete access to two major resources to support their learning, the teacher and peers. Ms. Scott perceived herself as a facilitator, and most of what I observed was consistent with that role. She regarded her main role as making it possible for students to accomplish their goals in their own ways and as a result of their personal efforts. Students were encouraged to work cooperatively and follow their plans to meet the goals of their group. Ms. Scott believed she was providing autonomy and hence empowering students by her efforts to shed power. Neither she nor her students adopted traditional roles in the classroom, especially with respect to the autonomy to make choices and participate in activities. Students were free to select their materials, make plans, build

their structures and continuously test and adapt them. There was sufficient time, too, for students to interact verbally and try out their ideas,
make mistakes, and endeavor to remedy them. Ms. Scott possessed knowledge of how to design a rigid and self-supporting castle using the materials that were available. She can be considered as a resource for learning,
a participant who was able to act in ways that others in the community
could not. However, she did not share her knowledge of structures with
the students, preferring that they interact with others and manipulate
materials in order to "discover" their own knowledge and test its viability.
Nor did she encourage students to learn from peers outside of the immediate group.

Ms. Scott did not prevent students from looking at what others had
accomplished, but neither did she make suggestions that they should examine others' structures, appropriate desirable practices and design features, and interact about progress, problems and the foci of present activities. The class was diverse with respect to what students could and
could not do and the situation was ripe for students to teach one another
and for knowledge to systematically diffuse throughout the classroom.
The degree of autonomy provided students in the classroom was such
that there was evidence of co-participation occurring between students
and also between Ms. Scott and students. The most compelling evidence
of co-participation in this classroom was that everyone spoke on many
occasions as they built their models, reviewed their plans, and produced
written artifacts for their castle books. Pronounced links to other areas of
the curriculum made it easy for students to see the relevance of what they
were doing and, because they chose the topic of study, the extent of the
commitment to participate was evident at all times. Interest rarely waned,
despite the evidence of disappointment and frustration. Even though there
was considerable diversity in the class in terms of the level of accomplishment, there was little evidence of students not participating or being reluctant to express a point of view.

Ms. Scott's acceptance of a role as facilitator was framed in terms of
her belief that learning is meaningful when students construct their own
understandings. It made sense for her to maintain an environment in
which students encountered problems they could solve by manipulating
materials and collaborating with peers. Ms. Scott believed that by not
telling the right answers or providing hints she placed students in situations that promoted meaningful learning. From my perspective the learning environments for students were relatively impoverished because they
were denied access to potentially valuable learning resources. Why would

the quality of learning be better when students interact with materials and a small group of peers rather than when they interact with peers or the teacher who can show or tell them what they need to know? I can accept that what is learned in the two situations might be different, but I cannot accept that the knowledge is in any way superior in either of the scenarios. Within any community, learning can be enhanced by facilitating interactions between learners and those who already know. Even though the students in Ms. Scott's class accomplished a great deal, it is my contention that they could have accomplished even more had they fully utilized the learning resources within the class. This analysis is consistent with Roth's conclusion that

> teachers can no longer expect students to discover canonical forms of knowledge (patterns, scientific laws, rules, applications of tools). One way of introducing students to specific, culturally devised forms of knowledge is through participation in culturally organized activities and environments in which this knowledge plays a role; that is, activities where students experience these canonical forms of knowledge used by someone who already has a certain degree of competence. (Roth, 1996a, p. 163)

None of the activities in this project were ideal for developing canonical knowledge of forces, equilibrium, and stability. All groups used shape and aesthetic appeal as guiding criteria rather than engineering or economic principles pertaining to their structures. The materials used by several of the groups were suitable for constructing very different representations of a castle. Within each group students began to build, making a structure that was constrained by their initial choice of materials but not making explicit what their structure represented or how their structure differed from those constructed by other groups. For example, the group using glue and popsicle sticks might have succeeded in building a castle if they had persevered and had sufficient materials. Their design regarded the popsicles as bricks or stones that were cemented together, the result being potentially distinctive from the approach adopted by the groups building with toothpicks or drinking straws. In each of these cases the attempts to build structures commenced with a frame for the walls and roof. The most successful group, which used newspaper and tape, built a shell of a castle that was self-supporting but that could not have supported a load. Use of large sheets to build an entire wall without subcomponents was a strategy that made their task easy and could have been linked to modern approaches to large buildings that attach intact walls to metal and concrete frames. Opportunities for discussing strength and rigidity were present in the newspaper castles because the students had rolled newspaper for added strength on the corners and their structure was freestanding and authentic in appearance. However, the development of canonical science was not facilitated by discussions within the group that extended beyond aesthetic appeal and the presence of features such as different types of rooms, a drawbridge, and a moat. The students' goals (i.e., to build a castle) were not related to learning canonical science and whatever they learned that might be classified as science was tacit and connected to the model itself.

I wondered if a more structured task would have been conducive to the development of a science-like discourse. For example, perhaps a more productive initial task might have been to build the tallest free-standing structure possible with 23 soda straws and 11 pins. This task could have been completed in less than an hour, and students would have had the advantages of seeing towers shoot up quickly and learning by observing others and comparing designs, building strategies and models. In this example of a possible activity, explicit attention could have been drawn to such issues as where people can sit in such a structure and comparisons easily could have been made to such towers as the Eiffel Tower, which may have shared some design familiarities with some of the students' structures.

Conclusions

This paper shows the presence of diverse ways of perceiving the learning environments of students. Ms. Scott perceived the learning environments as close to optimal and she could defend the viability of her perceptions. I perceived that some elements of the learning environments were conducive to learning and others would not support the learning of science. Two criteria characterize the differences between Ms. Scott and myself, and between my competing characterizations of the learning environments. First, there is an issue of grain size. At a macro level, the learning environments involved students in discussion and manipulation as they solved problems and pursued their own goals. At that level of analysis, the learning environments of students approached what might be regarded as optimal. At a micro level that focuses on the discourse of the community, there is evidence to support an assertion that some learning occurred and that the community evolved to a state that was more science-like than previously was the case. However, an analysis of the discourse also brings into the foreground the biggest limitation to the learning of science in this class, the knowledge limitations of the teacher and her beliefs that students could discover what they needed to know through the pursuit of their goals in a materials rich environment. The study highlights the significance of the teacher in mediating learning environments in a classroom. Students are not equally adept at learning given science content using the resources provided to support their learning. The notion that one type of learning environment can or should suit all learners is one that has little utility, and it is long past time for researchers to acknowledge this in their studies of learning environments.

To what extent will the experiences of building the castles provide a foundation on which canonical knowledge can be built at a later time? According to neural network processing theory, it is feasible that the knowledge constructed by participating in a community of castle builders will extend considerably beyond what can be spoken or written about. For example, the feel of a rigid structure, the balance of a three-dimensional structure that is in equilibrium, or the look of a structure that is robust are all parts of the habitus of expert castle-builders. Good castles look and feel right. In addition, the association of successful castle-building with the doing of science can be associated with the construction of a vector of neural loadings that project a set of feelings that doing science is enjoyable, manageable, challenging, and a way of life that is an option for the doer. For this set of feelings to remain viable it would be necessary to reinforce it with subsequent experiences with doing science throughout K–12 schooling. It is unlikely that just one experience of this type would lead to a sustaining set of feelings that would shape the construction of self in relation to the doing of science.

Discourse theory suggests that co-participation is most likely in a region that is close to the border of the intersection of the set pertaining to the discourse of the teacher and the set pertaining to the developing discourses of students. Referred to as border pedagogy, the theoretical frame implies that borders are the sites for effective learning when co-participation involves the use of a shared-as-negotiated language that evolves toward a canonical form of discourse. When viewed from this perspective, the sequence of lessons on castles seems to fall short. For the most part, the discourse of the students and the teacher did not resemble a canonical discourse of engineering science.

The materials environment for each of the small groups was constrained, perhaps to too great of an extent. Furthermore, because there was no whole-class sharing of what was learned there were few opportunities for students to learn from one another, not only about science but also about the problems they faced, how they tackled them, what questions they would like answered, and how they might adapt their investigations to get answers to the questions that puzzled them. The goals of the activities were mainly directed toward cooperative planning and building and using given or selected materials to build model castles. Failure to pose framing questions or to practice inquiry resulted in a sequence of activities that appeared to follow a script in that plans were developed and models were built and re-built until students built a pleasing model. Within each group there were opportunities for self and informal peer evaluation; however, there were no systematic inter-group peer evaluations or a need to provide evidence to convince peers about the efficacy of particular design features. There did not appear to be agreed-upon criteria for deciding whether or not models were suitable.

The children were young, and it is understandable that the ways in which they could represent their knowledge were limited. However, apart from the models they built, which were destroyed if they were not pleasing, there were no requirements to record what was learned or to present evidence for learning. The failure of students to maintain a journal and to retain early models meant that all of the knowledge was in the doing and was not available as a resource to support the learning of others in the class. Furthermore, since so much of what students learn from an activity sequence such as this is represented in an interaction between the models and a particular student, it is useful to have an established convention of discussing what is known in terms of physical evidence.

Although the teacher had a goal of giving students autonomy she did not emphasize a recursive relationship between autonomy and responsibility. Accordingly, the students did not share responsibility for reporting or recording what they knew, there was no evidence of an awareness that groups had a responsibility to make satisfactory progress, and there was no explicit attention on students helping one another to learn. The groups functioned as cooperative units that worked together to meet goals that did not include inquiry as a priority or the generation of canonical knowledge of science. Although each of these were goals that Ms. Scott valued, there was little evidence in the interactions between students that they were explicitly striving to attain inquiry-related goals or to systematically build a canon of knowledge for which they could provide evidence.

In this study, the goals of the teacher and students were to build authentic castles. The class was set up to allow students to collaborate in the building of rigid self-supporting structures that looked like castles and contained features of castles. The participation of students in the sequence of activities was consistent with the practice of science in many regards, even though there was little evidence of science in its canonical form. Students were able to fully employ their language resources to plan and build, to access materials, and to put their knowledge-in-action to the test. In addition, they had the freedom to draw, write, talk, manipulate, observe others, and, if they wished, to destroy what they had produced. Throughout the unit on castles, doing science was an emotional and human experience for the children. Students were stimulated, excited, happy, frustrated, angry, and disappointed. But they persevered and achieved success in the sense that all built many models of castles and all could discuss the strengths and weaknesses of their designs. The knowledge derived from their activities was accessible to students in many ways, including being able to talk and write about what they had learned.

Co-participation was evident in terms of language usage in continuous discussions, and the access all students had to materials and the manipulation of those materials to meet their goals. What is evident from my intensive analysis of co-participation is just how much more was possible in this class. Even though the accomplishments were commendable it also is apparent that a more proactive role by the teacher and a conscious effort by students to teach one another and to learn from the efforts of others would have led to a rich harvest of learning. As it was, the groups in the class were islands of activity separated from one another by a sea of cognitive isolation. If the teacher and students had structured activities such that those with knowledge could teach those without, it is highly likely that goals more closely associated with canonical science could have been accomplished within the community.

The final remark about goals and accomplishments raises an issue of the place of canonical science in a Grade 2 curriculum. There is no doubt that a teacher with the requisite knowledge of science could have mediated in a process of students developing many concepts associated with structures and forces. However, the teacher in this study did not have the background knowledge in science to have accomplished much more in terms of teaching canonical science. What she did demonstrate was an impressive ability to get the best out of students in terms of their making sense of their structures using their own language, of coordinating oral with written texts (pictures and notes), and of promoting an attitude that knowledge should be put to the test. The correlation of knowledge claims with evidence was present in this classroom, but in an unexpected way. The knowledge in question was represented as an interaction of individuals with artifacts, and the viability tests consisted of an integration of observation, manipulation, discussion, and emotion. What I observed was authentic science practiced by young and inquisitive minds. Unlike so many of the abstract and decontextualized canonical propositions that characterize science in other places, the science of this classroom was a human endeavor, subjective in form, essentially non-propositional, and inextricably linked to the practices of a community and a characteristic discourse. That discourse consisted of the natural language resources of students, manipulative skills, and a range of beliefs, values, and commitments that was reflected in a resolve to succeed. The students would not compromise as they persevered to solve problems that at times appeared to be insurmountable. Despite the frustration of ever-present challenges, as Ms. Scott concluded in her narrative, these students did appear to . . . live happily ever after.

Without a comparison case it might be concluded that Ms. Scott's science class is as good as it gets or as good as we can expect in the circumstances. However, the following case of Ms. Mack illustrates how a teacher is able to access professional development activities to improve her own knowledge of science and employ resources within the community to enhance the learning of science for young, highly motivated children. If the following case is used recursively with the examples provided in this chapter, it is apparent that learning of a different type was possible in Ms. Scott's class. However, for that learning to occur it would have been necessary for a different set of teacher and student roles to have been enacted.

Metalogue

Issue 1: What Should School Science Be?

K: I have oscillated in my feelings about this study. Ms. Scott was recommended to me as an exemplary elementary science teacher. When I first entered her classroom I gasped in amazement. It was alive with exciting displays, animals, and events. What a learning environment! This is the kind of classroom I would want my kids to be in, and Ms. Scott was exactly the teacher I would want for my children. But my first take on what happened was that the students participated in a series of craft lessons. There is nothing wrong with craft lessons, I hasten to add.

M: I agree, craft lessons are OK if their purpose is to develop craft-related practices. But, and this is the central issue of the book, engaging in some engineering activity does not in itself constitute science, and much of the discourse may not bring out what is important in a canonical science context.

K: So what I was expecting was a visible display of science as argument. Ms. Scott understood that as a goal, and I thought that the coordinated use of data to support knowledge claims about structures and forces would characterize what would happen. When it did not, I had to search for the science in the activities. So there was a discrepancy between my initial impressions in the classroom and writing about what was missing from the classroom. It was a story of missed opportunities. But as I presented my stories about what I had learned from this study, I began to reflect more on what students were doing and began to argue for this as an authentic way for young children to engage in science. My present feelings about the activities are that what happened reflected the community. This was a community in which the autonomy of students was valued above most everything else, and manipulations with materials were regarded as the essence of science. The verbal interaction that occurred was to be initiated by students and to involve the design and building of the castles. From the teacher's perspective, the science was in the manipulation mainly and in the verbal interaction to a lesser extent. Students should be able to describe what they had done, but there was less of a focus on what they had learned and the evidence for what they had learned.

S: This was a Grade 2 class, right? In Australia, the first eight years of a child's life are considered the domain of early childhood education (ECE). The emphasis in these years, as far as I understand ECE, is the pedagogy of play. Accordingly, I was and remain impressed by the classroom activities in Ms. Scott's class. Through playful activities, such as the ones described here, children can manipulate material resources and use their developing language games to describe these experiences to others. Traditional discipline boundaries are blurred and teachers infrequently label academic subjects in ECE settings. There are many opportunities for ECE teachers to guide conversations toward canonical language games within the context of these activities. We saw the beginning of this process in Ms. Scott's class. If our sole focus was the development of scientific language games, then I can appreciate why some scientists might be disappointed with the missed opportunities for scientific learning here. However, I believe that if all Grade 2 children had the same opportunities to engage in these craft-like activities, substantial progress toward scientific literacy could be made. So in this case we have competing referents. Ms. Scott appeared to be primarily interested in whole-child development across a wide range of domains through activities guided by the pedagogy of play. On the other hand, she also was interested in the children's scientific learning. Given the suggestions made in the chapter, I think that Ms. Scott has just about got the right balance. It would be interesting to see some follow-up lessons in Ms. Scott's class. Perhaps she might have drawn on the children's experiences with these design activities to move the conversation toward cultural reproduction. I get the feeling that this lesson could be the start of grander things to come.

M: In a sense, this brings us back to an issue raised earlier: When one considers the world as revealing its secrets to anyone who cares to look, then it makes sense to have children just do the building activities. From that perspective, one would expect children, in some yet-to-be-known way, absorb the knowledge already embedded in the world. But of course, from my perspective, this makes little sense, for viable knowledge has to have aspects both of the world and the individual. It lies in the interaction between the individual agent and the world as s/he perceives it.

K: Also, there was less of a focus on what issues were to be resolved in a cognitive sense. The issues to be resolved were mainly framed around the building of a structure in terms of arranging and connecting materials. So I would conclude that, although there were some examples of science-like discourse, the essence of the community was not science-like and the interactions between the participants in the community were not directed toward the emergence of a scientific discourse. However, the learning environment was a good one and students showed great benefit from the activities. I have the feeling that Gitte would have enabled more of a scientific discourse to emerge from these activities.

S: I agree, but Gitte's agenda was probably more specific. Marilyn Fleer's[2] views would support Gitte's position nevertheless. Marilyn's research in ECE settings has shown that young children can develop canonical language games when the teacher structures activities around the interactive approach for teaching science. I think her thesis was that if children developed ideas that were consistent with canonical science at an early *age*, they would be less likely to develop resilient "misconceptions" before undertaking more formal studies in science.

Her short-term results were impressive, but I would find the thesis more convincing if supporting longitudinal data were available.

M: I really get a strong sense from Ken's description that Ms. Scott's classroom is exemplary in many ways and an exciting place of learning. But I was also thinking of Gitte and the ways she could frame questions that started with children's interests. Out of children's accounts of what they had done, and where they were in their design project, Gitte always allowed issues to emerge that did in fact address canonical scientific knowledge. In a sense, the children had what we might call an authentic experience of what science might be.

K: I think that authenticity needs a reference point. It seems to me that there are at least two points of reference that pertain to the activities in this chapter. First, it is possible to look at the discursive characteristics of canonical science and compare them to the activities that occurred in this class. That leads directly to my earlier comment that what happened was far short of science even though there are vestiges of science-like discourse and some examples of science permeating a set of interactions. A second perspective looks at the discourse of the students and the trajectory of change during an activity. Is the discourse headed in a direction that is increasingly science-like? That perspective led me to describe much of what happened in the classroom as being authentic science within a context of children's science. For example, the students identified many problems and planned to overcome them. When they built their castles they put them to the test. I argued that this was science-like in that it involved empirical tests.

M: It may be worthwhile for us to think about the notion of "science-like." On the one hand, science-like could mean that children talk like or parrot scientists. On the other hand, it could mean that children have had opportunities to develop (or are familiar with) discursive resources that they can draw on in appropriate conversations. This might then lead to situations where in some contexts, such as an independently written essay, the child may not seem to use a particular discursive resource (e.g., "force," "strength," "stability" in Ms. Scott's classroom). But the same child may actually participate competently in science talk in another situation, where others ask questions and talk about scientific issues.

S: I get very positive feelings about this chapter. I think that there is great potential for Ms. Scott to move the classroom discourse in a direction that is more science-like during and after subsequent design activities. General elementary teachers should now be able to see what needs to be done to turn some exciting design activities into opportunities for more science-like discourse.

K: I have concluded that there is much more that can be done with students of this age to build a discourse that is scientific. In the next chapter Ms. Mack shows how to structure the learning environments of her students and use a wide variety of resources to facilitate the development of scientific discourse.

Issue 2: How Can Teaching Mediate in the Process of Building Canonical Science?

K: Ms. Scott regarded herself as a facilitator of learning. That in itself does not say as much as we might think because what Ms. Scott had in mind when she said facilitator and what I have in mind are clearly very different constructs. For Ms. Scott, the roles associated with being a facilitator appear to be associated with staying on the sidelines and allowing students to follow their own interests and initiating activities within their groups. Facilitating did not involve a proactive stance with respect to the learning of particular scientific ideas or following a prescribed path. Unlike Mr. Hammett in the previous chapters, Ms. Scott did not model being a scientist and did not co-participate in ways that were overtly scientific.

M: The metaphor of the "facilitator" is interesting, for I often view myself in terms of a facilitator who assists his graduate students to become members in a community. But I think the difference between myself and Ms. Scott is that she sees herself as someone sitting on the sidelines, whereas I consider myself as part of the game. So I facilitate all the while my students and I engage in a joint activity. In an earlier metalogue, I also described how my physics students and I wrestled jointly with problems to which we did not have the answer. Again, I not only felt like a facilitator of the process of inquiry from the sidelines, but I also felt like a facilitator in the center of the action.

S: Widespread use of descriptors such as "facilitate" has led to unwarranted criticism by those who oppose the apparent hegemony of constructivism in the science education literature. The critics take the view that (constructivist) teachers provide material resources with which children can engage in practices that their teachers then view from the sidelines. But, as we can see, (constructivist) researchers and teacher educators can hold different views about the activity level of teachers within classroom conversations. Teachers do have an important and direct role to play in the development of children's scientific language games. Michael orchestrated an effective balance between cultural reproduction and cultural production with Grade 6–7 students, but Ms. Scott was dealing with a younger cohort of children and she was interested in whole-child development across a range of domains. Under these circumstances, her practices are quite defensible. Nevertheless, Ms. Scott's facilitator metaphor does not embrace fully the images and practices we associate with its use. Maybe we should use it less frequently or at least clarify our meaning whenever it is used.

K: What might Ms. Scott have done differently in an effort to facilitate the learning of science? Much of what might be done is dealt with in the next chapter. However, context is so important in this discussion. The first concern of Ms. Scott was that the subject matter being studied fit with what the students were doing. They had been studying Germany and Ms. Scott had many books on castles, some of them showing castles in Germany. This was a good way to connect science to social science and literature. Hence the selection of the subject matter for the activities was constrained by the value that learning experiences should be connected across a curriculum and that interdisciplinary approaches are desirable. A second concern related to the manner in which the topic on castles was introduced. Because she wanted to connect to the social sciences, she had them design a castle in much the same way that Mr. Hammett had his students design their inventions in the previous chapters. The students had as resources books that portrayed castles as they might have been in countries throughout Europe. They were not looking at castles constructed from materials like those they would use in their constructions (e.g., drinking straws, toothpicks, etc). Instead they saw pictures of stone walls, moats, and drawbridges. It is not surprising then that the students had as an initial and ongoing concern that whatever they built should look like a castle.

S: I think this highlights one of the difficulties of an integrated curriculum. Sometimes there is a tendency for busy teachers to force unnatural links between subject domains. Maybe a different story would have provided a better integrative device by which the use of straws and other material resources available would have been more authentic. How does "The Three Little Pigs" sound?

M: I also think that this is an interesting way of bringing in canonical design and engineering. The pictures provide some strong images of what a castle looks like. From the activity of building something that looks like a castle can then emerge many of the same problems that are inherent in building castles of a much larger scale. Therefore, concerns that are central to engineering, structure, material strength, stability, and so on also become central in the children's activities.

K: This really leads me to my next point, that the materials were not all that suitable for building models of castles if the goal was to build something that looked like a castle. In that regard the students who used rolled newspaper had a decided advantage. Also it is not surprising that most students did not have it as a goal to learn about forces, stability and ideas about engineering science. Finally, Ms. Scott herself was a resource for the entire class that was underutilized in terms of providing cues for the development of a science-like discourse. Her decision to be on the sidelines led directly to students being restricted in the range of resources they could draw on to show what they knew and could do. They were restricted to their own verbal descriptions of what they were doing, models that in most cases could not be built to look authentic, and verbal cues from the teacher that were encouraging, supportive, and polite but rarely were directed toward accessing and appropriating a science-like discourse.

S: Teachers need to constrain student choices of material resources in design activities. Inappropriate selections can lead to unwanted frustration and limited success. It might have been more helpful for the teacher to specify newspaper as the material in the design brief. Also, it is useful for students to be assigned more demanding briefs gradually. For example, Mr. Hammett's students designed a 10-second marble machine before attempting the more demanding brief of a machine for a purpose.

M: Our conversation really puts into relief something that has been more or less latent throughout the cases: What is the degree to which science education in schools should take the form of cultural production versus cultural reproduction? I do not think that this is a question that can be answered on logical grounds. It requires fundamental choices about the kind of values we bring to the educational enterprise.

Notes

1　The voice in this chapter is that of Ken Tobin.

2　See Fleer, 1994.

Chapter 8

Learning to Teach Science as Inquiry

Developmental approaches to the teaching and learning of science, many based on stage models for the development of reasoning, may have contributed to teachers underestimating students' abilities to build canonical science knowledge. Throughout the 1960s and beyond there was a tendency to regard elementary-aged students as concrete operational thinkers or pre-operational in their logical thinking and to structure science programs around activities involving the manipulation of materials. An unintended consequence of materials-centered approaches to the teaching and learning of elementary science is that teachers adopted a hands-on metaphor for the science curriculum but were uncertain of how to move beyond manipulation of materials to the development of science concepts. Abstract ideas were labeled as formal operational, were designated as most appropriate for high school learners, and often were not seen as appropriate goals for elementary learners. In addition, the belief that a teacher's most appropriate role was to remain in the background became fashionable; many teachers felt serve their students as facilitators who were available when called upon to answer questions or to provide materials. Only rarely did such teachers model science in action, help in building ideas, or judge whether or not solutions to problems were viable. Often the social aspects of learning were not fully exploited by curriculum planners, teachers, or teacher educators. To a certain extent, the teaching of Ms. Scott fits closely with the metaphors of teacher as facilitator and students as explorers.

The main issue raised by the activity sequence on castles concerns whether Ms. Scott's students were capable of learning more. As was seen in the previous chapter, Ms. Scott's failure to assume a proactive role with respect to the learning of science resulted in activities that failed to reach their potential in terms of her students' learning of science, even though the activities were well managed and the students enjoyed themselves and were persistent in their manipulations of materials. However, because the teacher's actions did not require the students to exhibit inquiry and pursue answers to questions, most of them built castles with the purpose of attaining goals that were not scientific in nature. This case study of Ms. Mack, an elementary teacher, explores the issue of scientific inquiry within a classroom community that established some of the conventions missing from Ms. Scott's class. However, before describing Ms. Mack's present-day practices, selected aspects of her biography as an elementary science teacher are provided. As is evident in the biography, Ms. Mack was not always able or willing to teach in ways that promoted the learning of science. The case study shows how a teacher who is typical of many elementary teachers in her attitudes toward science and her practice of avoiding the teaching of science was able to change her attitudes and practices over a relatively long period of time. The manner in which Ms. Mack linked her knowledge of teaching reading and writing to the teaching of science and how she became an apprentice with respect to practicing scientists and science teachers is highlighted in the study. Finally, the study explores how Ms. Mack was able to provide her students with access to a larger repertoire of resources to support their learning by including parents as co-teachers, co-researchers, and co-learners. In so doing the community became a resource to support learning.

Biography

The following biography develops several themes that are salient salience to the development of teaching roles that are appropriate for elementary science. Ms. Mack is a teacher who is curious about her experiences, and from early in her career she showed a willingness to study her practices and learn from them. Poor experiences as an elementary and high school learner of science were reflected in her initial attitudes toward the teaching of elementary science. However, her natural curiosity catalyzed some changes in her approaches to the teaching and learning of reading and writing. As she developed new roles for teaching these subject areas she used ethnography to study what was happening in her classroom, developed coteaching strategies with her educational assistant and with parents, became committed to a philosophy that less content coverage could result in more learning, employed problem-solving strategies applicable for whole-class activities, and developed close links between in-school and out-of-school learning. In addition, she expressed a strong commitment to providing students with autonomy and showed respect for their ideas and high value for their participation at school and at home. Her emerging roles in teaching reading and writing provided a solid foundation for the teaching and learning of science.

Avoidance of Science Teaching

> For twenty-one years in urban and suburban settings, I denied my elementary students the joy of doing science because I never experienced it and feared the unknown. (McGonigal, 1998, p. 1)

Like many teachers at the elementary school level, Ms. Mack was afraid of science and had a history of avoidance that dated back to her own experience as a student. Even though her transcripts showed success in science at high school and college Ms. Mack was able to obtain good grades without actually engaging in serious efforts to learn science. She graduated as a teacher without a strong background in science and a perception from her science methods course that

> the discovery approach was only toying with me, the student. I did not like being asked to discover something which my instructor already knew and participating in an investigation with a pre-determined outcome. (McGonigal, 1998, p. 3)

Ms. Mack summed up her own attitude toward science at the beginning of her teaching career:

> For me the world of science was not a place to explore, question, investigate, and learn, but rather a place where to survive, I copied, memorized, fabricated, and avoided. (McGonigal, 1998, p. 4)

The initial approach adopted by Ms. Mack to the teaching of science was largely to avoid it and, once or twice a month, to get her students to copy facts into their notebooks. Some observations of the learning of her own children were catalysts for change. When her twin daughters were five years old she noticed they were reading at a level that surpassed that of most students in her Grade 2 class. Ms. Mack's efforts to find out what the kindergarten teacher was doing to promote the reading proficiency of her own children created a context for her to pursue graduate studies in reading and literacy. She enrolled in a course with the kindergarten teacher, and together they learned how to create "literate environments" that enabled students to participate in authentic language activities. Her active participation in studies associated with whole language enabled her to understand how to become a problem solver with respect to her own teaching and to involve her students in problem-solving activities:

> I was no longer a teacher who merely covered curriculum; I became a facilitator of learning who watched kids, listened to kids, and learned from kids. (McGonigal, 1998, p. 8)

Ms. Mack began to apply what she was learning about her own learning to her classroom. Notably, she began to use a problem-solving circle in which students, as a whole class, participated in discussions designed to solve problems that pertained to the whole class or individuals in the class. This strategy was to be used at a later time to facilitate Ms. Mack becoming a science teacher.

Experiences as a parent enabled Ms. Mack to see the benefits of having her children engage in activities out of school that were designed to extend their school learning. At the same time her efforts as a teacher-researcher provided her with important insights into the ways in which her students participated in class activities. She noted that

> in this journey the tools of the educational qualitative researcher (ethnographer) became the tools of an effective teacher. I listened to tapes of classroom engagements and transcribed them. I collected and viewed students' writing samples with the hope of uncovering patterns. I began to interview my students, trying to understand the meaning they were making from a given interaction with a text, with a peer, with a social context called "school." (McGonigal, 1998, p. 10)

As a reflective practitioner Ms. Mack was now convinced of the value of involving parents, children, and herself in designing curricula and she did all that she could to make the curriculum relevant to students and allow them to participate in authentic activities in which they were interested. However, science still was not a major part of the curriculum. She noted that "Because I taught transitional first grade, water, sand and block play sufficed for science" (McGonigal, 1998, p. 12).

Accountability for Teaching Science

When Ms. Mack began to teach Grade 4 she realized that science could no longer be avoided. At that time she arranged for her teaching assistant to teach science and used the hallways as the site for science activities. She observed that the topics her fourth graders were to study (e.g., circuits, pendulums, sight and sound, etc.) were beyond her understandings and increased her anxiety about science and her determination to avoid teaching it. However, Ms. Mack's avoidance of teaching science was noted by her principal, who took action to address the problem by requiring an evaluation of her science teaching. Ms. Mack was asked to schedule an appointment with the district science supervisor who would rate her science teaching on a scale that extended from exemplary through to unacceptable. The action of the principal and the scheduling of the evaluation some six weeks hence enabled Ms. Mack to approach her dilemma as a problem-solver. She wanted to obtain an exemplary rating and decided to involve her students in offering advice about how to solve the problem. Ms. Mack set up a whole-group problem-solving circle to address her problem. She explained that

> I told my class that in six weeks I was to be observed teaching fourth grade science by the science department head from the high school. I confessed to my students I had no idea how to do it. My biggest concern, which I shared with the class, was that I did not know how to manage twenty students simultaneously doing a hands-on science activity. (McGonigal, 1998, pp. 14–15)

Negotiating Roles for the Teaching and Learning of Science

Ms. Mack was able to develop suitable teacher and student roles in the time she had prior to the evaluation because of the high levels of cooperation she enjoyed with her class, a history of collaborative problem-solving in whole-class problem circles, and the availability of an educational assistant. The students recommended that the educational assistant help Ms. Mack to set up a suitable curriculum and made suggestions about a methodology that took into account many of the logistics of setting up a science program. Having a history of participating in a curriculum in which the students enjoyed significant autonomy with respect to suggesting curricular ideas and collaborating in groups was an advantage because the class had extensive experience in conducting open discussions to solve problems. Ms. Mack adopted the following managerial aspects of the curriculum when she assumed responsibility for the teaching of science:

- an optimal group size of two to increase participation of all students in the class
- a timeout place (the reading corner) where students could go when they needed time for their own thoughts or to work individually because of the distractions of working in groups
- use of an overhead projector for students to share ongoing results and ideas with the entire class
- a system of shared responsibility in which one student from a group reported results and the other student provided an elaboration of the initial report
- opportunities for students to repeat activities
- opportunities for students to engage in extension activities after an activity was completed

- procedures for disseminating materials using cafeteria trays
- a central place for sharing materials brought in from home for use in extension activities
- freedom for students to move around the classroom to observe what others were doing, discuss with other students, and obtain materials
- an awareness on the part of students that freedom and responsibility were interconnected

The need to get evaluated and Ms. Mack's desire to receive an exemplary rating set a context in which she was ready to assume the responsibility to teach science seriously. The subsequent success she enjoyed was a catalyst for her further efforts to learn to be a better teacher of elementary science.

The environment set up in Ms. Mack's class had similarities and differences from that described for Ms. Scott's class in the previous chapter. The similarities include the use of group activities, materials, and the ideas of students. Some of the differences include explicit provision for intergroup communication of results, overt responsibility of all students for their learning, and opportunities for students to enrich the materials environment and extend their investigations of problems to be solved. Although neither Ms. Scott nor Ms. Mack had strong backgrounds in science, the opportunities to build canonical ideas about science were enhanced in Ms. Mack's class by the provision for social interaction among peers in small groups and at the whole-class level, regular sharing of what was being learned, active involvement of an educational aid, and encouragement for students to repeat activities and participate in extension activities. However, Ms. Mack was aware of her limitations and resolved to improve her preparedness to teach elementary science.

The approach to science teaching that evolved at this time also gradually acknowledged the benefits of getting parents involved in the science curriculum. Initially the parents and students created a theme that became a foundation for the curriculum and later provided extension materials for the program. However, this tentative beginning was to flourish in later years as Ms. Mack continued to grow in her capacity to teach elementary science.

Building Knowledge of Science and Science Teaching

Ms. Mack had begun to teach science and with the assistance of her educational assistant and highly motivated students had adapted her strategies from the teaching of reading and writing to institute a program that appeared solid. However, she was aware that she could do better and that her lack of a strong background in science was detrimental to the learning of her students. This section describes some of the efforts Ms. Mack made to address what she considered to be a deficiency in her professional knowledge.

Building Expertise

In the following summer Ms. Mack attended a two-week summer institute on the teaching of science. Initially she did not volunteer for the program, but when no other teachers stepped forward to participate Ms. Mack acceded to the wishes of a parent that she participate in the program. The institute was standard in that participants met daily for seven hours and spent most of the time in hands-on activities from the fourth-grade curriculum. For the first time Ms. Mack was an active participant in science as she built models, observed, measured and participated in authentic inquiries.

During the workshop Ms. Mack learned how to maintain a "Wonder and Discover" book, a place for students to write their questions to be investigated at some later time. She also used a "Working Dictionary," where definitions arising from the activities were placed and revised as learning occurred and was refined. Of significance was Ms. Mack's own connection of what she experienced in the two-week workshop with what she knew from her previous studies of how to teach and learn reading and writing. Making these connections enabled her to adapt her strategies for teaching reading and writing to an investigative approach to the teaching of science.

Consistent with her valuing of additional adult support, Ms. Mack requested that her educational assistant also participate in the two-week course. Her participation enabled the two of them to plan and co-teach a science curriculum that was organized around 10 clusters of ideas, was taught every day, involved students in problem solving, and incorporated a "Wonder and Discover" book in which students wrote their questions and described what they had accomplished.

Increasing Competence to Teach Science

Over the following two summers Ms. Mack returned for additional professional development programs aimed at first-, second-, third-, and fifth-grade science. Her motivation to be a resourceful teacher enabled her to become quite expert in the teaching of science across the elementary grades. Ms. Mack identified the following underlying principles as essential to the effective teaching and learning of science:

- The curriculum needs to be constantly refined and responsive to the interests and knowledge of her children.
- No company-produced kits are to be used in the science program. Instead use recyclable materials gathered by teachers and students and stored in an "Inventor's Box."
- Students are to be involved in ongoing self-assessment of their science learning. Use portfolios and science notebooks in a comprehensive approach to assessment.
- The science program consists of activities from across the disciplines of science and includes physical, earth, and space science; technology, health; and math as well as studies of plants and animals.
- The program emphasizes inquiry and scientific habits of mind as students explore open-ended problems and tasks.
- Science is accessible to all students.

After three years of teaching science Ms. Mack felt much more comfortable with the approach of being a co-investigator, and she converted her classroom into a science-centered learning environment. To the extent possible she also endeavored to link her other subjects to science. For example, in reading and writing she explored different ways of viewing the world as a naturalist, a paleontologist, a meteorologist, an astronomer, and an environmentalist. She used biographies, autobiographies, non-fiction picture books, poems, and fiction to support each of the topics. In addition, current media, such as television, radio, and newspapers, were used to augment the studies. Similarly, social studies was integrated with the science curriculum by studying the flora and fauna of the local state, geological formations, meteorology, and environmental issues. However, Ms. Mack wanted to improve her knowledge of science. She commented that

> I was truly learning to love teaching science. I soon recognized how weak my science content knowledge was and wanted to begin to take physics courses at the local community college. However, calculus was required for the courses, so I first began taking math classes. (McGonigal, 1998, p. 30)

Collaborating with a Scientist
Ms. Mack volunteered to participate in Project Lab, a staff development program in which elementary science teachers collaborated with practicing scientists. The program enabled her to work for 10 days with a scien-

tist who volunteered to participate in the program. His company released him from most of his regular assignments to act as a mentor for the teacher in Project Lab. Ms. Mack addressed her goals for participating in Project Lab in the following way:

> Since I was making a transition from fourth grade to first grade, I decided to study water. I originally thought I would investigate every chemical aspect of water; however, I had to narrow my focus to the pH factor. I am embarrassed now when I look at my product because it highlights how little I knew about chemistry. At that stage of my career making a pH indicator with red cabbage was new knowledge for me. Now I see that experiment in every child's kitchen chemistry book in print!

During her project, Ms. Mack gained insights into the manner in which science was done. She appreciated the importance the scientist attached to his notebook, to safety, and to the necessity of being persistent. She noted that "this chemist would puzzle over a problem for months, exploring, collecting data, analyzing data, making a change, until he finally got close to the results he wanted."

Ms. Mack's interest and expertise in elementary science was recognized by the school district, who sent her to a national meeting of the science teachers association to select a program to be used throughout the district. During that meeting of science teachers Ms. Mack realized that the term "science inquiry" was used differently by different textbook writers and educators. She resolved at that point to find out more about the term and sought out a mentor in New York City.

Working at the Elbows of Professor Dean

Ms. Mack came to the workshop with a set of values that gave priority to problem-solving, providing autonomy for students to learn from one another and collaborate through the sharing of resources, using parents to support learning at home and in the community, and using whole class activities to create a community and ensure that knowledge and practices are disseminated. In addition, she was an accomplished classroom researcher and used ethnography to explore the quality of teaching and learning in her classroom. Ms. Mack was at a stage in her science teaching where she was ready to learn how to make manipulative, problem-oriented activities more scientific. She wanted to learn about inquiry. Co-participation with Professor Dean enabled her to experience an approach to the teaching of science that extended her current practices and exposed her to ways of thinking that catalyzed a re/construction of her science curriculum. Professor Dean was an ideal mentor for Ms. Mack because his beliefs about teaching and learning were similar to hers and his values were reflected in the structure and implementation of the workshop. Through her active participation as an advisor, Ms. Mack practiced inquiry and learned how to adapt her workshop practices to her roles as a teacher of Grade 1 science. The most salient aspects of the workshop, as far as Ms. Mack's approach to science teaching is concerned, are discussed below in subsections related to the structure of the workshop, investigations, role of prior knowledge, student presentations, and questions.

Structure of the Workshop

Professor Dean believed that a teacher can only plan a half day in advance because classroom activities need to be responsive to what the learners know and want to learn next. Accordingly, an advisory group that met twice a day for a half-hour to plan morning and afternoon activities planned the structure of the four-week workshop. Each of the planned activities was to be connected to observations of the previous activities in which students had engaged. This approach to planning reinforced other practices that were signs of how important it is for teachers to tailor the curriculum to what students know and can do.

Each morning and afternoon consisted of a two-hour period in which students pursued activities, followed by a half-hour in which results were shared in a larger group or whole-class setting. Although each advisor was responsible primarily for the learning of a group of seven advisees, Professor Dean expected all advisors to be aware of what all learners knew and could do. At any time an advisor was expected to report on the performance of any of the 33 students. As an advisor, Ms. Mack was responsible for monitoring the learning of all students and for coordinating at least one whole-class discussion each day.

At the conclusion of the day's activities the mentors would remain behind for an hour to debrief on what happened. At that time they would critique one another's performance in interactions with individuals and in small- and whole-group activities. Hence the activities in which Ms. Mack participated as a mentor were intended to engage her as a researcher and to provide self and peer evaluations on a regular basis.

Investigations

The investigations in which the participants engaged were significant in that they shaped those that Ms. Mack planned for her students in the next semester. Not only was the subject of the investigation important but so too were the enacted roles of the teacher and students. The first investigation required students to explore the properties of unknown liquids, and the second involved structures. Because of its salience to the Grade 1 curriculum enacted by Ms. Mack, details are provided here of her participation in the structures investigation.

The task required participants to build a free-standing structure that would hold up a large unabridged dictionary and suspend weights. Newspaper, paper clips, pins, and one roll of masking tape were the materials provided. The questions written by Ms. Mack in her journal included:

Which paper is best to use?
How is it best to roll the paper?
Would it be better to use long rolls or short thick rolls?
How do we hold the rolls together?
Should we only fasten the rolls together with paper clips, or should we also
    use masking tape?
How shall we attach the legs?
Should we use feet?
Should we put feet on both ends of the legs?
What should we do to prevent the legs from twisting?
How should we place the braces?
What role is prior knowledge playing in the way we are handling the materials?

In her own class a sequence of investigations on structures was framed by Ms. Mack's opportunities to participate in this investigation and the questions about which she was curious.

Role of Prior Knowledge

As a result of her participation in the workshop, Ms. Mack changed her views on how to take account of students' prior knowledge. She realized that to take seriously the idea that students learn on the basis of what they know already she had to structure her teaching roles to ensure that what they knew that was wrong would be a source of capital on which learning could build. Ms. Mack noted that

> I thought the teachers were to activate prior knowledge in order to facilitate learning by first identifying what students knew, so that they didn't waste time covering known material. I found out that teachers needed to identify prior knowledge because often it was incorrect or culture specific and blocked learning. (McGonigal, 1998, p. 44)

The significance of this idea was salient to Ms. Mack's own learning of science and to the way she preferred to implement the science curriculum for her class. She was very aware of the importance of knowing exactly what her students did or did not know; she perceived what they did not know, or were ignorant of, and initiated learning activities accordingly. Thus, not knowing was seen as an integral part of learning rather than a deficiency to be overcome. In her classroom it was acceptable for both the teacher and the students to not know. What was not acceptable was to not know and fail to do something about it.

Student Presentations

The final activity required participants to prepare a 10-minute presentation to inform the larger community about what they had leaned from their investigations. Presentations were followed by five minutes of probing by peers and advisors. The presentations not only provided an opportunity for participants to share what they knew but also to relate knowledge to evidence. Ms. Mack adapted her Grade 1 curriculum to allow children to communicate what they had learned and could do with peers, older children, and parents with the assistance of a presentation board on which they assembled selected evidence. The correlating of knowledge with evidence became a central part of Ms. Mack's thinking about science.

Questions

Ms. Mack was influenced by many of Professor Dean's values, especially those associated with the significance of questioning. She eventually incorporated into her teaching Professor Dean's beliefs that questions assume a critical role in science; that teachers respond too often to the questions they assume their students are asking rather than to questions the students actually ask; and that it is important to listen carefully to questions as a teaching strategy, take time to clarify the questions of students and help them find the answers, and understand the difference between "why" questions and "what if" questions. Ms. Mack also appreciated the significance of playing with materials as a means of identifying questions and the importance of writing down questions as they occurred.

Ms. Mack valued the role of whole-class activities as places for participants to wonder and question. In her adaptation of the workshop to her own Grade 1 class, whole-class activities assumed a central role for students to share and collectively problem-solve. This approach was readily incorporated into her whole-group problem-solving circle that she had developed in her teaching of reading and writing. Her uses of whole-class activities also provide a striking contrast to the approaches adopted by Ms. Scott, whose whole-class activities were more teacher centered.

Enacting Science Inquiry in the Classroom

The impact of Ms. Mack's participation in the workshop on the planning and implementation of her Grade 1 science program was considerable. This section explores the enacted science curriculum in terms of the physical environment, parental involvement, investigations, learning from others, the independent inquiry, writing a book, extended inquiry, and the evidence for student learning.

Physical Environment

Just as Professor Dean required participants to think first about the use of space to promote learning, Ms. Mack began to think about how she could arrange the physical space of her classroom to promote inquiry. She acquired a rich array of materials and placed them in plastic bins that would be accessible to her students. A hands-on program was a necessary but insufficient condition for the type of science program she envisioned. The materials would be in abundant supply and students would be encouraged to augment from home whatever Ms. Mack could provide. Even when individual activities were pursued, all students would be asked to search for materials that might be useful.

Parental Involvement

An integral part of Ms. Mack's approach to the teaching and learning of science was, to the maximum extent, to involve parents in the program as co-teachers, co-researchers, and co-learners. Her approach went far beyond keeping parents informed and included home visits on several strategic occasions during the semester. The first of these occurred prior to the beginning of the semester and was intended to get to know the parents, speak to the child in the presence of parents, and provide an overview of what approach was to be taken during the forthcoming year. The importance of speaking to the child in the presence of parents was that it modeled attentive listening and attended to questions about which the child was curious. Ms. Mack also invited parents to ask questions, showed them a child's portfolio from the previous year, and explained that during the year each first-grade student was to undertake an independent science inquiry.

> I told both the student and the parents that I was not sure how to do it, and I wasn't sure that anyone really had discovered how to manage it. We would be researchers and learners together. (McGonigal, 1998, p. 50)

Ms. Mack often used the reading and writing program to develop science themes. Because she had amassed a large number of books on insects and spiders, she decided that this year a thematic unit on insects and spiders would be her starting point in the reading and writing program. She informed the parents of this decision and asked students to select a book on insects or spiders to read with a parent before school began. The links with science became very strong when in the first two weeks an opportunity arose for a family trip to an insectorium on a Saturday. During the excursion parents and children collaborated in activities such as mounting butterflies, watching a video about insects, touring the museum with a guide, and eating barbecued mealworms.

The involvement of some parents assisted Ms. Mack to imagine how each child in the class could undertake an independent inquiry. While the class was involved in a six-week study of weather, Andrew developed an interest in the internal structure of balls, such as those used to play golf and baseball. He planned an investigation and, with the assistance of his parents, undertook the project at home. Ms. Mack assisted the parents to know how to be mediators of learning in an inquiry investigation, and the mother worked closely with Ms. Mack and debriefed her regularly. With the assistance of Ms. Mack, Andrew's parents compiled a list of suggestions on how to be an effective mentor for science inquiry activities. As a way to initiate the independent inquiries, these suggestions were sent to parents along with two chapters from a book on primary science and the nature of scientific inquiry.

Ms. Mack was aware of the worth of staying in good touch with parents to show them that she was interested in what they did at home to promote the learning of their children. For example, after a week in which the class studied structures every day, the mandated curriculum required the class to study meteorology. After four days of no structures Denise's mother wrote to Ms. Mack to let her know that Denise was building structures at home and was disappointed that the activity at school was not continuing. Immediately Ms. Mack arranged a home visit to observe Denise's structures. The visit was a sign of the value Ms. Mack attached to Denise doing activities of this type at home without being asked and the active involvement of her mother in facilitating the home activities.

Ms. Mack's approach was very thorough. She did not leave it to chance that parents would know intuitively what to do regarding the teaching of their children. Her approach appears to have been successful with Denise's mother. The following excerpt from a report suggests that Denise's mother was a co-learner along with her daughter as she mediated her learning:

While this process was time consuming, it was a tremendous learning process for both Denise and me. She learned about structures and how to investigate/learn, and I learned how to let her direct her own learning.

Investigations

The Grade 1 science curriculum began with a problem-solving task that required the students to add to a cone shaped party hat so that the added part moved when the wearer walked. So that students could imagine themselves as scientists Ms. Mack gave them lab coats and goggles to wear whenever they worked on their investigations. From the first activity Ms. Mack worked at establishing a culture that would value the linking of evidence to assertions. Each student walked across the room to demonstrate to others that his/her model worked as intended. If necessary students modified their hats until they passed the peer-review test. Also Ms. Mack required science notebooks in which each student would draw a diagram of the hats they invented. In this way she established a practice that could facilitate the use of evidence to support claims about what was done and learned. Maintaining and using records became an important part of this community of learners.

Ms. Mack wanted to connect classroom activities to the home and home activities to the classroom. Accordingly, the initial activity was adapted to include parents in an open-ended way. As a home activity, each student was required to adapt a styrofoam hat so that an added object would make a noise when the wearer moved.

The next activity involved chromatography. Students were to bring a leaf from a tree they were observing as a part of a family science activity. After rubbing the leaf onto a coffee filter, the students used alcohol and water to see what colors may have been hidden in the leaf. Ms. Mack felt that the most significant aspects of this activity were the manner in which the data were displayed and the attention that was focused on meaning-making.

So that students could experience a longitudinal study, the class undertook a two-month investigation of the growth of peanut plants. During this study, students followed their interests in an emergent way. For example, an investigation was conducted to determine which plants insects ate and whether insects caused plants to die or were attracted to dead plants.

A fourth activity involved structures and drew on Ms. Mack's experiences with Professor Dean. Its implementation was strongly influenced by the summer workshop experience and reflected the task as it was set up by Professor Dean and the list of questions compiled by Ms. Mack when she participated in that program. When she enacted the structures activities in her own class, Ms. Mack commented that "I then brought in straws and tape and asked students in pairs to see how high a free-standing structure they could build" (McGonigal, 1998, p. 53). Initial activities involved students building straight up with the straws connected in long chains. Not understanding the meaning of free-standing, all groups attached the structure to the floor with masking tape. In subsequent activities ladder-shaped structures appeared and then a three-legged stool. During a whole-class discussion students noticed that different structures had different numbers of straws touching the floor. This observation led to the development of a chart to relate the height of structures to the number of straws touching the floor. Following that activity, students made structures with square bases, built cubes, and then incorporated cubes into larger structures.

After the initial set of activities the class began some studies of meteorology. However, consistent with Ms. Mack's philosophy of encouraging students to follow their own interests, the class returned to the topic of structures because of student interest. A request from one student for a clay slab into which he could insert his straws led to a change in direction for many of the students, who then used clay in their structures. When the straws moved in the soft clay, the students requested clay that would harden. This is one of many examples of students being able to adjust their activities based on what they observed others doing. Learning from others was encouraged in the class and, because of the whole-class sharing, procedures that were tried by one group quickly permeated the classroom if they appealed to others. Similarly, questions and suggested solutions were readily disseminated throughout the classroom community.

Ms. Mack required students to document in their science notebooks their progress and any problems they encountered. The necessity for students to record aspects of their activities required them to focus on the most important issues that occurred and to identify what needed to be done to make progress. Unlike the students in Ms. Scott's class, who had no such requirements, the assignment focused the practices of all students and set a context for building a vocabulary to communicate with others about what was done and learned.

Three critical differences were apparent in the approaches adopted by Ms. Mack and Ms. Scott. First, the materials and the task provided a basis for between-group collaboration and an interest in what other groups were doing. Second, students had the freedom to interact with other groups and the structure of the activity included opportunities to report to the whole class. Third, whole-class activities led by the teacher allowed her to listen to the students' questions, suggest activities that they might try next, and assist them to see patterns in the results of their investigations.

Learning from Others

Ms. Mack had a vibrant science program underway, and in many respects it was consistent with the values of Professor Dean and her own evolving beliefs about the constituents of an effective science program. What was missing still was the independent inquiry she had promised parents. A conceptual breakthrough occurred for her when a student showed an interest in the internal structure of a baseball. With Ms. Mack's assistance, the student designed a study to be undertaken at home while the class continued with their studies of meteorology. Andrew's investigation included the structure of a variety of balls, many brought in by peers and even by a custodian. When he had finished, Andrew brought a presentation board to school with all the balls he had opened mounted inside plastic bags and attached to the board. Thus Andrew served as a model of an expert on the structure of balls. His demonstration of knowledge not only showed students what he had learned about balls and how he had conducted his inquiry but also how to use a presentation board and how to act as a scientist in relating evidence to claims about what he had learned from his investigation. Ms. Mack also assisted the students to act as critical peers by encouraging them to ask questions to probe for more information. This strategy enabled her to make the point that even experts do not know everything there is to know about a topic and the desirability of explaining when you do not know the answer to a question.

The Independent Inquiry

> I told students that next week I wanted them to have a topic that they could investigate and on which they could become an expert. Some students knew immediately what their inquiry would be. Denise wanted to continue her study of structures. (McGonigal, 1998, p. 59)

Parents were important resources in the independent inquiry undertaken by each student. Each child developed a focus question that they would investigate at home, and parents were introduced to the topic during a visit to school when they discussed their child's progress during the marking period. While they were at the school they observed the board used by Andrew to present his findings and developed an understanding of their roles in assisting students to present evidence of their progress and learning. In addition, so that each activity would maintain a focus, Ms. Mack arranged for each family to provide a weekly progress report to her.

In Denise's book called "Structures: My Science Inquiry" (Piserchia, 1998) Denise's mother commented that:

> I have to admit that when this whole science thing began, I had my doubts as to whether it would be worthwhile. I did not want to "take over" Denise's inquiry, but found it somewhat frustrating not to just do it myself. For me, this started out as a lesson in self control. I watched Denise scotch-tape straws together into a mass and somehow wondered how this would become a learning process. I made suggestions which she rejected, reminding me that this was her project, not mine. (Piserchia, 1998, p. 37)

Denise's mother was tempted to assume control of the activity and do it herself. However, she controlled her temptation and allowed Denise to learn by doing. The following excerpt from a report from the mother provides insights into her perceptions of the benefits to her daughter from being involved in the home investigation.

> When Denise decided to make a teepee, I again had all sorts of suggestions which she appropriately rejected. She made a series of tripods and piled them on top of each other. When it toppled, she figured out how to make a square base to hold it up. . . . When it worked, she was so proud especially because she did it herself. (Piserchia, 1998, p. 37)

The decision to access additional resources to supplement her learning was Denise's. She recognized the limitations of the available resources and requested assistance. The following comment from her mother suggests that she was able to discern what was likely to be of assistance to her and what was not.

> From then on, we both learned a lot. We went to visit an architect because Denise asked if we could go to a "structure museum." She rejected my suggestions that we go to Home Depot, because she liked the idea of talking to someone who designs structures. . . . The architect taught her (and me) about beams and columns, tensions and compression, and foundations. I was very proud of how well Denise digested the information. (Piserchia, 1998, p. 37–38)

The role of Denise's mother was significant in that she was the recorder of what Denise had learned. So often students are limited in recording what they know by their inability to write and spell. Having a recorder enabled Denise to describe what she learned and produce several progress reports and an impressive book because she was not limited by writing, spelling, and fatigue. Denise wrote a first draft of the text with the assistance of her mother as editor. The following week, Ms. Mack printed a copy of the text and Denise took the book home and illustrated it. These inscriptions were representations of what Denise knew and served later as sources for the re/construction of knowledge and also for her peers and the teacher to learn from Denise's reports of what she had done and learned.

Record-keeping was a feature of the approach adopted to science, whether it was undertaken at home or at school. For example, in addition to a photographic record, Denise and her mother completed three progress reports in which evidence was provided of what was learned in the preceding week. An example of a progress report is provided in the following note from January 9, in which Denise noted that "you can put the teepees on top of each other with a square base and it will stay up." She also noted that "if you bend the straws in half, it works better for a tower." In terms of evaluation she noted that "the bottom teepee had 2 parts that are bending. I put new straws next to the bent ones." In another example on January 16, Denise noted that "I put braces on the structure to make it stand up. It worked." And she acknowledged that she learned "that you use straight pins to hold the building straws together. Bracing helps buildings to be stronger."

An important part of the independent study was a home visit to see what had been done and what the family had learned. Together Denise and her parents told Ms. Mack what had been learned. During this presentation Ms. Mack modeled how an adult should value the student as a learner. She also took notes so that she would be prepared during the school presentation should the child become anxious and need some questions or comments to retain an appropriate focus.

Ms. Mack was committed to students learning from one another's investigations. She scheduled a presentation during which each child could describe to the entire class the findings of his/her independent research. One 30-minute presentation was scheduled a day. The parent and child would set up the presentation board that was to serve as the focus for the oral presentation and subsequent interactions. The use of the presentation board appears to have been a source of pride to the student as well as a suitable way to show what had been learned and to focus on the inquiry skills of providing evidence for knowledge claims.

> When her presentation board was finished, Denise was so proud of her work and couldn't wait to do her presentation. That in itself is amazing to me, I have always been nervous and anxious when faced with a presentation-type situation. That

my six-year-old could be excited about and looking forward to hers was truly incredible. (Piserchia, 1998, p. 38)

To focus attention on the presentation the students in attendance were required to complete a worksheet that included responses to the following questions: What did the student do? What did you learn? What new investigation could be done using the material? Ms. Mack compiled a list of the responses to these questions as students read them. The compiled list was then given to students to take home as a record of the peer interest in the presentation. In addition, the educational assistant transcribed the presentation, and a copy of the transcription was included in the student's portfolio and another copy was sent home to parents.

On March 4, Denise presented what she had learned (Figure 8.1). She had her models and a pasteboard with photos of her structures. As she described what she did, she re/constructed her knowledge with the assistance of the models and photos, which were referents for the use of her emerging language and gestures. Denise's presentation consisted of descriptions of what she learned from the building of her nine structures and responses to mediational texts from Ms. Mack. During the presentation, Ms. Mack was prepared to provide scaffolding if the students lost focus and needed her assistance in presenting what they knew. Toward the end of the presentation, Denise responded to questions from her peers and at that time her responses tended to be longer. In contrast, her responses to questions from Ms. Mack tended to be relatively short and factual. However, the presentation made it obvious that Denise knew a significant amount of canonical science as a result of her activities. Also, having the pictures and the models she had built provided a context in which Denise could re/construct her knowledge and produce the oral texts that were compelling evidence of what she knew. The models and pictures were referents for the re/construction of knowledge. Denise used the terms she had learned from her meeting with the architect (e.g., "This is a beam, the things that go across like this. The top ones that are across can be beams too." She also used the terms column, brace, and cube in appropriate contexts.). It is likely that, had Denise manipulated her structures, she might have been able to re/construct even more knowledge about equilibrium and stability. Denise's knowledge of structures appeared to exist not just in her body but in a form that was distributed across the interaction between her body and the structures she had built. In the presence of particular concrete referents Denise could re/construct knowledge that was learned over a period of three to four weeks of investigation.

Figure 8.1 Denise/Catlin during her presentation with structures and poster board about here

During the presentation Ms. Mack interacted with Denise to draw out what she knew. An example of an exchange between teacher and student is provided below.

Ms. Mack: Did you put a roof on this so that it would look good or did you put the roof on because it would make it sturdy?

Denise: I put the roof on because I was not sure it would look much. . . . If it had plain. Tension on the building, there has to be a little bit of tension pressing up on the building. Pressing it down. But, there can't be too much either or it will fall down.

The two excerpts presented above may be examples of co-participation. At first sight it appears as if Ms. Mack's mediational efforts led Denise toward a canonical discourse. However, when Ms. Mack previewed a draft of this chapter she was adamant that Denise was leading her. What is evident, however, is that the interactions between Denise and Ms. Mack were more substantive and focused than Denise's interactions with peers, whose comments elicited longer texts of a social nature. What this tends to do is to reinforce the significance of border pedagogy whereby both the teacher and the student cross into the community of the other as a canonical discourse is built, driven by co-participation.

When the presentation was complete Denise accepted questions from her peers. These questions served several purposes. First, they were a part of Ms. Mack's efforts to promote inquiry and reflected her valuing of questions as a key to productive learning. Second, they provided students with a need to listen to presentations and make sense of what was happening. Third, the presenter was required to make sense of questions and relate them to the activities on which the presentation was based. Examples of some of the questions and Denise's answers are provided below.

Q: How do you make a structure?
A: You decide what shape you want it to be and if it's like a building like houses that you live in, you just pick one and just build it up and you got to get compression and tension in it and then if it starts to fall, put braces in it, and then it's done.
Q: What gave you the idea of doing structures?
A: I like seeing structures that are real high like skyscrapers and I just like structures.

Parents were amazed at the results and complained at not being able to attend the presentations. The students met on the mat to consider this problem and decided to present again to their parents and to their fourth-grade mentors. During these subsequent presentations the fourth graders were asked to respond to the first-grade scientists by writing them a letter. The issues addressed in the letter were: What s/he learned; what additional investigation might be done; and what memories the presentation brought forth.

Writing a Book

Ms. Mack requested that each student write a book about his/her first science inquiry. A picture of Denise with some of her structures decorated the front page of Denise's book along with a gold circle of excellence placed there by Ms. Mack (See Figure 8.2). The book consisted of fourteen pages of illustrations and descriptions of what she did during her project, four pages of facts she learned, two pages of questions she still had, one page of description of why she selected the topic, three pages that described where she got her materials, two pages of places she visited, four pages of people she needed to thank, two typewritten pages of

Figure 8.2 The Cover of Denise/Caitlin's science inquiry book.

response from her mother, one page of Denise's response, and a four-page glossary containing definitions of the terms she had learned from the architect.

The provision of questions and sections in the book also provided a scaffold that enabled Denise to record what was relevant to the attainment of inquiry skills. Ms. Mack wanted to emphasize science inquiry; her planning and efforts to mediate the learning of students constrained their learning environments such that the interactions of students and their parents resulted in products that reflected the use of inquiry.

Extended Inquiry

An impressive aspect of the science program was the manner in which whole class activities led to home investigations that resulted in presentations that enabled extension activities to be planned for the whole class. A good example of this is the way in which the whole class studied structures on several occasions, enabling them to construct a considerable knowledge base from their investigations. For example, Ms. Mack decided that a fair test should be the next focus of inquiry by the whole group. After Denise made her presentation the whole class was again asked to build a structure. This time Ms. Mack asked the class to control variables. Each team was given only 20 straws and 20 paper clips, one new roll of clear tape, and only 30 minutes to work. The students were asked to identify the variables they were controlling, and they again measured the height of the structure. This time student pairs were asked to create their own graph to display the measurements.

The students requested that they be given shorter straws because they thought that the length of the straws influenced the height of the structures that could be built. They repeated the activities with 20 coffee stirrers. Many students could build sturdier structures using the coffee stirrers, but the height was shorter. Because of the focus on height the extent of the sturdiness was not considered empirically, but an interesting discussion ensued and students agreed that further investigation was needed.

What Did Denise Learn?

Ms. Mack used an approach to science teaching that encouraged active listening, and her emphases are apparent in the presentations of the students and their books. During the presentations students were to explain what they had learned, what they had done, what questions still were to be resolved and, perhaps, what they wanted to learn next. Denise's descriptions of what she did and the accompanying sketches provide evidence that she learned a considerable amount as a result of her investigations. The sketches of the models show a move toward three-dimensional structures that used a diversity of materials in imaginative ways to build a variety of structures. She obviously began with an interest in structures in the real world and used this as a source of learning. She visited buildings such as houses, office blocks, and bridges as well as construction sites. The terminology she had learned from the architect is used in her book (Piserchia, 1998, p. 11). Denise noted that "at the new house I saw beams, columns, braces and a foundation." This text is placed beneath a sketch of what she saw.

On pages 16–19 Denise explained and illustrated what she understood by a foundation, tension, compression, and a brace (Figure 8.3). In addition, the questions she posed suggested that she not only still retained her curiosity about the natural world and its structures but also that she was wondering about the manner in which structures were constructed and how they could be designed to support added weight.

The display used by Denise during her presentation (Figure 8.1) and the range of structures she built during her independent inquiry is evidence of her knowledge of structures. Similarly, in the many other photographs of Denise's structures it is evident that she not only could describe and sketch the technical terms such as brace but that she understood about compression and knew how to design a structure that is self-supporting and does not topple.

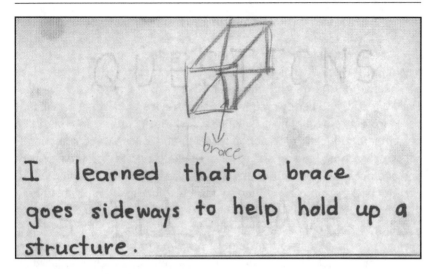

I learned that a brace goes sideways to help hold up a structure.

Figure 8.3 A sample entry exemplifying bracing.

During a summer camp involving peers of a similar age, following the completion of Grade 1, Denise incorporated some of her knowledge of structures into two models she built from clay. She was the only participant to build three-dimensional objects from clay and, as is evident in Figure 8.4, her models incorporated triangles and circles, echoing numerous comments in her book, in which she inferred greater strength to circles and triangles.

Figure 8.4 Models that include triangles and circles.

Conclusions

If Ms. Mack had been left to herself it is likely that she would still be not teaching science. Two significant interventions occurred to change her perspective on the role of science and her own ability to teach it effectively. First, due to her own curiosity about the learning of her class compared to that of her younger daughters, Ms. Mack enrolled in a graduate class that introduced her to action research and to learner-centered strategies for teaching reading and writing. Students became problem solvers and she became a co-learner and action researcher. Her learning about ways to teach reading and writing set a context for her learning about how to teach science. Second, her principal, noting Ms. Mack's avoidance of teaching science, held her accountable for her actions. Rather than placing her in a no-win situation he gave her time to prepare and then arranged for an evaluation of her science teaching by an external science supervisor. With the incentive to pass the evaluation Ms. Mack developed strategies to teach science in a problem-oriented manner that involved students in much the same way that Ms. Scott involved students.

After an initial draft of this chapter was written, Ms. Mack and I approached the principal to obtain his perspectives on the viability of my interpretations. Interestingly, he noted that when he first wanted to evaluate Ms. Mack, he regarded her as an outstanding science teacher. He provided the following two reasons for his actions:

- to document the exceptional science instruction that was occurring in his building for the benefit of the district science supervisors who believed that little science was taught in the school
- to move the hallway activities back into the classroom.

From Ms. Mack's perspective, her belief that the principal had "caught her out" was the catalyst for a concerted and sustained effort to learn to teach science. However, from my perspective, the principal's revelation is cause for concern and raises the question of the extent to which school decision makers and policy makers can accurately assess the efficacy of teaching and learning science. It seems as if there should be someone in the administrative hierarchy who can determine whether or not teachers are enacting a curriculum that takes account of the needs of learners. The contradiction inherent in the fact Ms. Mack was not teaching science to an appreciable extent and the principal's selection of her as an example of fine science teaching is indeed ironic. If the reform of school science is to occur, as so many policy makers intend, it is apparent that principal education will need to be a critical part of a systemic program of staff development.

Once she began to teach science, Ms. Mack developed a love for the subject and began to improve her knowledge of science and the teaching of science. Many of her strategies for teaching reading and writing and her ethnographic skills enabled her to fine-tune the teacher and student roles that characterized her elementary science curriculum. Her involvement in workshops reflects standard approaches to staff development in intensive summer programs. That Ms. Mack participated in so many is commendable and reflects her very professional attitude toward her own growth as a professional and her dedication to do what it takes to facilitate the learning of her students. What is of most significance in the staff development repertoire in which she engaged is her participation in two mentoring projects, one with a scientist and the other with Professor Dean. By this time she had an impressive knowledge of how to teach science and was an ideal participant for a mentoring relationship. By working at the elbows of these experts Ms. Mack learned a great deal, and what she learned was reflected in changes to the enacted curriculum. The learning and change demonstrated by Ms. Mack was impressive and has implications for the education of prospective and practicing teachers. Efforts should be made to include co-participatory activities with mentors in all programs for teachers.

Throughout her biography and descriptions of the investigations of the Grade 1 class and the independent inquiries it is evident that Ms. Mack's action research was a key to instructional improvement. She was willing to use research as a vehicle for reforming her curriculum and to enlist the support of parents, students, and an educational aid as co-researchers. Her research was formal in the sense that she kept extensive records that she carefully analyzed. In addition, she planned with an expectation that her research would yield solutions to problems she wanted to solve. The way she told parents about the independent inquiries to be undertaken by her students and then used research to ascertain how to best structure this as a home activity that became an in-class activity is a model for all teachers to emulate.

The students were motivated to participate in science, and a structure was provided so that as they participated they engaged in inquiry activities that were likely to promote canonical science. From the beginning of the year, Ms. Mack established conventions for the class. Some of these that are particularly salient are that whole-class activities would occur periodically to enable students to share what they were doing and learning. In such presentations all students were responsible for sharing, and incentives were provided to encourage listening. An important part of the classroom culture was the use of evidence to support all claims. Through a series of progress reports the students were provided with opportunities to review what they had done, describe the problems they were encountering, and explain the questions they wanted to pursue next and the answers they were getting. When the science activities were undertaken at home the parents were involved in preparing progress reports.

An impressive part of Ms. Mack's approach to the teaching of science is the manner in which she was able to promote lifelong learning by blurring the boundaries between investigations undertaken at home, in class, and in the community. Ms. Mack was aware of her own knowledge limitations and endeavored to involve students in learning from a variety of resources that included parents. This approach to learning science in the home enabled students to pursue their own interests, but Ms. Mack was careful to link the activities of the home with the activities of school so that students could learn from one another and also so that they would feel that their projects were valued by others, including parents, the teacher, and peers. Accordingly, the teacher visited homes, presentations of home projects were undertaken in class, and reports were used to create an information flow across the boundaries of school and home.

Ms. Mack's concern for the adequacy of her own subject matter knowledge has been a positive driving force for her during the past several years. Initially those concerns prevented her from teaching science, but as she accepted her professional responsibility to teach science regularly she initiated an ongoing program of professional development that reflected commitment to the learning of her students and a growing awareness that it is not necessary to know everything. While teaching science she employed the best practices from her approach to the teaching of reading and writing and also implemented the curriculum in ways that recognized the significance of the home as a resource to support learning. In setting up a program that relied on outside resources Ms. Mack did not abrogate her responsibilities. On the contrary, she structured activities so that they would reflect her priorities for the program and she educated parents so that they could mediate the learning of science in appropriate ways. Not much was left to chance, and the students operated in an environment in which their teacher knew what they were doing, how their activities related to their interests, what they wanted to do next, and what difficulties they were facing. At all times she showed a strong interest in their learning and modeled this interest to parents so that they would realize the importance of listening to their children.

Metalogue

Issue 1: Learning to Teach Science

M: Ms. Mack's science teaching provides a good example of what you can do if you do not have the science background that Gitte and I have. It is still possible to do some very interesting and authentic science lessons.

K: In the initial stages of her career Ms. Mack didn't teach science, a situation that is all too common in elementary/primary schools around the world. When something comes up to upset the schedule, science is frequently the first subject to not be taught. The impetus for changing this circumstance seems to have been grounded in Ms. Mack's progression toward becoming a researcher in her own classroom. Progressively she emphasized teaching strategies that focused on the goals, needs, and strengths of learners. However, it was the action of her principal that catalyzed the changes that led to Ms. Mack's realization that she had to assume responsibility for the science education of her students. Even though there is an irony in the fact that the principal may have selected Ms. Mack to be evaluated because he felt she was the best teacher of science, his actions serve as a reminder of the importance to science education of having active involvement from the school administrators.

S: The key to Ms. Mack's successful transition to effective science teaching was that she took responsibility for her professional development. Too often I hear teachers rationalize their less-than-ideal enthusiasm for science teaching by citing external factors such as budget constraints, limited material resources, and lack of professional support. Although these can be impediments to good science teaching, waiting for these factors to improve will not lead to change. Flooding classrooms with resources also will not lead to change. Effective science teaching involves much more than assigning well-designed activities and sharing cute ideas or teaching tips. This chapter demonstrated the sort of professional commitment needed to improve science teaching in the elementary school. Teachers without strong science backgrounds can indeed become better teachers.

M: Ms. Mack has tenaciously pursued her goal of learning science and learning to teach science. Sometimes I wonder if other teachers construct themselves as secure enough to engage in a similar journey. In such cases, the model of coteaching that I have recently been thinking a lot about may help these teachers because they automatically share the responsibility and find some comfort in enacting change with someone else. They also have the possibility to talk through difficulties and share in bringing about new ways of teaching.

S: Coteaching can indeed be a form of on-the-job professional development. It is possible for a teacher with little experience in science to team up with (and learn from) one with a stronger science background. By planning and trying out alternative ideas together, the inexperienced partner can experience the support needed for moving outside her comfort zone of teaching as usual. This is the sort of professional partnership teacher educators have been supporting in relation to the pre-service practicum.[2]

K: What is important in Ms. Mack's case is that she transported her competence from another area into that of teaching science. She assumed more and more responsibility for planning the science program by leaning on her knowledge of how to teach language arts. The roles of students and her own role as a mediator of learning were similar and emphasized student participation in the social construction of knowledge. However, Ms. Mack was aware that she needed to know more about science and the resources to support the teaching and learning of science. The chapter lays out a gradual progression in her thinking about her roles as a science teacher and the differentiation between those roles and the role of being a language arts teacher. Inevitably, Ms. Mack realized that she had to know more about inquiry, which she perceived as being a critical ingredient in making science activities as distinct from any other classroom activity (such as language arts).

S: Teachers can learn about inquiry firsthand when they become a teacher-researcher of their own practice—preferably with a peer- or a university-based collaborator. Ms. Mack differed from most other teacher-researchers in that she also engaged in science-related projects with Professor Dean. This was a better-than-usual model for professional development.

M: I have to come back to Ken's comment about inevitabililty. It is not clear to me that Ms. Mack's realization was an inevitability. All too often we seem to encounter people—not only in teaching—who appear to resist such realizations and the need for the necessary changes.

K: It was different for Ms. Mack in that she also realized that her own knowledge of science needed to be increased. She learned valuable aspects of doing science by actively participating alongside several mentors. After she had participated in numerous summer workshops she reached a stage where her background and approach were not unlike those described in the previous chapter for Ms. Scott. However, she was able to move beyond that stage by co-participating with scientists and thereby extending her personal discourse to be more science-like. Her close work with Professor Dean set the stage for her to be able to implement an inquiry-oriented science curriculum.

Issue 2: Enacting an Inquiry-Oriented Science Curriculum

K: Ms. Mack appears to have made a major conceptual leap when she realized that it is important for students to actively generate questions as they participate in science. Her emphasis on the students generating questions conveys a value to students that suggests that their own curiosity is significant in her classroom. However, she went beyond just having students generate questions. She ensured that she listened to them and endeavored to assist students to find answers to them.

S: Children's investigatable questions are the central feature of the interactive approach to teaching science. Young children sometimes find it easier to make statements, so teachers need to listen carefully to children before modeling how such statements can be transformed into research questions. The next crucial phase is for the teacher to work with the children in the design of investigations that address the particular question. This is where the notion of what constitutes a fair test comes into play.

M: There is something about being able to engage in an area, and become familiar with it, and thereby be enabled to engage even further with the area. I found that even Grade 8 students, in a period of 10 weeks, developed to the point where they could ask research questions involving three dependent and three independent variables. However, in most schools, activities are changed over at the ring of the bell, children are jerked out of their activities and asked to do something entirely different. I would not be able to even start writing a single page in such conditions. But of course, Ms. Mack had organized her classroom in ways that allowed children to find a coherence throughout the cycle of investigations.

K: It is important that Ms. Mack emphasized to student presenters that they had to cover set criteria each time they spoke orally to the class. First, she asked them to describe what they did. Second, they were to explain what they learned and to provide evidence to support what they learned. Third, they were to list the questions they had that still needed resolution. Finally, they were to discuss what they wanted to know next. Each of these steps is of critical importance and makes it possible for others to learn from an oral presentation of a peer. Too often in classrooms at all levels the verbal presentations of students are not of a type that are conducive to others learning from what is said.

S: This is an area that Mr. Hammett could work on in order to move conversations to more science-like discourse. I think the structure of these reporting sessions is a great model for other elementary teachers.

M: That it is important to provide some structure that supports children's growth is one thing I learned from working with elementary teachers. All too often, I simply jumped in as a teacher and did not worry about providing enough structural support that allowed students to develop in the way I wanted them to. In this sense, Tammy provided such structures that allowed Gitte's questions to have the impact on the classroom that they had. Just having conversations, even if they are about animals, nature, or engineering, does not mean that they are actually scientific conversations.

K: If I have concerns about the quality of student talk in classrooms I am an order of magnitude more concerned about the quality of the listening that occurs. Do students know what to do when they are expected to be listening? Ms. Mack's idea of students writing in their "Questions and Wonder" books is an important step forward. Just as speakers had a set of tasks to attend to while speaking so too did the listeners had to describe in their "Questions and Wonder" book what they had learned, what questions they had for the speaker, and what they would like to learn next about this topic.

M: It is interesting that you address listening as an important aspect of teaching. In a recent study, this is what I described to be the essence of my questioning—listening to children prior to asking dynamic questions that develop the conversation rather than finishing because the question-answer-evaluation cycle has been completed.

K: Within the structure of a prescribed curriculum Ms. Mack was able to allow students to undertake independent investigations pertaining to their own interests. I think this is extremely important. If students have an interest in an area and can undertake long-term investigations then there is an increasing likelihood that what they do and learn in science will have personal relevance. In these circumstances there is an increased probability that the students will be able to access and appropriate language games that are science-like.

S: So enacting an inquiry-oriented science curriculum involves much more than assigning activities or copying good ideas. Teachers need to establish a climate in which children ask questions that they wish to investigate and are prepared to work with others to design investigations and report their findings and where students welcome the scrutiny of results from their peers.

Issue 3: Blurring the Boundaries between School, Home and the Community

M: An important aspect of Ms. Mack's class was that the parents were also involved. Tearing down the walls that seem to separate formal learning from learning more generally is one of my main referents for thinking about the problems of schooling. In my recent work, I have been writing and speaking about the need to de-institutionalize science education, making science and science learning part of the community and changes of the world in which we live.

K: Ms. Mack visited the students' homes even before the year commenced. She informed parents and students about the goals of the course and got them started on activities that would set the tone for the enacted curriculum. Some activities would start at home, be followed up in class, and then be further developed at home. Similarly, some activities commenced at school and were continued at home. The boundaries between learning at home and learning at school were blurred and Ms. Mack consciously set out to get parents involved as resources to support the learning of their children. She got to know the students and parents in their own homes.

M: People have purposes and goals and as they attempt to achieve them, they learn. Perhaps Ms. Mack was able to provide parents with new goals, to be better at parenting and to grow with their children. In this way, parents too might have been learners: increasing their understandings of science, parenting, and their children's knowing and learning.

K: When Ms. Mack visited the home she modeled how to listen to students and respect their knowledge. She also set high expectations for the parents. She sent home two articles to educate parents about science teaching and how to be facilitators. Also she encouraged parents to provide materials for the use of the entire class and to speak to the class about areas in which they had expertise. In addition, the parents were to take their children to the community and allow them to access relevant experts to support their independent inquiries.

Ms. Mack's conscious efforts to have students access resources to support their learning from outside the classroom minimized the potential disadvantages of having a teacher with limited knowledge of science. It also set another stamp on the type of community that was being established. This was a learning community with very wide boundaries, one that included places, phenomena, and people from the community at large.

S: Extending the classroom boundaries to embrace the community provides additional challenges for teachers who may be ill prepared for new roles. I remember becoming frustrated at times when I was teaching in a rural community. Students (and even parents) occasionally brought in various rocks and plants from home for me to identify. Now I wasn't much of a geologist or a botanist and I had limited access to suitable keys. Also, if a teacher encourages parents to present information to the class, how does one deal with situations in which the parents convincingly reinforce alternative conceptions? These are just two problems that illustrate my point. Nevertheless, I think that if the emphasis is on working through investigations together, rather than on the teacher positioning him/herself as an authority figure, the impact of these problems could be diminished.

M: It might have been interesting to do with the parents what you did with the students and engage them in an inquiry together. This would have been great modeling for different approaches to teaching. This also would have extended what we normally understand when we talk about the schooling of our children.

S: In this respect, the Family Science Project in Australia had great potential. This project conducted initial and follow-up leadership workshops for parents and teachers, guiding them through innovative activities using strategies that encourage socially and personally relevant learning in the physical sciences. Mr. Hammett, for example, completed such a program and now encourages parents to work with their children, at home or in class, on various design projects and science activities.

Issue 4: Was This Scientific Inquiry?

K: Did Ms. Mack's students participate in a science inquiry? I raise this question only for the sake of Ms. Mack, who still worries that inquiry is an elusive concept. Like so many concepts, inquiry is holistic and does not lend itself to being defined operationally. I would answer the question by saying yes. But I do want to add some caveats as well.

First, I think science inquiry is supported by a habitus for the community as a whole. There is considerable evidence in the chapter that the participants knew what to do and what not to do when science was being practiced. Second, I believe that habits of mind are a key part of inquiry. In this class there was evidence of curiosity, persistence, and open-mindedness about learning from experience. Third, children used evidence to support claims to have learned particular things from independent inquiry. Taken as a whole, I argue this to be an example of scientific inquiry.

M: Inquiry, like so many other concepts, loses its life when we squeeze too hard for its meaning. Maybe if we consider inquiry to be a quest, a search with a passion for knowing, then we realize that the children in this class engaged in it. To me, science has always been associated with passion, a passion for knowing and understanding, a passion for being a lifelong learner. Part of this passion is linked to the pleasure arising from the construction of new representations.

S: Children are more likely to persevere with the repetitive trials needed to address particular research questions when they own the questions and the design. This is where the passion comes into play. The tasks don't seem to be dreary to those who have had a hand in the design of the investigation. Also, when children know in advance that they need to convince their peers of their findings, they are more likely to build in rigorous procedures into their designs.

K: In this, the presentation boards are an important part of setting up a learning environment to support inquiry. First, the kids own them, they are the fruits of their labor. Second, the boards enable students to represent their knowledge in the presence of artifacts and to include inscriptions, actual models, oral description, and gestures in their representations of what they had learned from an independent investigation. The coordination of explanation and evidence takes the form of an argument that is often a part of science in its many forms and forums.

M: The presentation board really brings together issues that we also saw in the class I was teaching, where the children constructed representations to make an argument about the past and possible future tug of wars they might have had with me, their teacher. I see in these activities a double function. On the one hand, children are engaged in the production of varied representations and in this already go beyond talk alone. On the other hand, the representation becomes both topic of the talk and the background against which they make sense using gestures and their entire bodies in the effort to communicate. Once we look at such productions, and experience them firsthand, we necessarily have to take a step back from the deficit models that often reign in science education research and in science teaching.

K: There was no evidence of using deficit models in either the teaching or the learning in Ms Mack's classroom. Her idea that what is not known is the first step toward coming to know was something she learned from collaborating with Professor Dean. Unlike so many science educators who see misunderstandings or wrong ideas as challenges to be directly addressed in conceptual change interventions, the wrong ideas or incomplete understandings were not critical parts of this learning community. Rather, the focus was on generating questions, providing evidence to support claims, and expecting to learn something next. This approach was a distinctive feature of a classroom in which what students knew and could do were forms of capital on which learning could build.

M: Your comment reminds me in a way of earlier attempts to teach general process skills, but I know this is not your intent. At the same time, there is something to being able to cope wherever you are, and in contexts such as the one Ms. Mack created, children develop the habitus of coping and making do. It appears to me that schools overemphasize the "right knowledge in the head" measure, according to which most of us would fail. For in our work, there are many situations when we simply pick up a book, a journal article, access the Internet, or draw on resources in some other form to make sure that the "facts" are right. What really counts is knowing how to tell good stories, stories others want to read and hear. Ms. Mack allows her children to develop such practices, which are more general than knowing the chemical formula for water or the parts of an atom.

S: I don't think we can ignore the significant role of scientific facts in scientific discourse or the conceptual change literature. Although I agree that it is important to establish a pattern of discourse that is science-like, the facts used should also be accurate.

M: Then we are right back where we began. Kids need to know the facts first, or at least second.

S: Okay, I can appreciate that the evidence available in a particular context might support an assertion that is inconsistent with canonical science. Under these circumstances, I might even accept that the assertion might be left unchallenged—especially when the teacher knows that a different outcome is not possible with available resources.

But it is a different matter when the teacher knows that the students' ideas are incompatible with canonical science and that teacher intervention might lead to a better understanding. This is what Mr. Hammett did when he knew that he could help Kerrin and Katrina understand the energy distribution in an electric circuit. It is important for teachers to continue to read and attend workshops conducted by scientists so that they can build confidence in their own scientific knowledge. Such a quest for a deeper understanding of science conveys to children the message that we are all learners and that learning does not stop on the way out of the school gate. What is inappropriate, in my view, is when the teacher overuses his/her authority in "telling" students about scientific facts for the purposes of enhancing students' low-level understanding of science.[3]

M: What we really need to pick apart is what "deeper understanding" could mean in the context of a discourse approach to knowledge. If we are focusing on language not as medium but as the only way that we can enact "knowing about," deeper understanding simply means talking a different talk, one that has a greater family resemblance with science. But we may have to return to this issue in our final metalogue on the topic of epistemology.

Notes

1   The voice in this chapter is that of Ken Tobin.

2   Such a professional partnership is described in Rigano and Ritchie, in press.

3   This point is elaborated in Ritchie, 1998.

Chapter 9

Concluding Metalogues

In this chapter, we further develop several themes that arose from the previous chapters and our metalogues: epistemology, the role of teaching and teachers, resources and artifacts, discourse community and participation, the nature of elementary science, and resources that support learning. In our view, these themes are central to any serious effort to re/construct elementary science. These metalogues are not thought to be end products in themselves but should be taken as launch pads for ongoing conversations among our readers.

Epistemology

M: A central but latent issue throughout our six case studies is that of epistemology. It is becoming quite apparent to me that knowing is not that which cognitivists treat as the hardware of the brain. Knowing cannot be reduced to a substance or structure that resides somewhere between the ears and underneath the skull; it has a number of dimensions, all of which are related to our being-in-the-world. For example, we describe how children's gestures, postures, graphical articulations, and talk make sense only if they are considered relative to and against unfolding conversations and against the physical, social, historical, and cultural settings within which these conversations occur. Jeff's utterances about forces and tensions that accompany his gestures over and toward the bridge artifact he presented to the class cannot be understood independent of the wheres, whens, and hows of the situation in which he and the listeners experience themselves. The knowledge that he enacts should not be thought of as something that he would or even could have brought forth on his own, like a trickle from what already exists in his mind prior to the event. Rather, the conversations unfolded as Jeff and his peers raised important issues at hand. It is in this context that claims and counterclaims, questions and answers, summaries and conclusions emerged as scientific processes that have to be enacted.

K: Another example of the distributed nature of knowledge is apparent in the example of Denise presenting her findings on structures to the class in conjunction with a presentation board on which she had inscriptions and artifacts to support her claims and guiding questions from Ms. Mack. The context in this case provided an opportunity for the re/construction of knowledge and its representation as oral text. The knowledge of structures was not just what was between Denise's ears but also what was constructed in the interactions involving Denise, the artifacts from the presentation board, and the structuring questions of Ms. Mack. In addition, a community of active listeners was composing statements about what they were learning from the presentation, listing questions that they would like to have answered, and recognizing what they do not know and would next like to find out. Her peers were to ask questions after her presentation, and these questions too provided a vehicle for the re/construction and re/presentation of knowledge about structures and forces. This context is a part of Denise's actions and her associated representations of what she knows about structures and forces. So where is the knowledge? There are many ways of responding to such a question, but from an epistemological point of view it is perhaps more important for me to emphasize interactions, the agency of teacher, peer discourse, inscriptions, and artifacts in Denise's ability to represent what she knows.

S: Without the student-student and teacher-student interactions the canonical knowledge would not have emerged in each of the classrooms studied. The teacher, however, establishes a climate for effective communication and learning. Michael, as the teacher interacting with Shaun and his peers, you were able to balance cultural reproduction and cultural production at the chalkboard in such a way that students eventually became fluent in the canonical discourse of science; that is, they learned to play the language games of science. So, knowledge is neither "out there," as in books or on the Internet, nor "in there," as in the heads of children and teachers. Rather, it emerges from the interactions between participants and material resources. In this sense, knowledge is situated in the community.

K: We could also say that our analytic frame is wide enough so that what we identify as knowledge forces us to look at individuals in community.

M: I agree. For example, although each of the student and student groups took major responsibility for the production of the artifacts, these artifacts could not be understood as concretions of ideas from the minds of the individuals, possibly negotiated by the group. But as I showed in detailed and extensive descriptions,[1] each artifact really emerged from the actions of the individuals in the material, social, configurational, cultural context of the setting. Teacher interdictions were enacted in different ways so that the same teacher utterance "you can't use any other materials" would, depending on the context, lead one group to use a heavy-duty cardboard pipe even if other groups did not use the same pipe. Thus, the setting was experienced differently by the individuals, thereby enabling the particular artifacts to emerge. But each artifact bore the marks of the multiple and multi-sourced influences on the design activity. Thus, even when students presented "their" artifacts, they already embodied in different forms the culture, materials, and practices that constituted this community. Thus, and in this sense, the epistemological position that we have taken here is one in which the window on cognition, knowing, and learning needs to set such as to include the multifarious details of the setting.

S: When you were talking about the emergence of artifacts, I was thinking about Emily's group, in Chapter 5. The materials in use evoked images of previous experiences and, when shared with other group members, they evoked images and ideas for them. This progressive evolution of ideas led the artifact to unfold as it did. The artifact embodied the knowledge of individuals and their collective experiences with the materials in the community.

K: I think that is particularly so in cases where verbal interaction is a key part of a learning situation. Different questions facilitate different actions on the part of a presenter who will, accordingly, re/construct different knowledge and to the extent that it is possible provide an appropriate representation. Similarly the presence in an environment of different peers, artifacts, and inscriptions will constitute different opportunities for the re/construction or re/presentation of knowledge. I view this as having serious implications for many activities, including initial teaching of a concept, review, and assessment of what students know. For example, in an assessment of learning, what are the triggers that will enable particular students to re/construct and represent what they know. Too often teachers and policy makers in particular regard assessment instruments as passive ways to measure what students know in valid ways. Such a perspective takes no account of the role of inscriptions as enabling devices in re/construction and re/presentation. To the extent that differing inscriptions are able to connect in different ways with what students know and can do, so too we can expect differences in the ways students are able to respond to assessments built around inscriptions. Of course that makes me think of performance tests that involve artifacts and inscriptions. In such cases the situation is just as complex, because artifacts such as equipment and materials will also interact with the individuals in characteristic ways.

M: Of course, our epistemology also constitutes teaching in a different way. Teaching itself is not simply an act in which some explicit skills are translated into action. Rather, teaching also involves sets of dispositions, a habitus, of enacting and thereby modeling the learner itself. Thus, in this perspective, lifelong learning is not a concept or even a metaphor. It becomes part of a way of being-in-the-world. There are no longer questions of location (school, university) or times (after work, during the school day) that delimit where and when learning is to occur. Rather, learning becomes something so ingrained that we no longer know otherwise.

K: When interactions are regarded as the units of meaning making the knowledge of an individual can be seen as distributed over the interaction. Just as a teacher might be needed to facilitate the initial construction of knowledge so it might be that a teacher is needed to enable re/construction and re/presentation of what has been learned. In this sense the term teacher could be applied to a peer or to the more conventional idea of teacher.

Teachers and Teaching

M: It has been an interesting experience to look back across the different case studies, being the teacher in one of them, and thinking about my peers and my own place in the world of teaching. We often place teachers into dichotomous categories, including those of beginner-experienced, traditional-innovator, or novice-expert, and in some instances, extend the dichotomies into gradients. However, when we think of the teachers in this study and the conditions in which they worked, such dichotomies not only break down easily but they are also not helpful in bringing about the kind of changes we might wish for elementary science education. For example, it is unreasonable to assume that Ms. Scott or Ms. Mack will one day develop my own expertise in physics, or even come close to it. But, as the case of Ms. Mack showed, this is may not be necessary. Even without content matter expertise, she was able to enact an authentic curriculum drawing on parents and children as resources to accomplish this feat.

K: You make a good point here. A key idea underlying Ms. Mack's teaching was her willingness to focus on the strengths and needs of the learner. Then she reached out to locate and use whatever resources she could to promote the learning of all of her students. Her use of parents and other community experts was just one example of how she did not rely only on what she knew. In addition, her focus on building autonomy and responsibility for their own learning produced a cohort of co-researchers who were willing to learn by listening to others, reading, and experimentation. When we view teaching and learning from the perspective of community it is interesting to note that the teacher always is regarded as a critical part of how learning progresses, but it is also the case that many more teachers are permissible than the traditional ratio of one teacher per class. Ms. Mack's class is one good example of how broadening the resources to support learning made it possible for astonishing levels of learning to occur.

S: Several years ago, I was a volunteer teacher in a large-scale research project in which my eighth Grade science class was videotaped for a term or so. The participating teachers were brought together on occasions where the researchers presented their preliminary results and we could discuss their findings. One of the conclusions that stood out for me was that the sort of science education experienced by students was very different, despite having a common curriculum and similar resources.

M: As we found out in a high school physics class, these experiences can differ considerably even within one and the same class.[2]

S: Now I respected each of the other teachers involved and there was never any mention that one teacher was perceived to be better or demonstrated more expertise than the others. What I learned most from my experience was that teachers do have different strengths and that they manifest themselves in the different learning environments observed. More important, however, individual teachers each demonstrate a unique blend of practices, some of which we might support and others that we might not, but all teachers have the potential to contribute to students' scientific learning. So there is not one fail-safe way to teach science, and teachers with a more limited science background can still make a very useful contribution to science teaching in the elementary school. It would not necessarily make sense for Ms. Scott, for example, to conduct a whole-class discussion at the chalkboard like Michael or attempt to assemble a gearing mechanism to drive a classroom-sized tennis ball machine like Mr. Hammett— I am not advocating a standardization of practices here. Teachers need to adapt teaching ideas to their own circumstances and personal theories.

M: A more differentiated concept of "authentic" science therefore has to be central to our discussion. As Ken points out as part of our chapter metalogues, authentic science has at least two distinct components: participation in the (methodological and subject matter–related) discourse of professional science and participation in activities which are personally relevant and meaningful. In Ms. Scott's classroom, we saw a lot of the latter and not much of the former type of authenticity. In the Grade 4 bridge-building class and the Grade 6–7 curriculum on simple machines, we saw a lot of both types. The key issue then is how authentic personal experience can be used as a process by means of which children can begin to participate in and appropriate more scientific discourses, which they then use for their own intentions while pursuing goals they have framed on their own.

S: The activities in Ms. Scott's class were just as personally relevant to the children as the activities of the students in Michael's class were to them. The challenge for teachers is to design personally relevant experiences that lead to scientifically authentic activities. I believe that the most effective sequence might be that which we saw in Michael's class; that is, a progression from activities that emphasize personal relevance, such as the tug-of-war contest, to those which accentuate scientifically authentic practices, such as the student-led conversation at the chalkboard. Ms. Scott and Mr. Hammett also first established personally authentic activities and there was some evidence that they provided the incentive to engage in scientific language games.

K: How does a teacher, or any participant for that matter, decide if an activity is science-like? I am guided somewhat in beginning to respond to a question like this by Deanna Kuhn's article,[3] in which she describes science as a form of argument in which claims about what has been learned are supported by data. So as a starting-out point,

I would design activities to ensure that all students participate in activities in which there is argument about the extent to which knowledge claims are consistent with data. But the presence of these arguments would be as a sufficient test of whether or not the activity was science-like. I think some habits of mind need to be present also. First, willingness to put knowledge claims to the test and to relinquish those claims or at least adapt them in the face of evidence. Intentionally seeking evidence to refute claims might be a component of a scientific-fair test and a characteristic of schools science. What I am doing is describing what should happen when students do science. In an elementary science program, there is bound to be more happening than the doing of science. For example, students probably would learn about science by studying the history of science and by learning interesting facts of science. I do think that a good science education would explore science in its cultural, social, and political contexts and in so doing explore issues of equity and power. Engineering science fits well into all of these contexts and that is another reason why curricular choices might consider more engineering examples as a vehicle for learning science.

Material Resources and Artifacts

M: All of the case studies were recorded in science classes in which teachers had planned technology and design activities as context. The case studies show how teachers work to achieve these contexts into opportunities to appropriate a discourse that sounded more like a science discourse than the children's everyday use of language did. Technology, and more precisely the artifacts, therefore constituted a central part of the setting by means of which children were introduced to science. However, the materials and tasks themselves did not lead to scientific discourse, understandings, and the like. Rather, they provided a context, the sort of stuff that could become the topic of conversations. The conversations—among peers, with the teacher, and with the parents—really constituted the settings that brought about the changes in students' and teachers' discourses. Whereas the materials and artifacts were used in constituting sites and topics, that was not sufficient for the discourse to become scientific. For example, as we saw in the classes that Gitte and Tammy or I taught, the kinds of questions raised and even the competitive aspects of a particular activity give a particular slant to the goals and purposes for the students involved.

S: As I have suggested previously, the conversations between partici- pants centered on their emerging inscriptions and artifacts. These artifacts, such as drawings, provided a focus or a material reference for the conversations. However, manipulating the material resources in the design of artifacts frequently created additional design prob- lems for the students. So these activities were much more than tink- ering exercises. Because the students were required to think with and about the materials in the design of their artifacts, the metaphor of thinkering was applied to their practices.

M: So in an important sense, the materials and resulting artifacts consti- tute both the focus of the activities and conversations but they are also the background against which the activities that the individuals and the learning community as a whole engage in make sense. Like the discourses, tools, books, rules, and practices, the materials and artifacts can be seen as resources that make possible particular kinds and degrees of participation in ongoing activities.

S: Another point we have not highlighted is that some of the children were first-time users of tools such as Stanley knives and wood saws. The design activities provided them with opportunities to develop particular practices from which they had been previously excluded. This was particularly noticeable with the female students in Mr. Hammett's class. In this sense, the design activities have the poten- tial of enriching children's lifestyles and alerting them to previously unknown practices and even career possibilities.

M: Interestingly enough, I made a similar observation in my Grade 6–7 class, and in other classes I taught. Girls especially, in part encour- aged and supported by me, wanted learn how to use real tools such as electrical drills, circular saws, and the like. In this sense, I do not think that tools and materials inherently bias against girls. But this is a matter other researchers are likely to have much more experience in writing and talking about than I do.

Discourse, Community, and Participation

M: One important concept in the case studies and in our conversations has been the notion of co-participation. I think we need to clarify this notion, for it might easily lead to confusion. Students co-participate even in the most horrible science lessons that we have seen or that we might want to imagine. Here, however, co-participation includes the notion that individuals do so willingly, generally with intent and pleasure, and have self-generated goals that motivate activities and the practices learned in the processes of completing them. I guess that the desirable forms of co-participation cover those instances of learning that we have described throughout this book. And when I think of coparticipation, I also contemplate the teacher as co-learner and co-investigator, in addition to coteacher, in the way Ms. Mack constructed her role. I guess, that some concept of democracy might be well suited as a descriptor for the kind of co-participation I would find desirable in my own classroom, one I would like to advocate in teacher education.

S: It is important for teachers to identify the children's ideas and questions so that they become the focus for the conversations and designs that might follow. Teachers should not feel excluded or sidelined from these activities, because we already have shown how important the teacher's interactions are in moving these conversations toward scientific discourse. I don't know about democracy. Perhaps an idealized form of democracy might be okay. I have some negative images of "democracies" in which decisions appear to be influenced by powerful interest groups and are made on the basis that the side that can muster greatest support wins on the day. I know that this is not what we are advocating here.

M: I think that we should seriously consider new modes of learning to teach, such as the model that I termed "coteaching." When two or more teachers work together, literally at each others' elbow, they are able not only to learn those aspects of good teaching practice that are easily describable in expressive forms, but also (and especially) those aspects that Bourdieu would classify as the tacit aspects of practices, dispositions, and more generally, the habitus. Although such notions as embodied knowing that cannot be made explicit are red flags to those who want to formalize teacher knowledge, my own studies of coteaching show that teachers usually come out of coteaching experiences with a sense of having learned a tremendous amount without having been conscious of the process. When they observe and compare teaching events from the beginning and the end, they often discover tremendous changes. Often, the coteachers adopt aspects of each other's practices so that, for example, Tammy's questions soon sounded like Gitte's, and Gitte's stance toward individual children was similar to that of Tammy, who had known them for a long time.[4]

K: Coteaching is an extremely good way to learn to teach. We have now adopted this model in our program for prospective teachers and we have seen signs of success in learning to teach in urban settings. However, I was thinking about the children from an elementary class learning to teach by co-participating in teaching at the elbow of any of the teachers involved in this study. As teachers, all were exceedingly good role models from whom any of the students could learn a great deal about how to be a successful teacher. I make this point because one thing every teacher could do tomorrow to improve substantially the quality of what is happening in their classroom is to recruit a fresh batch of enthusiastic teachers. In so doing there would be more opportunities for all students to receive more assistance from teachers, albeit peer teachers. On the positive side, the evidence suggests that the peer teachers benefit a lot from teaching their peers and that it is highly likely that peer teachers will use a discourse that is more accessible to the existing knowledge of peers.

S: Traditional classrooms can be insular sites that cut off learners from the rest of the world and isolate teachers from their colleagues. By expanding the classroom boundaries, we are likely to see more authentic learning activities and greater opportunities for coteaching. Although she did not seem to involve other teachers, other then Professor Dean, Ms. Mack did involve parents and children and therefore reintegrated herself in a learning community.

M: Discourse, community of practice, and participation are some of the key concepts in much of recent research. However, in the context of most school situations, these concepts also have their limitations. However, Ms. Mack brought about a context in which "community" encompassed more than just the classroom. Learning communities of the kind I envision, and which I attempt to foster in my ongoing research, go beyond the walls of institutionalized forms of learning. Participation then is no longer separable from other everyday activities as it is presently experienced by teachers and students who often have two distinct lives: at school and after school. Once the concept of learning is expanded from the context of schooling, and it becomes a concept that is more akin to education more generally.[5] In a sense, then, I am advocating that we transgress and transform currently existing boundaries that confine learning to particular institutions and individuals and assign to others the role of teachers. But at the same time, I do not want to suggest that we need to move to another simplistic model that institutes new boundaries. Rather, we need to think of a context of learning in which boundaries can and are continuously transgressed and redefined according to the needs of the current context. Only if we think of our theoretical concepts as open in the sense that they are under continuous re/construction and transformation will we come close to providing an appropriate context for knowing and learning knowledge that is appropriate and viable in the next century. We can conceive of communities as providing the "safe" but also changing grounds for the learning associated-transformations to occur.

S: Many elementary classes I have visited already have extended the "walls" into the community. Parental involvement in classroom activities has been encouraged for many years now in Australian schools. Perhaps we see most evidence of this in reading programs. Unfortunately, science has not attracted the same level of commitment by teachers and parents. Nevertheless, teachers such as Mr. Hammett offer some hope. Mr. Hammett organizes occasional visits for his class to the local community (TAFE) college, where the children have opportunities to use more elaborate equipment than is possible in his classroom. Also, visits to science education centers and the like are becoming more popular. Another tangible way that Mr. Hammett has reached out into the community is through the Family Science Project. Families are invited to continue working on classroom-initiated activities, like what happened in Ms. Mack's class. Parents can co-participate with their children on these science projects, and the children can then share these experiences with their classmates the next day. In this way, the classroom and home boundaries merge. It is not unusual to find parents and children working alongside each other before school in Mr. Hammett's classroom. Another exemplary elementary teacher I have observed recently coordinates an organic vegetable garden enterprise. Science lessons focus on growth and nutrition of plants as well as the control of insects without pesticides. Produce is sold to parents and local residents. These are some ways that teachers can weaken the boundaries between learning science in class and in the community.

M: Communities such as those you describe and such as we have seen here in Ms. Mack's class provide the ideal setting for the kind of conversations in which learning is a byproduct. Such conversations, as Jacques Désautels and I have argued, are recursive and reflexive occasions for epistemology as practice.[6] These conversations continually evolve by developing themes. But every now and then, the conversations step one level up and make previous accomplishments—themes, knowledge, understandings, and practices—the new topic. Conversations then are not just relegated to learning about some science topic but become occasions for learning to learn.

Re/Constructing Elementary Science

M: I think that we should not neglect to make the title of this book a topic
of our conversations. Apart from playing on the word "construction," which is also, and in a very material way, the activity in which
all the children engage, we have explicitly provided images for science
classes that are quite distinct from what is common. We are also
addressing, at different levels and in recursive ways, re/constructions
of what a suitable epistemology for school science might look like. In
a most general sense, knowing and learning are processes that should
be distributed across individual agents, communities, and artifacts. If
we consider knowing and learning as always and already occurring in
some context with specific social, cultural, and material contingencies, we also have to rethink what it might mean to evaluate learning
and how to re-conceptualize the notion of ethics and accountability.

S: As the children engaged in thinkering with the available material resources, they progressively constructed personally (and sometimes
socially) relevant artifacts as well as scientific or engineering knowledge. But this was only made possible by the skillful teaching moves
on the part of each of the teachers. These case studies provide us
with rich images of what can be done in elementary science classrooms; they also help us to identify what more needs to be done.
Much of our metalogue conversations have been concerned with authenticity. The design activities were personally relevant experiences
for the students and, on occasion, they became springboards to scientifically authentic activities. How appropriate would it be then for
teachers to turn around and administer pencil-and-paper tests of students' scientific knowledge?

K: We have learned a great deal from this set of studies. First, and speaking
for myself, I can say that I learned that very young minds are capable
of attaining very high standards of learning when the conditions are
set for them to succeed. I want to begin with Ms. Mack because I
know the details of the enacted curriculum a little better than for the
other teachers. Initially the program was planned to intersect with the
activities in other subject areas. Then, before school started, the teacher
set a context in which home studies would support the formal curriculum.

M: So she informed parents from early on that there were important
activities related to science coming throughout the year?

K: Yes. She selected certain literature to provide a springboard for the
study of insects and spiders, and then a longitudinal study of a tree

was planned. She announced to parents and children that she had planned independent studies to be co-guided by adults in the home and by herself. Although the details were not known at the time, Ms. Mack put the parents on notice that the students would be undertaking research on science. From this point onward the science program was implemented in a serious way that for the most part allowed students to develop interests and follow their interests.

M: I can imagine that children developed a passion for their projects, and perhaps for science?

K: Science and passion, as I like to think of it, were rarely separated. It is apparent that the participation of all was active and oriented toward learning. What made the program a success in my mind was not so much that science was done regularly and was at the center of the curriculum, but that the science was relevant to the passions of the students and was directly connected with language arts. The reading, writing, drawing, and speaking components of the enacted curriculum enabled high-quality outcomes to be attained by all students. In this class, success led to further success and the students developed skills that will serve them in many contexts for the rest of their lives. That science could provide a vehicle for lifelong learning is an impressive testimonial to the flexibility of science to be central in the curriculum. So, in my way of thinking about science in a re/constructed way, I want to see the doing of science become the staple of school science. I am not advocating doing science 100% of the time with no time for learning interesting facts and studying historical and political events associated with science.

S: So what do you advocate and envision?

K: I can envision re-enactments of historical events such as the discovery of fission or the history of measuring time as being wonderful sites for dramatic re-enactment. Joan Solomon has shown that historical drama can easily be constructed around "fictional" dramas such as the trial of Galileo. I envision activities of this type being a part of an elementary science program that has as its main goal the development of a science-like discourse through the independent research conducted in communities of co-learners, co-teachers and co-researchers. By the way, I would add to the list provided by Ms. Mack the idea of children as teacher educators. Ms. Mack showed in vivid detail how a class of primary students was able to help her to become a better science teacher and co-construct an appropriate curriculum. So in the re/construction of elementary science, I see a closer connection of science with other components of the school curriculum, a much greater emphasis on the use of language to promote the learning of science through interaction, and an expansion of the roles of teacher and learner to take into account of the desirability of ensuring that the students are at all times engaged in the study of something that is meaningful to them and of high interest.

M: David Hawkins also often related science and emotion, didn't he?

K: When David Hawkins planned the criteria for deciding whether or not particular topics would be selected for inclusion in the *Elementary Science Study* he involved a criterion that the topic should consist of activities that were potentially enjoyable for children. Although the Elementary Science Study came and went, the idea of potentially enjoyable activities is one that we should consider. Since I am most interested in teaching science in urban settings, I now turn to this issue to consider what content might be selected for inclusion in a curriculum. Rather than begin with authentic science defined as authentic when compared to canonical science, as happens in the National Research Council Standards, why not start with what students know and can do and what they would like to know next? I am thinking that it might be good to begin with something that is local, such as noises, smells, or other types of pollution in the streets close to their homes. Selection of a topic such as this immediately makes the science relevant to the world outside of the classroom, just as engineering does, and it is political too. Once there is an understanding of what is causing the problems, attention can be directed toward finding solutions. For example, how can oil spills on roadways be cleaned up and prevented from re-occurring? How much trash is swept into storm drains and what are its effects on life in urban communities? What causes bad smells in local communities, are they harmful to residents, and what can be done to remove them? Starting points such as these have potential relevance to the lives of the students and will involve a great variety of data and the study of technology. I also have a hunch that a curriculum built around problems having social relevance will likely be one that generates passion and that can result in a different form of literacy and the potential for using school science.

S: Ken's vision for an ideal elementary science curriculum is enacted in some classrooms each day across the world. Sadly, our student teachers see too few cases of such practice. Our challenge as teacher educators, then, is to alert teachers to the possibilities for effective and authentic learning of science and encourage the adoption of coteaching opportunities that might lead to more widespread use of scientific or engineering classroom activities.

K: Our different studies have shown that school science can indeed be elusive in many elementary classrooms. Let me begin with Ms. Scott, who taught science in a manner that was warm and active. Her approach was guided by beliefs about child-centered learning and the need to have opportunities to manipulate and speak about what was happening. She also included design and other aspects of writing in her ideas about what constituted good science teaching. Yet the study showed that despite the warmth of the learning environment and the richness of the problems to solve, a scientific discourse was lacking for the most part. In contrast, Ms. Mack showed how it was possible through her own learning to move beyond the patterns of interaction that were visible in Ms. Scott's classroom. By structuring the learning environment in particular ways that included blurring the boundaries of the classroom and the communities in which students live their lives, Ms. Mack was able to promote practices that were science-like.

M: In other words, what happened here was brought about by the task and the collective activity involving parents and students and students and teacher, the in-class discourse and home discourse overlapped. These discourses not only had family resemblances but were identical in many respects. In this case, we can think of students such as Denise as the initial border-crossers. These crossings have the effect that the discourses in the original communities change, bringing about a closing of the gap between them and the perception of blurring you are talking about. The children's discourses, then, are subject to continuous evolution—one can speak of an emergent phenomenon in which, really, the origins of particular discourse elements are blurred.

S: Students need to become comfortable in their use of scientific language games in and out of classroom contexts. I think this happens when children start to talk about personally relevant ideas and artifacts, which the teacher can then move progressively toward more science-like discourse.

K: I also think that this emergent discourse was authentic in that it began with what students knew and could do and gradually included additional insights and practices. What happened in her classroom was constrained by her explicit and conscious efforts to emphasize such factors as active listening, substantive speaking, and informative writing. In addition, a habitus led to participation of a type that sustained inquiry and modes of co-participation associated with what she referred to as inquiry. No longer an elusive entity, inquiry was practiced in her science classes and provided the context in which her students could become scientifically literate, even though she did not regard herself as being particularly knowledgeable about science.

M: This brings to my mind a recent discussion on an electronic network in which "inquiry" was the central topic.[7] It was my impression from this discussion that what is considered inquiry and how it comes about was external to the activities of students and teachers. That is, inquiry was a method that was to be imposed on communities. But I think that there is a problem in the sense that inquiry is considered to be something external to the activities of those involved. This is the general criticism ethnomethodologists voice when they look at science education. They are much more at ease with the notion of inquiry as an emergent and enacted phenomenon, as you just described.

K: Mr. Hammett provided another window into the nature of elementary science. Although his background knowledge of science was stronger than that of Ms. Mack, his way of teaching did not lead to much evidence of canonical science. The case studies show ample presence of active participation in interesting tasks of types that are engaging to students. However, the interactions with students did not lead to the learning of what might be regarded as science. As I have described earlier, I think of what happened as falling short of science and regard it as a promising springboard for the learning of science.

M: Yes. I got the sense that in Mr. Hammett's classes, there were many seeds for the kind of science education to be enacted that we have been envisioning in the course of our conversations. His content background and experience positioned him well to bring about the situations that can lead to an occasioning of science. But at the same time, there were only glimpses that he assisted children in making the next steps in the way we have seen in Gitte's or my own class.

K: I agree; in the studies involving Gitte and Michael we see examples of how engineering science ideas do provide opportunities for the development of a scientific discourse. What is so different here is that both teachers have strong science backgrounds and know how to mediate in the process of the students' constructions of science.

M: But in this, they do not differ much from Mr. Hammett.

K: Yes, but what is also apparent to me from these studies is that both of these teachers were able to use their own language resources to connect with their students in such a way that the science-like discourse was constantly evolving. Not only that, they were able to make it possible for the students to experience science by participating in engineering-type problems and then interacting with the artifacts, inscriptions (such as a design document), and others (such as peers and teachers).

S: As I have said before, Mr. Hammett had a different agenda than Michael and Gitte. In this respect, his goals were closer to those of Ms. Mack. That is, Mr. Hammett was enacting an integrated curriculum in which language development through the design activities was just as important as scientific learning.

M: It may well be that Gitte and I differed from Mr. Hammett in the purposes we had for the engineering activities and the level to which we saw them as opportunities for bringing about the kind of scientific discourse. Gitte and I had talked a lot about what we wanted to achieve. Thus, the engineering activities were, in our planning, only vehicles for our real goal, which was to foster the development of a scientific discourse. So both of us also set up many situations in which the students argued their designs or completed more guided activities that more easily lend themselves to bring about changes in discourse. Here, the particular materials chosen can help to bring about just that kind of discourse domain related to a particular concept. For example, I might have used balanced levers and asked children to find out "What happens if . . .?" and answer similar questions of their own interest, but related to the balance beam provided. The materials then serve as constraints on the type of discourse that is likely to emerge.

K: But you can make such choices because of your background and intimate knowledge of physics. Because of the relative strength of their backgrounds in science and their beliefs about learning in communities, you and Gitte were able to constrain the learning environments of their students in ways that promoted learning. In an important sense Gitte and Michael provide images of where teachers such as Ms. Mack might end up if they continue to learn over the duration of a career. In a similar way, teachers such as Ms. Mack provide models for improving the teaching of science in classrooms that are not unlike those of Ms. Scott.

S: Mr. Hammett also could have made those choices, albeit to a lesser extent, and he did so for some children with some concepts. Whole-class discussions were used infrequently by Mr. Hammett. When they were used, they tended to be opportunities for the children to share ideas and report on their progress rather than occasions for Mr. Hammett to move the conversation toward more science-like discourse. Of course, Mr. Hammett could have done more in terms of encouraging greater use of canonical language games. In fact I know that he will appreciate reading our different perspectives and will be keen to take his classroom conversations to a different level. In this sense, the design activities have not only provided a springboard to canonical discourse; Mr. Hammett's participation in our project as a co-learner is likely to lead to changes in his practice as well. I very much look forward to the transitions that might follow in his class.

K: Elementary science has to be more than hands-on activities with materials. Similarly, it cannot be accurately described as hands-on and minds-on. What does such a phrase mean? As we look at what has emerged in our six studies described here, it is apparent that elementary science is supported by a habitus of practices such as is the case with practicing scientists. The habitus, of course, extends beyond what can be described with language. However, it is evident that the habitus supports participation that is associated with raising questions, obtaining data as answers to those questions are sought, analyzing and interpreting data, and communicating about what is learned from the investigations. These are only examples and are not just a re-listing of the process skills of the 1960s. Nor are they the habits of mind that are spoken of in Project 2061. Instead, the habitus supports participation that includes the conventions of the community and prevents others that would be considered taboo. Our research also suggests that the habitus sustains the co-learning, coteaching and co-researching of all participants.

M: You know that I have been critical of the notions "hands-on science" and "hands-on, minds-on science" because they are misleading. Even if we take the metaphor that a mind can be put onto something—to which I want to take exception—because children are where they are, they will not arrive at the canonical science some teachers think children can evolve. Learning science through induction, as the curricula in the 1960s and 1970s envisioned, could lead to nowhere. Furthermore, I am not aware of any firm evidence in past research that "hands-on," that is, a sensorimotor activity, in and of itself can lead to a scientific concept, a formal thought. Only in some of my recent work could I show this relationship between, for example, activities, gestures, and scientific discourse.[8] Scientific language, like any language and including inscriptions, is a form of representation that uses arbitrary symbols and arbitrary grammars that cannot be inferred by looking at nature or artifacts.

errors in the lectures we observe. Books, the Internet, videos, etc. appear to be less prone to the kind of inconsistencies produced in lectures. But, we should not all of a sudden use texts as the ultimate and sole sources of knowledge. Rather, I think we need to use all of these sources as starting points to move our classroom conversations on and in doing so create possibilities for the evolution of new discourses.

K: Another source of written texts is the textual material written by students after participating in activities such as those that are best exemplified in the classes of Mr. Hammett, Ms. Scott, and Ms. Mack. These written texts are likely to use a language that is accessible to peers, and the topics for the text is likely to be familiar in the sense that previous oral and written communication has already made students familiar with the main ideas. It is conceivable that over a number of years, numerous books on pertinent topics, each authored by students such as Denise, will fill the shelves of the elementary school libraries and constitute a resource for the learning of science.

M: In this, you provide a concrete example for the ideas that Jacques Désautels and I recently developed to promote epistemology as practice. In this practice, conversations become recursive and reflexive processes in which the results of earlier conversations themselves become the topic of future conversations. It would be interesting to see what kind of elementary science would be enacted if future students of Ms. Mack were to pick up and build on what Denise, her peers, and her parents have produced and then move beyond it.

K: Finally, many sources of children's literature can provide starting places for the learning of science. These take the form of many genres, and I would not want to deal with any of them in detail. My main point in mentioning them is that even at a young age there exist many books that can catch the interest of students and capture their attention in ways that are every conducive to participation in science and/or engineering.

S: The selection of materials and tasks is obviously critical in facilitating the learning of science. Tasks and materials are both part of co-participation. If students cannot engage the tasks or are unable to use the materials in ways that facilitate their goals then co-participation is impossible. Accordingly, the selection of materials and tasks is a critical part of the conduct of elementary science.

M: This became quite clear in a recent coteaching experience in which my partner used a Mickey Mouse label to help children remember the chemical formula and structure of water. Later, this Mickey Mouse image of the water molecule was used by the students to make inferences that, while logically correct, led to a conclusion that was inconsistent with science. Ms. Mack was quite taken when she read our description of this teaching sequence, because she had not realized how easily the resources we teachers provide can lead to results that we do not desire.

K: Quite clearly, a teacher can do the selection or students can do it. Ideally the selection will be a negotiation that takes into account the interests of the student as well as their existing knowledge. As I visit classrooms I see too many students with their heads down and little to no intention to participate. What is wrong with the system? Then, when I look at what the students are supposed to be studying, I am left with the feeling that perhaps my head would be down too! Given that there is so much that could be learned and so many problems to be solved in this day and age, I cannot understand why the science to be learned cannot intersect in a very direct way with the interests and passions of the students. The feelings of students are important and can be connected to the science to be learned in a very direct way. If the students have an intense interest in a particular task or project, then it seems to me that motivation to learn might be less of an issue than it appears to be in most classrooms. In the instance of Ms. Scott's class, the materials were inappropriate for the task in most of the cases, except perhaps for the use of newspaper and sticky tape.

M: In this way, her materials were a little like the Mickey Mouse model I talked about earlier.

K: So in all cases, the tasks were inappropriate for the goals of the activity, which were associated with the coordination of evidence and claims about structures and forces. Not surprisingly, students became frustrated when they were unable to use the materials to meet their goals and were also unable to change the materials they were using.

M: In mediating students' frustrations, Gitte and Tammy really were outstanding. There were frustrations, although this was not salient in our descriptions of the activities. But developing ways to deal with frustrations when learning does not proceed is also an important aspect of knowing how to learn, and incidentally, one that many adults have not acquired.

K: The negotiation of a shared discourse is easy to talk about and much harder to do. So what is involved in this process? First, in an ideal learning environment the discourse needs to be dynamic and evolving. Second, if a new discourse is to be negotiated, one that is ideal for enhancing the learning of a child, the child should either be reading or listening in a meaningful way. Active listening and reading are very important skills, and many students need practice at developing both. If a science program is to be effective it is imperative for close attention and valuing to be associated with active listening and reading. More is needed. The speaker or writer needs to provide a substantive and meaningful text from which a learner can provide information that is pertinent to what it is she wants to learn. When active listening is combined with substantive speaking and the discourse of the speaker can be accessed and appropriated by the listener, then co-participation is possible and can lead to meaningful learning of science. In these circumstances, the trajectory of an emerging discourse within a community can become more science-like over time. My impression is that this was occurring in a number of the studies that were presented in the book.

M: I often thought during my coteaching experiences with elementary school teachers that they had evolved better ways of producing such classroom-wide practices. It is in such situation that I learned a lot by coteaching. As a high school teacher, I was not too concerned with bringing about a particular set of practices such that it became a habit. Well, this is not quite true, but I thought it was easier for me to say to high school students, "This is the kind of practice I would want us to evolve." My coteaching partners, however, seemed to be much more at ease with bringing about such practices as listening.

K: The interactions that occur in classrooms should go beyond within-group conversations and interactions between the teacher and students. Too often the groups within a classroom act as independent islands of activity. However, it is essential that effective between-group communication be planned so that each group can benefit from the activities of others. Many different strategies can be used to promote between-group interactions, but too often they do not occur and, even worse, there are occasions when such interactions are considered to be disruptive or even cheating.

S: As an onlooker to this lively conversation, I have checked off just about all possible resources that could be used in a classroom to support science learning. What stands out is that it is not the list of resources but how a teacher uses the resources that really counts. Even though each of us has slightly different readings of the case studies as presented here, none of us would advocate an anything-goes approach, which has been wrongly attributed to constructivists.

Instead, I have learned that teachers need to constrain the resources for students in science and engineering activities in order to foreground the goal of canonical discourse. This requires an active co-participatory role for the teacher in science classroom learning by which the teacher purposively links the children's primary discourse with the secondary discourse of school science. We can learn from the teachers in our study about their ongoing dilemmas in dealing with competing referents through observation, discussion, and writing. The stories we tell of these insights might then help other teachers enact challenging science experiences for elementary school children.

Notes

1   See for example, Roth, 1996a, 1998a.

2   The study was conducted in a suburban high school physics class of a large Australian metropolis and showed considerable variations in the experiences of individuals to the extent that the students, and teacher, appeared to have been in different classes (Roth & McRobbie, 1999; Roth, Boutonné, McRobbie, & Lucas, 1999).

3   See Kuhn, 1993.

4   Coteaching often leads to situations in which teachers, without noticing, appropriate practices, mannerisms, and even gestures typical of their partner without noticing it (e.g., Roth, 1996d; Roth & Boyd, 1999; Roth, Masciotra, & Boyd, 1999). The sort of silent pedagogy in operation here is embodied in the harmonizing tendencies that living under the same condition produce (Bourdieu, 1990, 1997).

5   In German, there exists the term of Bildung and an associated genre of novels, "Bildungsroman" (a novel that describes the learning trajectory of an individual throughout his or her entire life). Here, learning is not relegated to one stage in life, but refers to the entire life span.

6   We have argued for an epistemology as practice in which students engage from the very beginning of their formal learning (Désautels & Roth, 1999). If students reflect on knowledge and knowledge representations, they will be empowered in the sense that they have the tools and experiences in deconstructing all sorts of signs, texts, and gestures. In a recent research seminar at the University of Victoria, I argued that if students had some such experiences in deconstructing signs and texts, they could easily deconstruct and thereby defuse situations that now lead them to school violence. In some situations, the question "What are you pointing at?" may take the stinger out of a raised middle finger.

7   The electronic conversation occurred in the fall of 1998 on the NARST-L list server.

8   See Roth, 1999.

References

Agre, P. E. (1995). Computational research on interaction and agency. *Artificial Intelligence, 72,* 1–52.

Amann, K., & Knorr-Cetina, K. D. (1990). The fixation of (visual) evidence. In M. Lynch & S. Woolgar (Eds.), *Representation in scientific practice* (pp. 85–121). Cambridge, MA: MIT Press.

American Association for the Advancement of Science (1993). *Benchmarks for science literacy.* New York: Oxford University Press.

Anderson, J. R. (1985). *Cognitive psychology and its implications.* San Francisco, CA: Freeman.

Association for the Promotion and Advancement of Science Education (APASE). (1991). *Engineering for children: Structures* (A manual for teachers). Vancouver, B.C.: Author.

Australian Academy of Science. (1994). *Primary investigations: Student book 6—energy and investigation.* Canberra: Australian Academy of Science.

Australian Education Council. (1994). *Science—A curriculum profile for Australian schools.* Carlton, Victoria: Curriculum Corporation.

Bakhtin, M. (1981). *The dialogic imagination.* Austin: University of Texas.

Bannon, L. J., & Bødker, S. (1991). Beyond the interface: Encountering artifacts in use. In J. M. Carroll (Ed.), *Designing interaction: Psychology at the human-computer interface* (pp. 227–253). Cambridge: Cambridge University Press.

Barton, A. C. (1998). Reframing "science for all" through the politics of poverty. *Educational Policy, 12,* 525–541.

Bateson, G. (1972). *Steps to an ecology of mind.* New York: Ballantine.

Bateson, G. (1980). *Mind and nature: A ncessary unity.* Toronto: Bantam Books.

Bateson, G., & Bateson, M. C. (1987). *Angels fear: Towards an epistemology of the sacred.* Toronto: Bantam Books.

Biddulph, F., & Osborne, R. (Eds.) (1984). *Making sense of our world: An interactive teaching approach.* Hamilton, NZ: University of Waikato.

Bijker, W. E. (1987). The social construction of Bakelite: Toward a theory of invention. In W. E. Bijker, T. P. Hughes, & T. J. Pinch (Eds.), *The social construction of technological systems* (pp. 159–187). Cambridge, MA: MIT Press.

Bond, A. H. (1989). The cooperation of experts in engineering design. In L. Gasser & M. N. Huhns (Eds.), *Distributed artificial intelligence* (Vol. 2, pp. 463–484). London: Pitman and San Mateo, CA: Morgan Kaufman Publishers.

Bourdieu, P. (1990). *The logic of practice.* Cambridge, UK: Polity Press.

Bourdieu, P. (1997). *Méditations pascaliennes* [Pascalian meditations]. Paris: Seuil.

Bowen, G. M., & Roth, W.-M. (1998). Lecturing graphing: What features of lectures contribute to student difficulties in learning to interpret graphs? *Research in Science Education, 28,* 77–90.

Brooks, R. (1995). Intelligence without reason. In L. Steels & R. Brooks (Eds.), *The artificial life route to artificial intelligence: Building embodied, situated agents* (pp. 25–81). Hillsdale, NJ: Lawrence Erlbaum Associates.

Brown, J. S., & Duguid, P. (1992). Enacting design for the workplace. In P. S. Adler & T. A. Winograd (Eds.), *Usability: Turning technologies into tools* (pp. 164–197). New York: Oxford University Press.

Brown, J. S., & Duguid, P. (1996). Keeping it simple. In T. Winograd (Ed.), *Bringing design to software* (pp. 129–145). New York: ACM Press.

Bucciarelli, L. L. (1994). *Designing engineers.* Cambridge, MA: MIT Press.

Kuhn, T. S. (1970). *The structure of scientific revolutions* (2nd ed.). Chicago: University of Chicago Press.

Lakin, F. (1990). Visual languages for cooperation: A performing medium approach to systems for cooperative work. In J. Galegher, R. E. Kraut, & C. Egido (Eds.), *Intellectual teamwork: Social and technological foundations of cooperative work* (pp. 453–488). Hillsdale, NJ: Lawrence Erlbaum Associates.

Lakoff, G. (1987). *Women, fire, and dangerous things: What categories reveal about the mind.* Chicago: University of Chicago Press.

Latour, B. (1987). *Science in action: How to follow scientists and engineers through society.* Milton Keynes: Open University Press.

Latour, B. (1992). *Aramis ou l'amour des techniques* [Aramis or the love of technology]. Paris: Éditions la Découverte.

Latour, B. (1993). *We have never been modern.* Cambridge, MA: Harvard University Press.

Lave, J. (1993). The practice of learning. In S. Chaiklin & J. Lave (Eds.), *Understanding practice: Perspectives on activity and context* (pp. 3–32). Cambridge: Cambridge University Press.

Lave, J., & Wenger, E. (1991). *Situated learning: Legitimate peripheral participation.* Cambridge: Cambridge University Press.

Law, J. (1994). *Organizing modernity.* Oxford, UK: Blackwell.

Law, J., & Callon, M. (1988). Engineering and sociology in a military aircraft project: A network analysis of technological change. *Social Problems, 35,* 284–297.

Lemke, J. L. (1990). *Talking science: Language, learning and values.* Norwood, NJ: Ablex.

Lemke, J. L. (1995). *Textual politics: Discourse and social dynamics.* London: Taylor & Francis.

Lemke, J. L. (1998). Multiplying meaning: Visual and verbal semiotics in scientific text. In J. R. Martin & R. Veel (Eds.), *Reading science* (pp. 87–113). London: Routledge.

Lin, H-s., Shiau, B-r., & Lawrenz, F. (1996). The effectiveness of teaching science with pictorial analogies. *Research in Science Education, 26,* 495–511.

Luff, P., & Heath, C. (1993). System use and social organization: Observations on human-computer interaction in an architectural practice. In G. Button (Ed.), *Technology in working order: Studies of work, interaction, and technology* (pp. 184–210). London and New York: Routledge.

Lynch, M. (1995). Laboratory space and the technological complex: An investigation of topical contextures. In S. L. Star (ed.), *Ecologies of knowledge: Work and politics in science and technology* (pp. 226–256). Albany: State University of New York Press.

Lynch, M., & Edgerton, S. Y. (1988). Aesthetics and digital image processing: Representational craft in contemporary astronomy. In G. Fyfe & J. Law (Eds.), *Picturing power: Visual depiction and social relations* (pp. 184–220). London: Routledge.

McGinn, M. K., & Roth, W.-M. (1998). Assessing students' understandings about levers: better test instruments are not enough. *International Journal of Science Education, 20,* 813–832.

McGinn, M. K., Roth, W.-M., Boutonné, S., & Woszczyna, C. (1995). The transformation of individual and collective knowledge in elementary science classrooms that are organized as knowledge-building communities. *Research in Science Education, 25,* 163–189.

McGonigal, J. (1998, May). *A teacher's journey. Destination: Science inquiry.* Haddonfield, New Jersey: J. F. Tatem School (Unpublished manuscript).

Mehan, H. (1993). Beneath the skin and between the ears: A case study in the politics of representation. In S. Chaiklin & J. Lave (Eds.), *Understanding practice: Perspectives on activity and context* (pp. 241–268). Cambridge, England: Cambridge University Press.

MicroSoft Bookshelf (1996/1997). Microsoft CD.

National Research Council (1996). *National science education standards.* Washington: National Academy Press.

Norman, D. A. (1991). Cognitive artifacts. In J. M. Carroll (Ed.), *Designing interaction: Psychology at the human-computer interface* (pp. 17–38). Cambridge: Cambridge University Press.

Packer, K., & Webster, A. (1996). Patenting culture in science: Reinventing the scientific wheel of credibility. *Science, Technology, & Human Values, 21,* 427–453.

Pickering, A. (1993). The mangle of practice: Agency and emergence in the sociology of science. *American Journal of Sociology, 99*, 559–589.

Pickering, A. (1995). *The mangle of practice: Time, agency, & science.* Chicago: The University of Chicago Press.

Pinch, T. J., & Bijker, W. E. (1987). The social construction of facts and artifacts: Or how the sociology of science and the sociology of technology might benefit each other. In W. E. Bijker, T. P. Hughes, & T. J. Pinch (Eds.), *The social construction of technological systems* (pp. 17–50). Cambridge, MA: MIT Press.

Piserchia, C. (1998, March). *Structures: My science inquiry.* Haddonfield, New Jersey: J.F. Tatem School (Unpublished manuscript).

Poole, D. (1994). Routine testing practices and the linguistic construction of knowledge. *Cognition and Instruction, 12*, 125–150.

Quine, W. V. (1992). *Pursuit of truth* (revised edition). Cambridge, MA: Harvard University Press.

Ramsay, B., Ryan, J., & Dick, B. (1995). *Using the technology profile.* Carlton, Victoria: Curriculum Corporation.

Rheinfrank, J., & Evenson, S. (1996). Design languages. In T. Winograd (Ed.), *Bringing design to software* (pp. 63–80). New York, NY: ACM Press.

Rigano, D. L., & Ritchie, S. M. (in press). Learning the craft: A student teacher's story. *Asia-Pacific Journal of Teacher Education.*

Ritchie, S. M. (1994). Metaphor as a tool for constructivist science teaching. *International Journal of Science Education, 16*, 293–303.

Ritchie, S. M. (1998). The teacher's role in the transformation of students' understanding. *Research in Science Education, 28*, 169–185.

Ritchie, S. M. (in press). The craft of intervention: A personal practical theory for a teacher's within-group interactions. *Science Education.*

Ritchie, S. M. & Hampson, B. (1996). Learning in-the-making: A case study of science and technology projects in a year six classroom. *Research in Science Education, 26*, 391–407.

Ritchie, S. M., Tobin, K., & Hook, K. (1997). Teaching referents and the warrants used to test the viability of students' mental models:

Is there a link? *Journal of Research in Science Teaching, 34*, 223–236.

Roth, W.-M. (1993). Metaphors and conversational analysis as tools in reflection on teaching practice: Two perspectives on teacher-student interactions in open-inquiry science. *Science Education, 77*, 351–373.

Roth, W.-M. (1994). Student views of collaborative concept mapping: An emancipatory research project. *Science Education, 78*, 1–34.

Roth, W.-M. (1995a). Affordances of computers in teacher-student interactions: The case of Interactive Physics™. *Journal of Research in Science Teaching, 32*, 329–347.

Roth, W.-M. (1995b). *Authentic school science: Knowing and learning in open-inquiry laboratories.* Dordrecht, Netherlands: Kluwer Academic Publishing.

Roth, W.-M. (1995c). From 'wiggly structures' to 'unshaky towers': Problem framing, solution finding, and negotiation of courses of actions during a civil engineering unit for elementary students. *Research in Science Education, 25*, 365–381.

Roth, W.-M. (1995d). Inventors, copycats, and everyone else: The emergence of shared (arti)facts and concepts as defining aspects of classroom communities. *Science Education, 79*, 475–502.

Roth, W.-M. (1996a). Art and artifact of children's designing: A situated cognition perspective. *The Journal of the Learning Sciences, 5*, 129–166.

Roth, W.-M. (1996b). Engineering talk in a Grade 4/5 classroom: A pre- and post-unit assessment. *International Journal of Technology and Design Education, 6*, 107–135.

Roth, W.-M. (1996c). Knowledge diffusion* in a Grade 4–5 classroom during a unit on civil engineering: An analysis of a classroom community in terms of its changing resources and practices. *Cognition and Instruction, 14*, 179–220.

Roth, W.-M. (1996d). Teacher questioning in an open-inquiry learning environment: Interactions of context, content, and student responses. *Journal of Research in Science Teaching, 33*, 709–736.

Roth, W.-M. (1996e). The co-evolution of situated language and physics knowing. *Journal of Science Education and Technology, 3,* 171–191.

Roth, W.-M. (1996f). Thinking with hands, eyes, and signs: Multimodal science talk in a Grade 6/7 unit on simple machines. *Interactive Learning Environments, 4,* 170–187.

Roth, W.-M. (1996g). Unterricht über einfache Maschinen im 6. und 7. Schuljahr—geplant und analysiert aus einer sozial-konstruktivistischen Perspektive des Lernens [Learning about simple machines in Grade 6/7: A social-constructivist perspective]. *Zeitschrift für Didaktik der Naturwissenschaften, 2,* 39–52.

Roth, W.-M. (1998a). *Designing communities.* Dordrecht: Kluwer Academic Publishers.

Roth, W.-M. (1998b). Situated cognition and assessment of competence in science. *Evaluation and Program Planning, 21,* 155–169.

Roth, W.-M. (1998c). Starting small and with uncertainty: Toward a neurocomputational account of knowing and learning in science. *International Journal of Science Education, 20,* 1089–1105.

Roth, W.-M. (1998d). Science teaching as knowledgeability: a case study of knowing and learning during coteaching. *Science Education, 82,* 357–377.

Roth, W.-M. (1999). Discourse and agency in school science laboratories. *Discourse Processes, 28,* 27–60.

Roth, W.-M. (2000). From gesture to scientific language. *Journal of Pragmatics, 32,* 1683–1714.

Roth, W.-M., Boutonné, S., McRobbie, C., & Lucas, K. B. (1999). One class, many worlds. *International Journal of Science Education, 21,* 59–75.

Roth, W.-M., & Bowen, G. M. (1995). Knowing and interacting: A study of culture, practices, and resources in a Grade 8 open-inquiry science classroom guided by a cognitive apprenticeship metaphor. *Cognition and Instruction, 13,* 73–128.

Roth, W.-M., & Bowen, G. M. (1999a). Complexities of graphical representations during lectures: A phenomenological approach. *Learning and Instruction, 9,* 235–255.

Roth, W.-M., & Bowen, G. M. (1999b). Decalages in talk and gesture: Visual and verbal semiotics of ecology lectures. *Linguistics & Education, 10,* 335–358.

Roth, W.-M., & Boyd, N. (1999). Coteaching, as colearning, in practice. *Research in Science Education, 29,* 51–67.

Roth, W.-M., & Duit, R. (1996). Knowing and learning in real time: Towards an understanding of student-centered science activities.

Roth, W.-M., Masciotra, D., & Boyd, N. (1999). Becoming-in-the-classroom: a case study of teacher development through coteaching. *Teaching and Teacher Education, 17,* 771–784.

Roth, W.-M., & McGinn, M. K. (1996, July). Differential participation during science conversations: The interaction of display artifacts, social configuration, and physical arrangements. In D. C. Edelson & E. A. Domeshek (Eds.), *Proceedings of ICLS 96* (pp. 300–307). Charlottesville, VA: Association for the Advancement of Computing in Education.

Roth, W.-M., & McGinn, M. K. (1997). Science in schools and everywhere else: what science educators should know about science and technology studies. *Studies in Science Education, 29,* 1–44.

Roth, W.-M., & McGinn, M. K. (1998). Knowing, researching, and reporting science education: Lessons from science and technology studies. *Journal of Research in Science Teaching, 35,* 213–235.

Roth, W.-M., McGinn, M. K., Woszczyna, C., & Boutonné, S. (1999). Differential participation during science conversations: The interaction of focal artifacts, social configuration, and physical arrangements. *The Journal of the Learning Sciences, 8,* 293–347.

Roth, W.-M., & McRobbie, C. (1999). Lifeworlds and the 'w/ri(gh)ting' of classroom research. *Journal of Curriculum Studies, 31,* 501–522.

Roth, W.-M., McRobbie, C., Lucas, K. B., & Boutonné, S. (1997a). The local production of order in traditional science laboratories: A phenomenological analysis. *Learning and Instruction, 7,* 107–136.

Roth, W.-M., McRobbie, C., Lucas, K. B., & Boutonné, S. (1997b). Why do students fail to learn from demonstrations? A social practice perspective on learning in physics. *Journal of Research in Science Teaching, 34,* 509–533.

Roth, W.-M., & Roychoudhury, A. (1992). The social construction of scientific concepts or The concept map as conscription device and tool for social thinking in high school science. *Science Education, 76*, 531–557.

Roth, W.-M., & Roychoudhury, A. (1993). The concept map as a tool for the collaborative construction of knowledge: A microanalysis of high school physics students. *Journal of Research in Science Teaching, 30*, 503–534.

Roth, W.-M., & Tobin, K. (1996). Aristotle and natural observation versus Galileo and scientific experiment: An analysis of lectures in physics for elementary teachers in terms of discourse and inscriptions. *Journal of Research in Science Teaching, 33*, 135–157.

Roth, W.-M., Tobin, K., & Shaw, K. (1997). Cascades of inscriptions and the representation of nature: How numbers, tables, graphs, and money come to represent a rolling ball. *International Journal of Science Education, 19*, 1075–1091.

Roth, W.-M., Woszczyna, C., & Smith, G. (1996). Affordances and constraints of computers in science education. *Journal of Research in Science Teaching, 33*, 995–1017.

Schank, R. C. (1994). Goal-based scenarios: A radical look at education. *The Journal of the Learning Sciences, 3*, 429–453.

Schank, R. C., Fano, A., Bell, B., & Jona, M. (1994). The design of goal-based scenarios. *The Journal of the Learning Sciences, 3*, 305–345.

Schegloff, E. (1982). Discourse as an interactional achievement: Some uses of 'uh huh' and other things that come between sentences. In D. Tannen (Ed.), *Analyzing discourse: Text and talk* (pp. 71–93). Washington, DC: Georgetown University Press.

Schön, D. A. (1983). *The reflective practitioner: How professionals think in action.* New York: Basic Books.

Schön, D. A. (1985). *The design studio.* London: RIBA.

Schön, D. A. (1987). *Educating the reflective practitioner.* San Francisco: Jossey-Bass.

Schön, D., & Bennett, J. (1996). Reflective conversation with materials. In T. Winograd (Ed.), *Bringing design to software* (pp. 171–184). New York: ACM Press.

Schrage, M. (1996). Cultures of prototyping. In T. Winograd (Ed.), *Bringing design to software* (pp. 191–205). New York: ACM Press.

Slaughter, S., & Rhoades, G. (1996). The emergence of a competitiveness research and development policy coalition and the commercialization of academic science and technology. *Science, Technology, & Human Values, 21*, 303–339.

Solomon, J. (1986). Children's explanations. *Oxford Review of Education, 12*, 41–51.

Sørenson, K. H., & Levold, N. (1992). Tacit networks, heterogeneous engineers, and embodied technology. *Science, Technology, & Human Values, 17*, 13–35.

Star, S. L. (1989). Layered space, formal representations and long-distance conrol: the politics of information. *Fundamenta Scientiae, 10*, 125–154.

Starling, G. (1992). Problem solving as a social process: A theoretical and empirical analysis. *The Social Science Journal, 29*, 211–225.

Suchman, L. A. (1990). Representing practice in cognitive science. In M. Lynch & S. Woolgar (Eds.), *Representation in scientific practice* (pp. 301–321). Cambridge, MA: MIT Press.

Suchman, L. A., & Trigg, R. H. (1993). Artificial intelligence as craftwork. In S. Chaiklin & J. Lave (Eds.), *Understanding practice: Perspectives on activity and context* (pp. 144–178). Cambridge: Cambridge University Press.

Suzuki, D. (1989). *Inventing the future: Reflections on science, technology, and nature.* Toronto: Stoddart.

Symington, D. (1986). I see but do I understand? Investigating. *Australian Primary Science Journal, 2*, 14–15.

Tobin, K. (1984). Effects of extended wait time on discourse characteristics and achievement in middle school Grades. *Journal of Research in Science Teaching, 21*, 779–791.

Studies in the Postmodern Theory of Education

General Editors
Joe L. Kincheloe & Shirley R. Steinberg

Counterpoints publishes the most compelling and imaginative books being written in education today. Grounded on the theoretical advances in criticalism, feminism, and postmodernism in the last two decades of the twentieth century, Counterpoints engages the meaning of these innovations in various forms of educational expression. Committed to the proposition that theoretical literature should be accessible to a variety of audiences, the series insists that its authors avoid esoteric and jargonistic languages that transform educational scholarship into an elite discourse for the initiated. Scholarly work matters only to the degree it affects consciousness and practice at multiple sites. Counterpoints' editorial policy is based on these principles and the ability of scholars to break new ground, to open new conversations, to go where educators have never gone before.

For additional information about this series or for the submission of manuscripts, please contact:

Joe L. Kincheloe & Shirley R. Steinberg
c/o Peter Lang Publishing, Inc.
275 Seventh Avenue, 28th floor
New York, New York 10001

To order other books in this series, please contact our Customer Service Department:

(800) 770-LANG (within the U.S.)
(212) 647-7706 (outside the U.S.)
(212) 647-7707 FAX

Or browse online by series:
www.peterlangusa.com